Agents of Atrocity

Agents of Atrocity

Leaders, Followers, and the Violation of
Human Rights in Civil War

Neil J. Mitchell

palgrave
macmillan

First published 2004 by PALGRAVE MACMILLAN™
175 Fifth Avenue, New York, N.Y. 10010 and
Houndmills, Basingstoke, Hampshire, England RG21 6XS.
Companies and representatives throughout the world.

PALGRAVE MACMILLAN is the global academic imprint of the Palgrave Macmillan division of St. Martin's Press, LLC and of Palgrave Macmillan Ltd. Macmillan® is a registered trademark in the United States, United Kingdom and other countries. Palgrave is a registered trademark in the European Union and other countries.

ISBN 1-4039-6274-X hardback

Library of Congress Cataloging-in-Publication Data

Mitchell, Neil J. (Neil James), 1953-
Agents of atrocity : leaders, followers, and the violation of human rights in civil war / by Neil J. Mitchell
    p. cm.
  Includes bibliographical references and index
  ISBN 1-4039-6274-X
    1. Political violence. 2. War victims. 3. Human rights. 4. Civil war—Protection of civilians. 5. Political leadership—Psychological aspects. 6. Control (Psychology) 7.
  Brainwashing. I. Title.

JC328.6M58 2004
323'.044--dc22
2003063229

A catalogue record for this book is available from the British Library.

Design by planettheo.com

First edition: August 2004
10 9 8 7 6 5 4 3 2 1

Printed in the United States of America.

To the memory of my father,
James Ferguson Mitchell.

Contents

Acknowledgments

My purpose in writing this book is to reduce political violence to its basic motivations and to do so in a way that is accessible to the general reader. There are some concepts that require some explanation, but as far as possible I have tried to use everyday language. The argument is a general one as it is built around concepts that have been successfully applied to other problems, and as it draws on examples that are culturally, geographically, and historically very different.

Beyond the obvious debt to historians, I owe a great deal to colleagues and students for their comments and criticism. In particular, I thank Caroline Beer, Alok Bohara, Christopher Butler, Jeff Drope, Tali Gluch, Wendy Hansen, Hank Jenkins-Smith, Jim McCormick, Karen Remmer, Carol Silva, Mark Peceny, and Maggie Toulouse. David Pervin's patient editorial advice consistently pushed me to try to write a more readable book. The University of New Mexico and the Department of Political Science provided the institutional support and encouragement for me to write this book.

Machiavelli, the Grand Inquisitor, and Count Tilly's Reward

The bastard theory of political violence has one central proposition: bastards do the violence. I add the refinement that there are different types of bastards. There is the bastard motivated by getting and holding power and the one motivated by the logic of his dogmatic belief system. Both use others to carry out the violence. Those carrying it out may be motivated by loyalty to the leader's mission but also by the private temptations of revenge, rape, and loot. The interests of the one who orders the violence and of the one who carries it out are not necessarily the same, as with any relationship between principal and agent, whether the Emperor of Japan and his army of rapists at Nanking in China in 1937, or you and your car mechanic, or you and your lawyer. Shocking, perhaps—but violence and depravity aside, there is a similar logic to these relationships and similar issues about who is controlling whom. The standard explanations of political violence that point to historical patterns of national or group conflict, the context of economic development, or the institutional, cultural, and demographic environment make us lose sight of the simple wisdom that it is bastards ordering and doing the violence.

On September 11, 1649, during the English Civil War (1642-1651), a royalist soldier in Drogheda, 35 miles north of Dublin, would have known this simple truth. Sir Arthur Aston, an Englishman, Catholic, and royalist, was besieged in this fortified town. He rejected a summons from the commander of the besieging army to surrender. Aston and his men at first resisted and then fell to the storm of cannon and determined troops. On that early autumn day, the successful commander, Oliver Cromwell, ordered that all of those who had fought be put to death, and that no mercy was to be extended to friars and priests. His troops killed between 2,000 and 4,000 defenders of the town.

On March 17, 1921, during the brutal Russian Civil War (1917-1921), a Russian sailor at Kronstadt would have known it. This offshore fortress and home port of the Baltic fleet, lying in the maritime approaches to St. Petersburg (Petrograd, Leningrad), was held by mutinous sailors demanding free elections and equal rations for all. Red Army soldiers under the great Bolshevik Civil War commander Tukhachevskii donned winter camouflage and stormed the fortress, then ice-linked to the land. His troops, stiffened with Communist Party volunteers, slaughtered many of the defenders. They took some prisoners at Kronstadt, but the secret police shot or drowned them in smaller groups over the following year. Priests died elsewhere in Lenin's Russia. Lenin, like Cromwell, had already killed a king.

And, on the morning of April 9, 1948, during the fighting preceding Israel's independence, a child waking up in Deir Yassin would have known it. Menachem Begin's Irgun forces and the Stern Gang killed about one hundred of the inhabitants of this village, situated on the western approach to Jerusalem, and paraded survivors through the city. The Jerusalem office of the Haganah, the predecessor to the Israel Defense Force, had approved the "dissident" irregulars' assault on the village and committed a few elite troops. Although the village had entered into and apparently observed peace pacts with neighboring Jewish communities, its hill location close to Jerusalem and the major Tel Aviv-to-Jerusalem road gave it strategic visibility.

These soldiers, sailors, and villagers knew that it was men doing the violence, not a context or an environmental factor. Commentators, in trying to make these events known and understandable to the rest of us, often lump together those who do these evil things, as if all bastards are equal. Reacting to the recent tragic events in the West Bank, Jose Saramago, the Portuguese Nobel Prize winner, likens refugee camps to death camps: "we can compare what is happening in the Palestinian territories with Auschwitz."[1] On one level the dead are dead, a tragedy is a tragedy, and the type of camp where one meets death does not matter. But even setting aside the scale of different tragedies, there are different motives at work, and all bastards are not equal.

Human rights violations during civil wars are nothing new. What is a change from the standard approach is to seek explanation for their actions from the individuals involved rather than from their circumstances or "objective conditions." I argue that the use of atrocities is selfish, rational, or logical. I argue that the leaders or principals who use violence against civilians and prisoners have two basic motivations. They are motivated by the self-interested pursuit of power or by the intolerant logic of a divisive belief system, or by some mixture of the two. Leaders order this sort of violence to destroy challengers to their power or to destroy those whom they see as on the wrong side of the political argument. The archetypal figures representing these two motives are Niccolò Machiavelli and the Grand Inquisitor; two figures who, like Oedipus and Electra, bring tragedy to the political family. Machiavelli's Prince is caught in the internecine conflict of Italian city-states, in a country subject to foreign invasion, and has the narrow aim of getting and maintaining political power. More mythically, the Grand Inquisitor, of Spanish origin but Russian exposition, is dedicated to his definition of the public interest in a self-consciously dogmatic way. One can hope that another type of leader exists: the antithesis of the Grand Inquisitor, the Tolerator may have to use violence yet abjures atrocity.

Machiavelli's argument, complete with detailed historical illustrations, is that atrocities and deception should be used in a calibrated way to get and to stay in power. It is the view from the top, not concerned with why citizens should consent to government but with how the ruler holds on to power. *The Prince* contains practical advice for the successful ruler, not wrapped in "pompous phrases" or "rhetorical embroidery," as Machiavelli says in dedicating his book as a gift to the "Magnificent Lorenzo de Medici," and not tied by a rigid view of right and wrong. His model is Cesare Borgia, duke of Valentino and a military leader who sought to unify Italy at the turn of the sixteenth century, a bastard son of Pope Alexander VI, a brother to the infamous Lucretia Borgia, and a man who murdered his own brother-in-law and perhaps his brother. While the Prince who wishes to hold on to power must be prepared to be ruthless and cruel, Machiavelli stresses that there are limits to the useful use of cruelty. Violence beyond a certain point harms the Prince's hold on power by increasing the popular antagonisms generated by killing, torturing, and imprisoning. There is a time for reconciliation, accommodation, and finding a scapegoat for the violence that has been done. Machiavelli's Prince is an archetype for a very influential view of what power requires.

By contrast, the Grand Inquisitor quite explicitly denies the power motive, except as power serves his ideals. His type is more dangerous, burning "infidels" out of love and duty. There is no end to the Grand Inquisitor's demand for victims. His victims are defined within the internal logic of his belief system, not by what they actually do to threaten his power and position as the Grand Inquisitor. Ironically, in Dostoevsky's story of the Grand Inquisitor, the one individual who commands spontaneous public support on the streets of Seville, and who does represent a real threat to the Inquisitor, is treated with kindness. His treatment is, however, exceptional. The Inquisitor's world is defined by collective identities that are confirmed as much by having nonmembers as members in a group, and there is no place for tolerance.

For an example of the Tolerator, we find not a single figure but more of a philosophical tradition. We can look to, for example, Germany at the end of the eighteenth-century Enlightenment. Immanuel Kant could imagine, so he says, a moral politician and could even look forward to a situation of perpetual peace, while acknowledging the hatreds that had previously accompanied linguistic and religious differences. Force and violence is legitimate to defend liberty, but even then there are rules governing the use of violence. Or we could look to France, where Voltaire argues that philosophy was driving out superstition and that "the human spirit awakened from its intoxication is astonished at the excesses it committed under the influence of fanaticism."[2] Or to England in the previous century to find philosopher John Locke arguing for toleration, although within some specific limits.

Beyond power and dogma, there is a third motivation for human rights violations. We need to consider the selfish gratification and enjoyment of those who actually do the atrocities. Like greed in general, the agent's selfish motivation for violence persists across time, cultures, and countries. We may point to dysfunctional cultures and to tribal rage and customary savagery to explain what happens in the Middle East, as Thomas Friedman does in *From Beirut to Jerusalem,* but there are more general dynamics at work. The principal, however motivated, relies on others to do the killing and to administer the torture. Neither the Prince nor the Inquisitor carries out the violence personally; they have implementers, or agents. In work on public policy that can be readily applied to the problem of human rights violations, scholars have addressed the problem of how those who make policy maintain control of those who carry it out. They use the concepts of principal and agent to denote the key policy participants. The principal-agent logic is familiar to us in everyday contractual relationships such as those formed in the real estate market. A house buyer is a principal, and the real estate agent or broker is an agent, and the former may question the motives of the latter. What is the best deal depends on your position in this relationship. A low house price suits the principal, while a high price suits the commission-driven agent. Scholars explicitly recognize that the relationship between principal and agent raises some general problems, namely that both principal and agent bring their own, possibly even conflicting, motives to the situation, that only the agent knows her true motives, that the agent may have more information about the issue or situation than the principal, and that she may be able to exploit these information advantages for her own selfish ends.

In the relationship between principals and agents, the principal can never be certain of complete control. If behavior from other bureaucracies provides a guide, the private interests of the agents and their ability to hide their interests and actions from the principal contribute substantially and systematically to the human toll of the bureaucracies of repression. For some agents, the violence may be simply a task to perform in order to achieve the leader's goal. For others, violence may be the raw end, not the means, and the agents seize opportunities provided by their offices and uniforms to supply personal gratification. The relationship between the leader or principal and his agents is crucial, and the complicated interactions between the principal, whether Machiavelli or the Grand Inquisitor, and the guards, the police, or the soldiers have important implications for the overall amount of violence. The central task of this book is to identify and organize the motives of both principal and agent in order to restore the focus to choice and to responsibility in the use of violence. Before describing what this approach offers over standard explanations of rights violations, it is important to recognize the absence of cultural and historical limits on the inimical interaction between principal and agent in the use of violence.

IMPLEMENTING VIOLENCE, FROM THE MIDDLE AGES TO THE MIDDLE EAST

As Shakespeare's Henry V laid siege to Harfleur in Northern France, he threatened the people of the town:

> I will not leave the half-achieved Harfleur
> Till in her ashes she lie buried.
> The gates of mercy shall be all shut up,
> And the fleshed soldier, rough and hard of heart,
> In liberty of bloody hand shall range
> With conscience wide as Hell, mowing like grass
> Your fresh-fair virgins and your flow'ring infants.
> What is it then to me if impious war,
> Arrayed in flames like to the Prince of Fiends,
> Do with his smirched complexion all fell feats
> Enlinked to waste and desolation?
> What is't to me, when you yourselves are cause,
> If your pure maidens fall into the hand

Of hot and forcing violation?
What rein can hold licentious wickedness
When down the hill he holds his fierce career?
We may as bootless spend our vain command
Upon th'enraged soldiers in their spoil
As send precepts to the leviathan
To come ashore. Therefore, you men of Harfleur,
Take pity of your town and of your people
Whiles yet my soldiers are in my command

—Henry V, Act 3, Scene 3

In these lines in awful graphic detail, we see the motivation of men under extreme danger left to their own devices. Brutalized by training and experience, "rough and hard of heart," facing their own oblivion, they are selfishly motivated by the violence itself, by revenge, by sex, and by the prospect of loot. This motivation, which Shakespeare likened to the force of gravity, can even overpower the power of the victorious commander, or so Shakespeare's Henry says. The commander's motivation on the other hand is strategic, to take the objective efficiently, minimizing his casualties. The town, believing Henry's threats credible, gave up without further fight, and so he instructed that mercy be used. In this case, just the threat of the unchecked selfishness of the agents delivers control of the town.[3] According to historical accounts, the citizens of Harfleur lost homes and property but avoided massacre by Henry's army, and the real Henry in his articles of war (the rules of conduct that he established for his troops) forbade rape and punished it with death. But the truly frightful consequences that Shakespeare's Henry attached to further defiance do not make the warrior king or for that matter his "happy few," his "band of brothers," simple heroes. This commander will take no responsibility or even admit much remorse for the actions of his agents and for the fate of Harfleur's virgins and infants. "What is it to me," he repeats. It is the town's responsibility for continuing to fight, and his soldiers are out of his control, his "vain command."

What was threatened at Harfleur was done at Magdeburg, Germany, in 1631. Count Johann von Tilly's troops stormed the town. Count Tilly commanded the armies of the Catholic League and the

Holy Roman Empire during the Thirty Years' War (1618-1648). He was born in Belgium and buried in Bavaria. Educated by Jesuits, as a boy he enlisted in the Spanish army and became a professional soldier. Dramatist, poet, and historian Friedrich Schiller (whose "Ode to Joy" Beethoven set to music) describes a May day in Magdeburg:

> Even a more humane general would in vain have recommended mercy to such soldiers; but Tilly never made the attempt . . . Scarcely had the savage cruelty commenced when the other gates were thrown open, and the cavalry, with the fearful hordes of the Croats, poured in upon the devoted inhabitants.
>
> Here commenced a scene of horrors for which history has no language, poetry no pencil. Neither innocent childhood, nor help-less old age; neither youth, sex, rank, nor beauty could disarm the fury of the conquerors. Wives were abused in the arms of their husbands, daughters at the feet of the parents; and the defenceless sex exposed to the double sacrifice of virtue and life . . . In a single church fifty-three women were found beheaded. The Croats amused themselves with throwing children into the flames; Pappenheim's Walloons with stabbing infants at the mother's breast. Some officers of the League, horror-struck at this dreadful scene, ventured to remind Tilly that he had it in his power to stop the carnage. *"Return in an hour,"* was his answer; *"I will see what I can do; the soldier must have some reward for his dangers and toils* [my emphasis]."[4]

A far cry from an ode to joy, the slaughter at Magdeburg was more extensive than required to achieve the strategic goal of taking the town, as a result of the soldiers taking their pleasure, or "reward," in the ensuing violence. The carnage lasted days, not hours, and only a few thousand of the 30,000 inhabitants survived.[5] The survivors were mostly women carried off to the attackers' camp.

Beyond its monumental cynicism, Schiller's story forces our attention on two actors: the leader, or principal, and the leader's agents. Count Tilly, removed from the red mist of battle, coldly times taking control in order to give the Croats and the Walloons the opportunity to do things that they want to do. His remark suggests that the agents who actually perpetrate the violations value the violations:

they want the joy of sex, violence, revenge, and loot as reward. Knowing this, leaders may use violations to both secure their power over the subject population and motivate their own agents. Schiller's Tilly does not want to be alerted to his duty or to be bothered about the interests of the civilians of Magdeburg until his men have had the opportunity to take care of their private interests. But notice too that in addition to the reward-seeking Croats and Walloons, there were "horror-struck" officers at Magdeburg. Not all are motivated by the normally forbidden pleasures, which is important as we think about preventing atrocities.

Schiller's account of Count Tilly's murderous passivity contrasts with some more sympathetic histories. C. V. Wedgwood credits one of Tilly's generals, Pappenheim, with taking the initiative to storm the city, and Tilly with rescuing a baby and trying to arrange ransom or marriages for the women that his soldiers had carried off, doubtless with something more temporary in mind.[6] More than just Tilly's historical reputation hangs on this question. Did Tilly lose control? Did he refuse control? If the latter, the perennial temptation for the principal is to claim the former, building insincerity into the relationship between principal and agent. What happened at Magdeburg highlights the critical and dynamic relationship between principal and agent, the propensity of agents to value the violation for its own sake, and the alarming potential for the commander to know and cynically manipulate this propensity.

After Magdeburg, three centuries on and further to the east, Cossack soldiers fighting against the Germans in World War I were allowed not one but two hours of Count Tilly's reward in a small Prussian town. Mikhail Sholokhov in his epic novel *And Quiet Flows the Don* writes: "The brigade commander, an estimable and honest general, had pointed with his whip to a little town lying under the hills and had told his regiment: 'Take it! For two hours the town is at your disposition. But after two hours the first man caught looting will be put up against the wall!'"[7] In fiction, at least, the estimable commander retakes control. In fact, wandering over the same territory at the close of World War II, Soviet soldiers, officers often included, behaved again with the "fury of the conquerors." As they rolled the Wehrmacht westward, the men of the Red Army raped hundreds of thousands of women, not just German women whose individual tragedies could be attributed to reprisal, but even women in areas of the Soviet Union liberated from the Germans.[8] No less furious were the Japanese soldiers who, late in 1937, exacted Count Tilly's reward in the city of Nanking. At their leisure, not for two hours nor two days, but for *six weeks,* these troops raped and killed Chinese civilians. Neither age nor sex, but only the actions of individual members of Nanking's international community provided relief. The violence was bad enough to nauseate a Nazi who heroically gave some protection for the Chinese. This rape was an alternative to the more organized rape of "comfort women," the sex slaves that the Japanese army took along with it, and at Nanking the more than willing soldiers and officers joyously engaged in violations, including beheadings, as a form of competitive sport.[9] In that city, the dead numbered in the hundreds of thousands.

In Europe, rape was an inducement for some Allied soldiers. It is reported that in the Italian campaign, the prospect of raping Italian women was the motivation of Moroccan troops under the command of the Free French officers.[10] According to one account, in one region in Italy these soldiers raped all the girls and women between ten and seventy years of age who could not escape to the mountains, and to a complaint from the Pope, the French commander General Alphonse Juin responded that the French articles of war "granted to these troops, in enemy territory, the right to rape and plunder."[11] The Pope might have referred General Juin to the Hague Convention of 1907, which prohibits plunder even after an assault and protects, in Article 46, "family honour and rights." France was a contracting party to this convention.

To bring us to the present era, in the Middle East, in 1982 in the Sabra and Shatila refugee camps on the outskirts of Beirut, Christian Phalange fighters sought the rewards of revenge and rape among the Palestinian civilians who had been corralled by Israeli armor. These fighters were permitted entry to the camps by the Israel Defense Force and Defense Minister Ariel Sharon. After the massacre, the defense minister claimed the Phalange got out of control.

From the principal's perspective, the benefits and enduring attractions of Count Tilly's reward are that it motivates troops, that it can be used as a threat to achieve objectives efficiently—namely, to gain the compliance of opponents without having to fight—and that the reward is powerful enough to support the principal's claim of vain command. The reward costs the leader no tangible resources, and he can deny responsibility. In each case described, no effort from the leader is required to get at least a substantial number of the soldiers to kill and rape. Effort is required to hold this motivation in check. Schiller's Tilly won't control. Shakespeare's Henry can't control, or that is his convenient claim. The perverse and tragic consequences that result from principal-agent logic are left out of general explanations of human rights violations, yet this logic is of a worldly significance sufficient to figure in fictional accounts and to recur from century to century, and in diverse cultures. It is also the subject of international law.

Recognizing the benefits that a commander may derive from Count Tilly's reward, international law has tried to do away with vain command. Article 3 of the Hague Convention states that a "belligerent party . . . shall be responsible for all acts committed by persons forming part of its armed forces." This responsibility was refined after World War II to hold the commander responsible, if the commander knew or should have known of atrocities committed by troops. General Tomoyuki Yamashita, a Japanese general fighting in the Philippines was tried in 1945 before the United States Military Commission in Manila, prior to Nuremberg and the Tokyo International Military Tribunal. He was charged as a war criminal and with having:

> unlawfully disregarded and failed to discharge his duty as commander to control the operations of the members of his command, permitting them to commit brutal atrocities and other high crimes against the people of the United States and of its allies and dependencies, particularly the Philippines; and he, General Tomoyuki Yamashita, thereby violated the laws of war.[12]

An enforceable legal doctrine of command responsibility was certainly centuries overdue, but in this landmark case they may have got the wrong man. General Yamashita was not present for the atrocities, did not have direct control of the naval troops largely responsible for the sack of Manila and the killings of approximately 100,000 civilians, and did not have the means to stop them.[13] Yamashita's defense team appealed the case to the U.S. Supreme Court, on due process grounds, questioning the jurisdiction of the military tribunal. The Supreme Court upheld the legality of the tribunal. Yamashita was hanged in 1946. The Yamashita case set a broad precedent for the doctrine of command responsibility with the concept that the commander "should have known" of the atrocities.

The International Criminal Tribunal for the Former Yugoslavia is employing a broad view of the doctrine. It has indicted for genocide, crimes against humanity, and violations of the laws and customs of war Radovan Karadzic, president of the Bosnian Serbs, Ratko Mladic, commander of the Bosnian Serb army, and Slobodan Milosovic, president of the Republic of Serbia. The July 1995 indictment held that they "knew or had reason to know that subordinates in detention facilities were about to kill or cause serious physical or mental harm to Bosnian Muslims and Bosnian Croats with the intent to destroy them in whole or in part, as national, ethnic or religious groups, or had done so, and failed to take necessary and reasonable measures to prevent such acts or to punish the perpetrators thereof."[14] Had the principal carried out appropriate punishments, it is some indication that the agents or "subordinates" really had been out of control, although, as we shall see, scapegoats can receive the most severe treatment from opportunistic principals. The tribunal's indictment describes the genocidal motive of the leadership and holds them responsible for the actions of their subordinates who carried out the genocidal killing. A genocidal (Inquisitorial) principal is less likely to view the control of agents and their reward-seeking behavior as a problem requiring his attention and correction.

As the indictment made clear, the responsibility of the leader is not limited to active and direct participation in the atrocities. Rather, Milosovic's indictment refers "to participation in a joint criminal enterprise as a co-perpetrator."[15] Among the individuals listed in this "criminal enterprise" was Zeljko Raznatovic, also known as Arkan. Arkan led a paramilitary group known as Arkan's Tigers, and Milosovic is held responsible for the actions of Arkan's paramilitaries over whom he "exercised effective control or substantial influence." The indictment is crystal clear in the principle it holds forth: "A superior is responsible for the criminal acts of his subordinates if he knew or had reason to know that his subordinates were about to commit such acts or had done so, and the superior failed to take the necessary and reasonable measures to prevent such acts or to punish the perpetrators." The doctrine of command responsibility attempts to structure incentives for principals to take proper control of their agents, countering the temptations of Count Tilly's reward by holding them criminally accountable when their troops commit atrocities. It basically seeks to affect the calculations of the leader by raising the possibility of punishment by the international community so that he or she will energetically take control of subordinates.

THE STANDARD EXPLANATION
OF HUMAN RIGHTS VIOLATIONS AND ITS LIMITATIONS

In international law individuals choose to commit violations, but social scientists have tended to focus on the economic, political, and cultural context of violations and have largely ignored individual choice and responsibility. Scholars are making good progress in mapping the general social, political, and economic landscape of countries where governments have committed widespread violence against people under their control.[16] There is some evidence that economic well-being leads to fewer human rights violations. It is plausible that economic scarcity creates social and political tension, and so increases the likelihood of rebellion and reactive government repression. The very poor with little material stake in the present may feel they have little to lose in rebellion. What is surprising is that the statistical evidence for the relationship between general poverty and violent governments is not more consistent, as relatively wealthy societies may deteriorate into violent conflict while poorer societies may be less violent than one would have thought. An analysis of human rights violations in India compared violations across the Indian states.[17] While some very poor states such as Bihar had a high number of violations as measured by deaths or rapes in custody, there were some relatively prosperous states with quite poor human rights records.

Economic relationships with other countries may have implications for human rights. Some scholars, like Noam Chomsky and Edward Herman, claim that the economic ties between rich and poor countries encourage violations in the effort to control unrest and emerging labor movements and to create favorable investment conditions.[18] But there is mixed evidence for such a relationship. Generally, trade with and investment from capitalist countries do not seem to encourage more repressive activities on the part of governments interested in establishing a safe and compliant investment environment. Nor so far is there clear evidence of the reverse: that trade and investment by themselves encourage good behavior from governments. China, representing a good proportion of all humankind, illustrates how a country can expand the volume of imports and exports and sustain repression.

Important political divisions can form along historical, cultural, ethnic, as well as economic class lines. Cultural and ethnic divisions result from a combination of physical, linguistic, cultural, and political differences. President Clinton's analysis of the war in Bosnia was, "Their enmities go back 500 years, some would say almost a thousand years."[19] We have little hesitation in attributing political violence and atrocities to "ancient hatreds," from the Middle East to Northern Ireland, although the ancients are not around to face the music. Of all the awful things the ancients did, they seem to return to haunt only some quite geographically circumscribed territories. Which is to say that the ancients do not do the violence, although the violence is done in their name and at the behest of groups, associations, and the political parties that political leaders create, who then revive, manipulate, and intensify cultural divisions and hatred.

The type of regime makes a difference, at least when representative democracies are contrasted with nondemocracies. Democracy is a collection of institutions, norms, and practices. It commonly includes universal suffrage, political participation, competition, regular and fair elections, elected representatives, decisions made by majorities, press freedom, and judicial independence. The widely held beliefs of the political community are part of contemporary conceptions of democracy. Emphasis is placed on social capital that is produced by trust and cooperation fostered by networks of participatory clubs and associations. Political scientist Robert Putnam's highly regarded work on Italy and the United States shows that a common set of electoral institutions can produce great variation in policy performance and the quality of governance.[20] He argues that widely shared values have a critical impact on the quality and efficiency of the delivery of public policies, and he contrasts the low social capital of the more authoritarian and repressive south of Italy with the high social capital of the more participatory north.

Drawing broad distinctions among types of nondemocracies—totalitarian, authoritarian, or military—has not added much to our understanding of human rights violations. Jeane Kirkpatrick, President Ronald Reagan's ambassador to the United Nations, was wrong to assert that at that time totalitarian (left wing) regimes were significantly worse than authoritarian regimes (right wing). She made this argument in an influential article titled "Dictatorships and Double Standards": "Only intellectual fashion and the tyranny of Right/Left thinking prevent intelligent men of good will from perceiving the facts that traditional authoritarian governments are less repressive than revolutionary autocracies, that they are more susceptible of liberalization, and that they are more compatible with U.S. interests."[21] Actually, when she was making this argument, totalitarian regimes tended to be heavier users of imprisonment as a means of political control than authoritarian regimes, yet they did not place significantly greater reliance on torture and killing.[22] And with the fall of the Berlin Wall, these regimes proved contagiously susceptible to liberalization.

In general, leaders in democracies seem to behave well. There are a number of mechanisms at work. Elected leaders are periodically accountable to their electorate. They are accountable for their policy decisions and for the implementation of policy by bureaucratic agencies. Winning reelection is an inducement for elected leaders to pay attention to the quality of policy being delivered in their name and to address principal-agent problems. Some evidence suggests that democracies experience lower levels of corruption, and by extension one would expect that to apply to the greediness of Count Tilly's reward and the particular form of corruption represented by the entrepreneurial violence of the agents. Further, democracies by definition permit freedom of association, and it is likely that groups and associations composed of concerned citizens will form to monitor government use of violence, providing an independent flow of information about agents' activities that compensates for the agents' information advantages, a flow that is public and therefore is difficult for the principal to ignore.

But even leaders in democracies will decide to violate the rights of their citizens under certain conditions. Where opponents use violence, democratic leaders may well choose to do the same. Their choice to respond violently to the threat is facilitated when their opponents can be isolated geographically or culturally. British governments deployed their fiercest soldiers on their own citizens in Northern Ireland without much in the way of electoral repercussions or damage to the government's general level of public support. India, the world's largest democracy, successfully and violently crushed Sikh threats in the Punjab in the 1980s and early 1990s, and seeks the same outcome in other northern border states, including predominantly Muslim Kashmir. And Israel, as we shall see, offers a diagnostic opportunity for investigating the repressive choices of democratic leaders, with public or external pressure occasionally acting as a restraint when the violence gets too visibly disproportionate to the tactics employed by the opposition.

Democratic institutions may inhibit the domestic use of violence on citizens by generally rewarding politicians who exercise restraint, but these institutions provide fewer guarantees abroad. Democratic governments, even if they behave relatively well at home, have supported governments that commit extreme violations and atrocities in other countries, and they have equipped and trained the security forces that do the violence. In December 1981, in El Salvador the American-trained Atlacatl brigade was reported to be responsible for the massacre of hundreds of civilians.[23] The government soldiers raped the young women and decapitated the men.[24] Soldiers machine-gunned the children through the windows of the convent in which they were detained. Some of the men were tortured, and three were stabbed to death. Operation Rescate ("Rescue") finished up in El Mozote with the Atlacatl brigade torching the village. The United States embassy in El Salvador doubted the evidence of a massacre. However, the *New York Times* and the *Washington Post* carried reports of the massacre on January 27, 1982. Even in the face of evidence of widespread human rights violations, President Reagan was saying in 1982 that, "the Government of El Salvador is making concerted and significant effort to comply with internationally recognized human rights."[25] As political scientist William Stanley says, "the strategy of mass murder enjoyed the tacit support of the highest levels of the U.S. government. The Reagan administration made its interests clear early on."[26] In fiscal year 1982, the government of El Salvador received 27 percent of all United States bilateral aid. Any doubts that an atrocity took place were eliminated in 1992, when bone remains of at least 143 people, 131 under 12 years of age, were uncovered in the convent. There was no evidence to suggest that these young children, whose average age was estimated at six years, were combatants. With the help of four forensic anthropologists from Argentina, a total of over 500 victims were identified from El Mozote and some nearby villages. The soldiers fired bullets made for the U.S. government at Lake City, Missouri, and used M-16 rifles.[27]

Both international and civil war increase the likelihood of human rights violations. While the relationship between war and violations is almost definitional, what is of interest here is that wars vary in the scale of tragedy associated with them. Even civil wars vary substantially in their consequences for human rights. Not all wars, nor all poor countries, have governments with equal propensities to commit violence. That being the case, we need to shift our thinking about the problem of human rights violations from a characteristic associated with an environment—be it war, level of development, or regime type—to one of choice and an outcome of decision making. There are explanatory, moral, and practical reasons for moving beyond the environment of atrocity constructed by the standard explanation, toward a focus on how and why leaders and their agents choose to commit atrocities.

Do not misunderstand: it is useful to know whether colonial experience, abject poverty, or demographic conditions come with government killing and torture. But this sort of scholarship has said little about the leaders themselves, about motives, about orders, about the bureaucrats that implement the orders, and about the targets of the orders, that is, the victims. Human rights violations are a policy—not the inhuman outcome of impersonal, slow-shifting economic, historical, international, or sociological substructures—and policies require policy makers.[28]An individual, Oliver Cromwell, made the decision to refuse mercy at Drogheda on September 11, 1649, and to offer it to most of his captives on the following day and most everywhere else that he fought, although his economic, political, and international environment was not conducive to good conduct. He fought amid the superstitions of a pre-industrial age and in a nondemocratic society, with no international bill of human rights. He draws our attention to the motives behind policies and the bastards involved, and not just the conditions under which violations tend to occur. While historians offer motives for particular tragedies, we need to think about them in a general way to account for violations recurring across cultures, through history, in diverse places, and often involving large numbers of perpetrators.

Attributing cause to culture or underlying levels of development is morally unsatisfactory and does not provide much policy leverage. To have accountability and to offer an analysis that has the best chance of being useful, the focus must be on individual decision makers and their officials and agents. If we treat the suffering of civil war like the suffering of a natural disaster, then we meet this calamity with resignation. If we think about violence as a decision, as does Schiller, then we can share Schiller's outrage. On a practical level, slowly shifting forces are not easy to manipulate. On the other hand, we can influence individuals. To influence choices, we foster core beliefs in the boy scouts or madrasses. To tighten control between principal and agents, we design institutions, structure incentives, and improve management practices.

COMPARING THREE CIVIL WARS

Rather than generalize about environmental factors and their influence on violations, my approach is to select some specific episodes to illustrate the motives at work. The focus on leaders, their management practices, and the process of making repressive policy in a situation that makes the option of choosing repression easy does not mean that these leaders had to choose repression. This was a choice and responsibility. In this way the book includes the players in addition to the set and the backdrop. After all, average per capita income, the absence of elections, or even an ancient's hatred have "disappeared" or tortured no one. Absent actors, motives, and victims, this standard explanation is Hamlet not only without the Danish prince, but without his dead father (his spectral motivation) and his mad girlfriend—no curtains for her father, either.

In examining the motives behind human rights violations, three civil wars—the English, the Russian, and the Israeli—provide the mass of illustrative evidence for the argument. Civil wars are moments when who rules is in doubt, when power is uncertain, and when societies are at an unusually high risk of the violence extending to prisoners and to civilians. Pithily expressed: "this is the law of civil war—slaughter all those wounded fighting against you." So wrote a Communist official of the Extraordinary Commission for Combating Counter-Revolution, Sabotage and Speculation (Cheka) on the eastern front in an article for *Izvestia* that appeared on August 23, 1918, entitled "There Are No Written Laws of Civil War."[29] Civil wars are intense conflicts. Institutional uncertainty or even meltdown, high stakes, and a society mobilized for violence increase the probability of human rights violations, although the very worst violations do not necessarily occur at these times.

Civil wars, then, represent historical markers for the likely presence of human rights violations on a horrific scale. Generally, civil wars suggest a common motive for atrocities; they provide the means to commit atrocities, and they generate the opportunities for atrocities. Civil war suggests a severe threat to government survival. Governments act on a common desire to retain power or office. Depending on the severity of the threat posed by the opposition, governments escalate violations, perhaps beginning with censoring press freedom, and building to internment and on to summary execution—or from rubber bullets to real bullets—in order to counter threats to their power. Civil war signals that the level of threat is severe, provoking severe repression. Further, during civil war the government has the means to commit atrocities as it mobilizes and arms large numbers of soldiers, police, and citizens. Finally, civil wars present governments with the best opportunities to lower the political costs of violations; violations can be obscured by the general fog of war, admitted but shrugged off with a *"c'est la guerre"* necessity, or framed as an unfortunate but appropriate response to the more bloodthirsty opposition. By comparing civil wars, one can approximate similar levels of threat to the regime, similar resources to commit violations, and a common relaxation of norms of behavior that occurs in war. Yet, here is the puzzle: despite these common features that can be linked plausibly to widespread violence, civil wars actually have had quite different consequences for the affected populations, measured by the scale and severity of the tragedy. François Furet, in his history of the French Revolution, puts it this way: "Situations of extreme national peril do not invariably bring a people to revolutionary Terror."[30] In the case of the French Revolution, he argues that the worst violence did not correspond to the greatest threats to the revolutionary regime. Heads rolled on Robespierre's convictions about the friends and enemies of the people, not as a result of military circumstances.

In defending Red Terror, Trotsky and Lenin suggested that the Russian Civil War should be viewed as a historical successor to earlier civil wars, like the English and the American wars. The Bolsheviks invited this comparison in response to criticism of their terror. Some historians adopt a similar position that terror and barbaric behavior, "the furies," are a necessary part of revolution and civil war: "if war is hell, then civil war belongs to hell's deepest and most infernal regions."[31] There is a strong correlation between civil wars and violations. Yet, as we shall see, the assumption that civil wars are uniformly marked by extensive human rights violations is wrong. And Trotsky was wrong; there is no "law of civil war," as his comrade put it. The Russian Civil War saw widespread torture and killing. Atrocities in the English Civil War were few. Both these wars were serious wars. They saw extensive conflict, attracted outside intervention, upended the existing monarchical structure of government, and stretched over a period of years. The toll of the Israeli War, which also attracted outside intervention, is substantially closer to the English Civil War than to the Russian.

What accounts for the differences in human rights violations across these civil wars? This book proposes a general answer located in the motives of the principals and in the institutionally shaped incentives offered the soldiers, the members of the security forces, and other irregular participants to the killing.

Human rights entail individuals being accorded rights stemming from their common humanity. These rights override individuals' random subjection to particular systems of government and law. In this book the concept of human rights violations has the everyday usage of killing, torture, and arbitrary detention and imprisonment by governments; in other words, the violations of rights that are sometimes referred to as negative or first generation rights. Governments continue to do these things, but nowadays there is broad acceptance that they represent violations of human rights, which has led to an international bill of human rights. While preceded by conventions on war crimes, the major impetus for this legal regime was World War II. At Nuremberg, in an international court, the United States, Russia, France, and Britain put human rights before national rights and sovereignty, although the behavior of their own troops was not open to scrutiny. With the concept of crimes against humanity, an idea first used by the British to condemn the Turks for their annihilation of Armenian communities in Turkey in 1915,[32] they extended the scope of international law from how governments treated prisoners and populations of combatants, to how they treated any population, including their own people, and no matter what national law prevailed. The United Nations Charter, the Universal Declaration of Human Rights, and subsequent and more specific international conventions outlawing genocide and torture and protecting civil, political, economic, and social rights provide the framework for an international regime protecting individual rights. There is now a code of conduct for governments, and there is also an incremental, uneven effort in seeing that the code is observed.

Philosophers have labored from hours before the dawn of these legal developments to construct a plausible theoretical foundation for these rights. They have sought a single moral argument that refutes the utilitarian contention that the good of the greatest number might have to come before the rights of the individual; they also sought an argument that tears down religious or cultural barriers to common standards of decent behavior and treatment. Whatever the sophistication of moral concern, nowadays the fact that most states in the international system have signed on to human rights conventions makes them accountable—even if at the dusk of this contractual activity philosophers have yet to complete the work of providing security for humanity from any particular government or custom.

This book adds a temporal as well as spatial dimension to the task of explaining human rights violations and their prevention. To understand why government officials violate human rights, it helps to examine events that occurred prior to the construction of the international legal regime, and even when sacking cities fell within the rules of war. The historical focus complicates accountability and condemnation, but it helps the process of sorting out the factors and mechanisms at work and clarifying the record of violence. Actually, condemnation is not quite the retroactive iniquity or "trick upon the dead" that it seems. True it is that the rules of war have changed and our value frameworks evolve. International contracts to improve ourselves are relatively recent, and nowadays we more readily question race or gender as a legitimate basis for discrimination. But as Theodor Meron says: "Henry's proscriptions, as described by Shakespeare, against molesting the inhabitants and taking any goods from them without proper payment were quite advanced for their era and are comparable to nineteenth- and twentieth-century texts such as the Lieber Rules, the Oxford Manual and the Hague Regulations."[33] Schiller, two hundred years ago, was as horrified as we are by the conduct of those Walloons and the Croats in the seventeenth century who exacted the double sacrifice of virtue and life. It is arguably as much a trick upon the dead to hold them unfit or too morally immature for judgment.

As the record of violence inevitably becomes part of the contemporary political assessment and debate, and the truth is difficult to disentangle, the passage of time clears some of the confusion and misinformation, although it may require the passage of considerable amounts of time. With the Israeli war, the release of recently declassified documents is assisting historians' understanding of events in 1948. The Russian Civil War is in sharper relief with the end of the cold war. The English Civil War remains contested, but nonetheless historians have achieved some consensus on the incidence of atrocities, even in Ireland. Since the English Civil War induced the birth of social contract thinking, which matured into arguments for limited government, there is something fitting in returning to this war in an effort to understand human rights violations.

In addition to uncovering the record on violations, the passage of significant blocks of political time between the cases also helps with the explanation. Any selection of cases is open to question and is an inevitably crude and inconclusive investigative technique. But there is fault to be found with the statistical measures used in large scale comparisons, and across this time span and amid all the changes in domestic and international institutions, the laws of war, the technology of repression, communications, and culture, we can search for the elements of an enduring and general explanation.

One civil war usually provides a career for a historian. This comparison of three civil wars is made manageable by approaching the subject with a narrow concentration on the atrocities and the motives of the political leaders involved. Visiting some of the more dramatic and heavily researched junctions in history with a new set of questions directed at the actors and institutions involved allows the insights derived from contemporary work on organizations, public policy, and policy implementation centering on the motivations of policy makers and those who implement policy to shed light on an important and pervasive problem.

A book about civil wars is spoiled for choice. Seventeenth-century England, Ireland, and Scotland, early-twentieth-century Russia, and Israel and Palestine are in some senses defining wars. The first represents a clash between institutions—monarchy and parliament—and over religious differences, the second between ideologies, and the third between national and religious groups. The English and Russian wars are very familiar to historians and the accumulated descriptions make them accessible to those without specialized knowledge of the periods. Israel's conflicts are contemporary, copiously documented, and of the utmost political significance, as the state has been central to international politics since its founding.

The wars themselves had different consequences for losers and bystanders, producing differences in what we are trying to understand. The English Civil War had relatively few atrocities, the Arab-Israeli conflicts more, and the Russian Civil War was murderous. In each case there was a severe external threat to government, which suggests that this factor alone does not account for the different levels of atrocities. There is great variation in other factors that are of particular interest: principals, agents, and accountability. Cromwell had his army, but Lenin's government created both an army and a specialized bureaucracy of repression. Lenin blamed history and foreign intervention rather than God, but also tried to distance himself from some of the more notorious actions of his government's security forces, notably the midnight murders of the Romanovs. Despite a tendency to credit God for both his disasters and his triumphs, Cromwell was willing to be held accountable for his actions. He led at Drogheda and wrote an explanation of his actions to the speaker of the House of Commons. And he led in the daylight execution of Charles I and wrote his name on the warrant. In Israel there has been a mixed record of deception and admission, including occasional prosecution. Taking responsibility has an obvious bearing for any effort at historical judgment, but as we shall see, it also provides useful information for evaluating explanations about the use of political violence.

In thinking about the relationship between the leader and the agents, I am treating violence as a policy and introducing what we know about policy formation and implementation to this problem area. Do the insights of scholars of bureaucratic behavior help us understand the actions of the men and women who staffed the Bolsheviks' Cheka?[34] Considering individuals as members of organizations helps us to understand sustained behavior, whether appalling or benign. The hope is that by examining the principal's goals, institutional incentives, and political control, we can get a better understanding of history's bastards. The Israelis began with divisions among their armed forces. The Russian Civil War achieved a high degree of specialization in the task of repression. The English Civil War put the principal on site with his agents, minimizing "authority leakage." Cromwell fought at Drogheda, led the assault on the fortifications, and ordered no quarter. Lenin was no soldier but killed far more.

The book begins with what we know about human rights violations and the argument that I am trying to develop. Taking as a starting point leaders, their perceptions of the world they were making, and the details of their institutional relationships, rather than the macro-institutional, cultural, or structural environment, is both an analytically and morally more satisfactory approach to this subject matter. The approach, however, is not biographical and psychological, where the search might be for the deeply personal source of inferiority, narcissism, or paranoia, perhaps in childhood experience or in a Richard III type of physical deformity. The motives at the core of the argument are general, involving interests and passions. How else is it possible to explain the large numbers of ordinary people who commit these violations? Violators are rational and selfish (power and pleasure) or are carriers of programmatic intolerance cultured in the political discourse of the day and transmitted by organizations. Victims either directly threaten the leaders' interests or are caught on the wrong side of the political argument, and satisfy the agents' desires. Chapter two describes the theoretical argument and contrasts it with the conventional approach to political violence and what others have said about the topic.

Chapter three discusses the Israel and Palestine case. Contrary to those who compare Jenin with Auschwitz, it is Machiavelli's motive and strategic calculation that is at work on the West Bank. The pattern of political violence in that part of the world and even some of the specific policy choices, such as punishing relatives and destroying their houses, go back not to the Nazis, nor even to ancient desert hatreds, but to the period of the Mandate when the British implemented such measures. One cannot help thinking that Machiavelli would have found as much to admire in Israel as he did in ancient Rome or in the Swiss cantons and German cities of his day. A core doctrine for Machiavelli was that military strength supports political strength, that good arms are the foundation of good laws. But even in those places that he admired, he observed the danger in prolonged military success and careers, and in territorial expansion, with corruption inevitably setting in.[35] In addition to long military and political careers, and even Israeli "Caesars," the great victory of the Six-Day War came with the administration of territorial conquests that would tax and divide both Israeli society and its military. From the birth of the state of Israel, under the overarching goal of safeguarding power against internal and external threats, the relationship of principal to agent is an important component of an explanation of the level and type of violence.

If this chapter on Israel and Palestine provides support for violence as a rational choice, the next chapters show what such a bare framework leaves unexplained. Chapter four examines atrocities in the Russian Civil War. Here the conventional wisdom fails to represent just how bad things were, as Count Tilly and the Grand Inquisitor combined to raise killing, imprisonment, torture, and rape above any rational threat-management strategy. The Russian chapter illustrates how the inquisitorial principal's beliefs and institutional choices led to very different outcomes in human rights violations.

Chapter five discusses the evidence for atrocities in the English Civil War. Power is only part of the narrative. This chapter shows how Cromwell's commitments and the institutions he set up generally worked to reduce political violence below what an opportunist, single-mindedly worried about threats to power, would have unleashed. In the English Civil War, violations were generally below the level expected, that is, below what a prudent prince who was worried about his personal power and position would have chosen. Even in Ireland, the violations were not at the levels that would be expected from dogmatic intolerance, given both the means of violence at hand and the absence of external constraints (informal norms of behavior, the United Nations, international human rights advocacy networks, bilateral foreign policy initiatives)[36] on actions that modern commentators find so important in the analysis of political violence. While around him and before him the Thirty Years' War raged, and while other Protestant commanders in Ireland created mayhem, Cromwell repudiated and resisted the leader's motivations for violations and denied his soldiers theirs. He repudiated the Grand Inquisitor and, while in some circumstances acted harshly, he generally resisted raising violations to the levels that Machiavelli would have advised. In stark contrast to Lenin, he cared sufficiently to monitor and regulate the behavior of his agents. This chapter illustrates the difference that leadership committed to toleration, even in civil war circumstances, can make. The worst atrocities are best understood from a principal-agent framework and as examples of the normally tight control breaking down.

Chapter six tries to anticipate some of the criticisms of the argument and puts it in the context of what we already know about this sort of violence. The purpose is to show the wide range of bastard theory and the three inexhaustible horsemen of political violence, Machiavelli, the Grand Inquisitor, and Count Tilly. It aims also to draw the implications for inhibiting atrocities.

This is a book that uses historical evidence to push and probe explanations of why governments behave badly. The goal is to lodge the argument in the historical material in a way that is plausible to the historian and at the same time theoretically interesting to the social scientist, while holding the attention of the general reader. Nobody may end up satisfied, but the key must lie in finding a way between losing the social science in the narrative and offending historical sensibilities in the effort to generalize.

The Principals and the Agents of Political Violence

Naming a principal and agent in the use of violence recognizes that there are actors involved and awakens us to the possibility of multiple motives at work. Principal-agent scholars examine lines of control between the two and have made important progress in specifying an underlying logic. But the control issue cannot be all there is to understanding policies. We not only want to understand the independent contributions of the agents, we also want to understand the overall policy of violence. Consequently, we must examine the motives of the principals as well as the motives of the agents, and how they interact.

For the principal, my starting place is Machiavelli's motive of protecting power and the rationality of using violence in response to threats from opponents. Yet, Machiavelli's motive illuminates only part of the darker side of government, as at times the violence expands far beyond a level suggested by a rational strategy to deal with opponents. In contrast to Machiavelli, the Grand Inquisitor is ideologically intolerant and committed to violence, irrespective of threats to his power. For the Inquisitor, specific forms and targets of violence flow from a more abstract set of core beliefs and commitments that serve to divide humanity into categories—religious, racial, ethnic, class, or other. For either the Inquisitor or Machiavelli, the agents who implement the violence may raise the level of violence beyond the principal's expectation. In order to understand atrocities, I begin with power, add commitments, and then incorporate the institutional working out of the tension between the agents' falling to temptation and seeking gratification and the leader's understanding of his command responsibility.[1] Following this path, I explore the motives of Machiavelli, the Grand Inquisitor, and Count Tilly and his men, for it is they who design and carry out violations.

MACHIAVELLI AND THE RATIONALITY OF VIOLENCE

Machiavelli argued that a political leader uses "cruelty" properly if he or she does so all at once, rather than in an ongoing way, and for "self-preservation."[2] Machiavelli puts leadership at the center of his political theory. He argues that leadership has to work with a realistic view of how human beings actually are, not how we want them to be, in order to be successful. They actually are selfish, ambitious, untrustworthy, and danger-avoiding, and a leader must work with these characteristics to gain and hold power. But if you do this, if you think the worst of others and act accordingly, you have no guarantee of success. Machiavelli recognizes that in the political world chance causes a significant share of what happens, and one is often up against other, more powerful actors. In the Italy of his day, events are sometimes beyond a leader's control, and the goddess Fortuna, the pope in Rome, or the French may intervene.

Even an effective leader like Machiavelli's contemporary Cesare Borgia may succumb to these forces. While Cesare achieved much, Machiavelli argues that he was undone by chance, in particular by the death of his own father, the pope; by his own untimely illness; and by the papal election of Julius II, who opposed Cesare. This bad luck interrupted a very promising career, as Cesare was a leader who understood the lowness of humans in their relations with each other and who possessed Machiavelli's idea of the "right stuff," what he subversively called *virtù*. A leader with *virtù,* who is active, martial, cunning, and not inhibited by ordinary standards of behavior, can accomplish a great deal: "Fortune is a woman, and the man who wants to hold her down must beat and bully her. We see that she yields more often to men of this stripe than to those who come coldly toward her. Like a woman, too, she is always a friend of the young, because they are less timid, more brutal, and take charge of her more recklessly."[3] Such energetic and brutal leadership is crucially important to political relationships and the fate of nations. Machiavelli concludes *The Prince* with an "exhortation to restore Italy to liberty," that is, as an Italian nationalist, hoping for the right man, one with *virtù* who, when the situation calls, can be sufficiently uncharitable, untrustworthy, and inhumane to liberate Italy from foreign power and "the cruel insolence of the barbarians."[4] An experienced Florentine diplomat, he wrote during the political turmoil of early sixteenth-century Tuscany, with warring city states, with foreign armies in the hills, and when the pope actually did field battalions. Having recently been dismissed and having personally suffered torture, he knew what he was writing about.

Getting and holding onto political power is the motive. Cruelty and treachery can be used well and therefore add to power and security, as when Cesare strangled his rivals at Sinigaglia. In December 1502, with the seasonally correct promise of peace and friendship, Cesare lured Vitellozzo Vitelli and Oliverotto da Fermo among others into negotiations in this city on the Adriatic and murdered them on New Year's Eve. The others survived a couple of weeks into January. Machiavelli, actually in Sinigaglia on a mission for Florence, describes in his diplomatic correspondence the capture of these rivals and speculates that "there won't be one of them alive tomorrow morning."[5] At two o'clock that morning, Machiavelli met with a cheerful Cesare, who joked about what had happened, and whose sang-froid made a lasting impression on his visitor.

Cruelty can also be used less well, or suboptimally, thereby contributing to a leader's insecurity. Machiavelli warns against persistent and continuous violations that keep injuries fresh in the minds of the people and undermine a leader's hold on power. Machiavelli says that the prince who does not use cruelty well, "either through fearfulness or bad advice, must always keep his knife in hand, and he can never count on his subjects."[6] Machiavelli had a notion of some ideal amount of brutality, and by exceeding or not attaining this quantity the prince endangers his hold on power. Cruelty is not pursued for any other goals or for its own sake, and it must be handled carefully as it carries potential costs in political support. Adverse effects on public opinion must be minimized. Consequently, Machiavelli recommends imitating Cesare Borgia's delegation of cruelty to his Spanish minister, Remirro de Orco. Cesare's wisdom was to be at one remove from the cruelty so others could take the blame. When violence had served its purpose and responsibility had to be taken, Cesare shielded himself from political damage by activating his dramatic version of the doctrine of individual ministerial responsibility:

> He determined to make plain that whatever cruelty had occurred had come, not from him, but from the brutal character of the minister. Taking a proper occasion, therefore, he had him placed on the public square of Cesena one morning, in two pieces, with a piece of wood beside him and a bloody knife. The ferocity of this scene left the people at once stunned and satisfied.[7]

The importance of the public square, public opinion, and a scapegoat is clear. The rational leader appears moral and acts the opposite. Machiavelli's psychology of selfishness, his identification of one goal—the power motive, his emphasis on efficiency by using the instruments at hand unrestrained by ordinary morals, his understanding that there is a point at which further use of repression can make the user worse off, his disinterest in the intrinsic joys of repression, and his focus on individual decision making continue to offer profound insight to contemporary rational-choice explanations of politics.

From this perspective, violations are a means of political control, implemented after weighing the impact on domestic and foreign economic and political support, a policy alternative to accommodation, one that is adjusted to the level of threat represented by the opposition.[8] "Opposition threat" has several important components: size, organization, goals, and tactics. Opposition likely coalesces around ethnic, ideological, economic, or religious divisions that characterize a society, and the larger the size and resources of the opposition, the greater the level of threat. For government leaders, the type and variety of organizations that are used by the opposition, whether cultural associations, political parties, or military organizations, imply different levels of threat. The goals of the opposition are more or less threatening to the government. Secessionist or revolutionary demands resolutely pursued are usually more intimidating and more difficult for a government to accommodate than demands for lower taxes. The tactics of the opposition and whether or not they are willing to resort to violence are a component of threat and influence the ease with which governments, particularly democratic governments, turn to violence in return. The government's choice of violence is dependent on the tactical choices of the opposition. War, whether civil or international, presents the supreme threat to national survival and so is expected to stimulate extraordinary levels of intervention and repression against suspect populations.

In trying to understand political action, Machiavelli's focus on power as an overriding and generalizable motive is a useful initial simplification that explains an important component of political violence, as well as all sorts of other political behavior. The leader or principal, whether democratic or authoritarian, responds to the level of threat presented by the opposition and makes predictable decisions unconstrained by moral compunction. Democracies experience lower incidences of human rights violations in part because political demands are generally managed, addressed, and diffused prior to reaching regime-endangering levels, and because there is a parliamentary road as well as a revolutionary road for the opposition to take. Machiavelli's view provides a useful starting place and has influenced the contemporary rational-choice accounts. So, violations are a form of government intervention to protect power and are a choice made by a ruler in response to the threat presented by the opposition, increasing as the level of threat increases. The level of violations is generally consistent with the threat posed and the tactics used by the opposition. Less plausibly, it is argued that the violations themselves provide no intrinsic value or utility: as two scholars have written, "The act of repressing itself provides no utility."[9] Power is the principal's goal, repression is a tool to achieve and maintain power, ratcheting up and down to counter the opposition's moves, and the agents faithfully carry out the principal's orders.

As Machiavelli pointed out, there are costs as well as benefits to repression. Internally, there may be costs in domestic support, and ill-used repression may stimulate further opposition. Externally, and this was not much of a concern in Machiavelli's day, the international system may levy costs, for example, by stopping foreign aid or imposing sanctions if violence and human rights violations are considered disproportionate.

That human rights violations and political violence may represent a rational strategy to deal with political opposition is the Machiavellian part of the story. But commitments and beliefs can interfere with the smooth and uniform operation of this strategy. Machiavelli recognized that some princes have principles, that they might be charitable or tolerant, and they may make the "mistake" of allowing these commitments to guide their decisions. Machiavelli sought to persuade the prince to respond rationally to those who seek to displace him. He is infamous for the wisdom of being cruel rather than kind, and feared rather than loved. He was concerned that the commitments and core beliefs of the leader may keep the violence below the level prudent for political survival. At the same time, Machiavelli counseled against prolonged and overly harsh repression, when the leader may boost violations far above what is necessary to stay in office even to the extent of jeopardizing personal power and continuance in office. Machiavelli recognized that a leader's use of violence may well deviate from the amount that is rational.

THE GRAND INQUISITOR

Political leaders are motivated by both interest and passion: by the desire for political support and power and because they have arguments, ideas, and agendas they wish to convert to policy. While they violate rights to get and protect power, they may also violate rights programmatically, in accordance with an ideological program or agenda, which was the Grand Inquisitor's motive for his bonfires.

In Seville, also in the sixteenth century, a different type of principal supervised the ritual burning of heretics. These Spanish fires, sanctioned by the pope at the request of the monarchs Ferdinand and

Isabella and set by the Inquisition under the control of Tomás de Torquemada, purified Catholic Spain of Jews, Protestants, Muslims, witches, and others. Whatever the reality of the Grand Inquisitor's actions, his spirit and motivation is given dramatic voice by Dostoevsky in his novel *The Brothers Karamazov*. Not power but the public interest is his motivation. In the Grand Inquisitor's view, ordinary people are not capable of meeting Christ's elitist standards of resisting temptation and freely choosing the good life. The Inquisitor, like Machiavelli, has arrived at a low view of humanity. But he differs from Machiavelli in that he puts what he considers the public interest before any selfish pursuit of power. As the Inquisitor sees it, through "miracle, mystery, and authority," he selflessly satisfies humanity's need for community in obedient belief. Freedom of choice, reason, and uncertainty are much too large a burden for ordinary human beings to put up with. They have an existential need for the group therapy and comfort of a simple dogma, providing a sense of purpose that they can share and something to live for, and that sorts the insiders from the outsiders, the faithful from the heretics and infidels. The Inquisitor has a view of history: "And this need for communality of worship is the chief torment of each man individually, and of mankind as a whole, from the beginning of the ages. In the cause of universal worship, they have destroyed each other with the sword. They have made gods and called upon each other: 'Abandon your gods and come and worship ours, otherwise death to you and your gods!' And so it will be until the end of the world, even when all gods have disappeared from the earth: they will still fall down before idols."[10] Dostoevsky's gloom contrasts with the Enlightenment's optimism about the progressive triumph of reason over "the hands of superstition which have for so long been reddened with gore,"[11] and registers the philosophical mood swing from the eighteenth to the nineteenth century. The Inquisitor suggests that collective intolerance is the human condition and that it will outlast Catholicism. People are irrational, fickle, social rather than individualistic, and aggressive, and they are not making progress.

Sigmund Freud seems to pick up on the Inquisitor's argument in *Civilization and Its Discontents*. He claims that having a group in common permits both collective self-love and fellowship, and an outlet for the inclination to aggression in the form of hostility to nonmembers. He describes national groups (the Spanish and the Portuguese, the English and the Scots), religious groups (Jews and Christians), and political groups (communists and the bourgeoisie), serving this function. These groups, even where the actual differences between them are slight, provide a means to bond together considerable numbers of people while identifying others as targets for the group's aggression. He expects "the narcissism of minor differences," his memorable phrase for this collective love and hate that is organized around objectively trivial differences, to continue differentiating.[12] Here is the psychofoundation for civil wars, which tend to be between groups within a quite similar geographical and cultural context.

Experience has confirmed the narcissism of minor differences with a vengeance. Experiments, referred to as "minimal group" experiments, reveal that people, without cultural or social ties or connections, are willing to identify with each other on the flimsiest of pretexts. For example, experimenters showed people a picture with dots on it and assigned them to either a group that counted too many dots or a group that counted too few. Similarly, researchers used artistic preference as the categorizer, dividing people into groups based on whether they preferred Klee to Kandinsky. When the subjects were told they shared this or that preference or characteristic with others, and without knowing anything else about the others in their group, they willingly discriminated on such a flimsy basis, sharing benefits with their group but not with the others.[13] As Paul Sniderman and his associates say, "if so superficial and contrived a distinction can elicit invidious differences, it is only possible to imagine the destructive power of deeper and societally reinforced bases of distinction."[14] The Inquisitor recognizes this need to belong and categorize, and he channels the unquenchable inclination to aggression.

Dostoevsky's Inquisitor loves humanity, not power. While the Inquisitor's "armies and Jesuits"—his agents in our terms—may well have filthy motives to do with money and power, he—the principal— is long-sufferingly aware of the needs and the limitations of people. The Inquisitor is a man of ninety, near death, and beyond selfishness. He provides dogma for the feeble-minded.

The Inquisitor's system and his use of violence rest on an intolerant political and religious agenda. His commitment to an agenda, not to office, starts and sustains him on the path of cathartic repression. The Inquisitor holds and protects his office because of his devotion to his argument about the human need for authority and community and what makes a livable world for ordinary people. His belief system identifies the outsiders and why they need to be eliminated. The Inquisitor expects that in time other agendas or idols will replace religious categories as the irrational motivation and justification for official killing, and produce a new list of victims. The Inquisitor's programmatic intolerance is historically renewable in religious, national, or political forms and implies a commitment to violence.

In historical Spain, the Inquisition's grand and elaborately staged auto-da-fé, or act of faith, was a ceremonial burning of victims held in the largest square. The first auto-da-fé was held in Seville in 1481, with six victims. The Inquisition's foremost and first victims were Jews, then Muslims, Lutherans and other Protestants (foreign and domestic), witches, and sexual offenders. Seville saw about seven hundred burnt between 1481 and 1489.[15] The church established Inquisitions in other major cities, on the Canary Islands, and Mallorca. One prisoner in Saragossa, incarcerated for an assassination of an inquisitor at prayer in the cathedral, contrived to kill himself by swallowing the shards of a broken lamp. He avoided the auto-da-fé.[16] Strangling prior to burning was a mercy for those who, in an act of desperation, accepted Jesus.

In *The Origins of the Inquisition in Fifteenth Century Spain*, B. Netanyahu presents evidence to show that by the time the Inquisition got underway, the targeted group was already assimilated religiously— that is, that they were already accepting Jesus. As a consequence of late-fourteenth-century and early-fifteenth-century persecutions, the great majority of Spanish Jews had already converted to Christianity. So he poses the intriguing question, "why did the Inquisition attack so fiercely a community that was essentially Christian?"[17] Their conversion and assimilation suggests that they represented little in the way of a real threat to other Spaniards. As Netanyahu points out, they could convert beliefs but not their ethnicity. It was race theory, the "otherness" of the converted Jews (or Marranos) as a people, that caused the Inquisition: "a theory based on racism appeared whose three major articles of faith were: the existence of a conspiracy to seize the government of Spain; the ongoing contamination of the blood of Spanish people; and the need to do away with these frightful dangers through a genocidal solution."[18] Netanyahu draws the parallel with Nazi race theory aimed at the elimination of Jews.

Thus violations result from core commitments and from an attachment to power. But of the two motives, the Inquisitor's is the more unrestrained. Love of humanity rather than "lust of power," in the Inquisitor's words, is likely to lead to the greater tragedy. As Machiavelli recognized, the rational leader motivated by power and without other conviction, realizes that there is a point at which cruelty becomes too costly, provoking opposition. This type of leader's awareness of costs as well as threats suggests that the violence can be regulated, even from abroad should the international society take an interest. If it cares, it imposes or threatens to impose costs. In the history of ideas, Machiavelli's celebration of reasons of state, his amoral policy recommendations, and his admiration for Cesare Borgia are sometimes thought to explain Hitler, but the latter is the Inquisitor's responsibility, now with a continental grasp, high-speed communications, and a vision of the German People or Völk for inspiration (what separates the Holocaust from other human catastrophes is not the willingness of executioners). The Inquisitor pursues his program with little regard to costs, sanctions, or shame, implying that in order to stop him, external force is the only effective response of a caring international community. Hitler pursued his irrational program even at the expense of what was necessary to maintain power, notoriously putting the supply of victims for his death camps over the supply of his armies in the field.

It follows that if commitments can cause these violent acts even to the point of self-destruction, moral commitments of the sort that Machiavelli was worried about could also lower violations, below the amount that is reasonable to safeguard personal power and welfare. It is unrealistic to view all principals as equally unencumbered morally or normatively, or with an equal capacity to choose freely among policy instruments (as if they are all Cesare Borgia). In responding to what opponents are doing, leaders vary in their moral willingness to use repression. They are more or less willing to employ different types of repression, even if they evaluate the level of threat similarly. As

Machiavelli recognized, the values that they bring to their office are critical: "Any man who tries to be good all the time is bound to come to ruin among the great number who are not good. Hence a prince who wants to keep his post must learn how not to be good . . . "[19] According to Machiavelli, leaders must swallow moral qualms about the use of imprisonment, exile, torture, and strangling in order to control the political situation, otherwise he or she will not last all that long.

We are accustomed to spacing the set of beliefs and values held by a politician or a political party on an ideological line stretching from the left to the right. The placement of a political leader on this line has a variety of connotations, but at the least it implies degrees of commitment to equality and belief about the appropriate scope of government. Moving leftward indicates an increasing commitment to equality and an increasing belief in the effectiveness of government. The conventional left-right spacing does not, however, locate the normative factor that is of most relevance to government propensities to employ violence, propensities that can vary tremendously within the left or the right. Here the focus is on the quotient of tolerance rather than equality contained in a political program or agenda. Tolerance is a willingness to live with others even if they do or say things that we find objectionable. It requires patience and forbearance, if not respect.[20] If we arranged tolerance positions vertically and not horizontally, classical liberals and parliamentary socialists or social democrats generally have the highest degree of tolerance, while Bolsheviks, fascists, and racists have the lowest. The antithesis of the Grand Inquisitor is the leader who refuses to violate citizens' human rights, even if such a refusal endangers his or her hold on power.

COMBINING STRATEGY AND COMMITMENT

We can represent the contrasting positions of Machiavelli and the Grand Inquisitor visually. Figure 2.1 simplifies the first stage of the argument by showing the amount of violations supplied at different threat levels by the variously motivated principals. Figure 2.1 includes the committed antithesis of the Inquisitor: the leader committed to tolerance rather than intolerance and opposed to the use of violence.

Fig. 2.1. Machiavelli and the Inquisitor

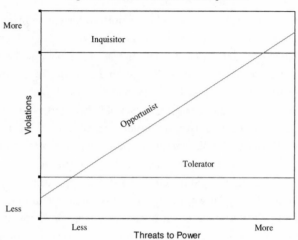

Machiavelli is worried about the antithesis, and any foolish attachment to values that might inhibit the use of cruelty and violence as the most efficient means of securing power. Figure 2.1 combines strategy and choice with commitments and beliefs and draws out the consequences for human rights violations.

Leaders are perfect opportunists or perfect ideologues. The Machiavellian opportunist or power maximizer strategically ratchets up the cruelty as threats to power increase. The choice of violations is adjusted to the opponents' actions. But the opportunist must also calculate the violations-inhibiting influences of other actors, including the domestic economic elite and the international system, with the result that there may be lower levels of violations at higher threat levels than would be anticipated from the simple linear relationship depicted in figure 2.1.[21] In some political communities, most obviously democracies, the general public may voice objections to their government's use of violence. After some level, the costs of adding further violations increase sharply, as the brutality mounts and these other actors are assumed to begin noticing and caring.

The Grand Inquisitor is just inelastically cruel. He seeks out "heretics" however submissive or assimilated. He pursues those who choose flight as well as those who fight. Violations are not an instrument to achieve or protect power, but a policy consequence of the Inquisitor's core values. His choice of violations is not strategic, not dependent on what others do, but a consequence of his beliefs and disproportionate to any threat. Figure 2.1 also depicts the normative antithesis of the Inquisitor, the Tolerator. He or she is inelastically tolerant, and would rather resign than silence one opinion.[22] The Tolerator prefers no power to power achieved through the instrument of violations. The degree of commitment to toleration is central to the analysis of repression rather than the usual focus in political analysis on left-right issues and the degree of commitment to equality, markets, or government intervention.

Although policy makers are as unlikely to be perfect opportunists as markets are unlikely to be perfect markets, nonetheless figure 2.1 is a useful abstraction for understanding the real world. There is a tension between the simplicity of the conceptual scheme and the complications of actual political events. Machiavellian leaders, subscribing to the basic motivation of using violence to respond to threats to power, will be more or less sensitive to the costs of the use of violence, and more or less willing to use the nastiest strategy. The choice of strategy or the slope of Machiavelli's line in figure 2.1. is dependent on perceptions of the opposition, their motivations and capabilities, as well as perceptions about political costs and moral sensibility. Analysis and ideology contribute to how leaders evaluate threats. To draw on an example from international relations, contrast the differing evaluations by presidents Jimmy Carter and Ronald Reagan of the external threat to American national security presented by the Soviet Union. President Carter placed human rights very publicly on his foreign policy agenda and did not evaluate the Soviet threat as serious enough to warrant the sort of military and surrogate military actions, and Star Wars defense that characterized the 1980s. President Reagan was influenced by Jeane Kirkpatrick's distinction between authoritarian and totalitarian regimes as he prioritized the Soviet threat and shifted human rights to a lower position on his policy agenda.

The Tolerator is depicted as inelastically tolerant in figure 2.1. Never mind how threatening opponents become and irrespective of what others do, the Tolerator holds firm. In real politics what is more likely is the policy maker willing to make pragmatic compromises in certain circumstances (faceless judges, juryless courts, imprisonment without trial) in order to safeguard the larger commitment to toleration. Cromwell was generally of this type. On the other hand, Lenin's agenda of having a proper revolution in order to create a brand new society pushed him to violations beyond what adverse circumstances and foreign intervention necessitated in order to hold on to power. As he defined a revolution, it had to be violent. There is also the Insincere Inquisitor, which in Dostoevsky's account is the crux of Alyosha's accusation as Ivan's story unfolds. The Insincere Inquisitor is the opportunist who recognizes the personal gain and the reservoir of political support to be tapped by dogmatic appeals to collective identities. Alyosha accuses the Grand Inquisitor of manipulating believers and being motivated by power. As his brother tells the story, filthy motives belong to the Inquisitor's agents, to the Jesuits, but not to the principal, who is suffering rather than enjoying power. As Alyosha's questions indicate, sincerity is very difficult to ascertain with any confidence. But opportunistic shifts in beliefs are suggestive, as, for example, when a former Communist like Milosovic discovers Greater Serbia.

AGENTS AND CONTROLLING
THE BUREAUCRACY OF REPRESSION

The agents who carry out the repression need to know why they are doing what they are doing. Policies require justification or a rationale, possibly including a precipitating event or incident that justifies a violent response. Even the Inquisitor, like other policy makers, will seize policy windows or opportunities for action.[23] Or rather than wait for the right moment to come along, he or she may open policy windows. For example, in Rwanda the shooting down of the president's plane immediately preceded the genocidal massacre of Tutsis. With the Hutu president's death, Hutu army officers took control, tuned the dial to "Radio Genocide" and broadcast that Tutsis were cockroaches. The incident did not require such actions; the officers created an opportunity to carry out the planned atrocity. This is not unusual: even with very high concentrations of political power, political leaders still carefully prepare the ground for policy actions. Consider the burning of the Reichstag in 1933, which the Nazis blamed on a Dutch communist in order to launch repression, or the murder of Sergei Kirov in 1934, which Stalin used to unleash terror.

Leaders justify policies and provide excuses for their actions to motivate their agents and perpetrators. They need to persuade their agents, with argument and evidence, that what they are doing is appropriate or even necessary. The Scottish philosopher David Hume put it this way:

> Nothing appears more surprising to those who consider human affairs with a philosophical eye than the easiness with which the many are governed by the few, and the implicit submission with which men resign their own sentiments and passions to those of their rulers. When we inquire by what means this wonder is effected, we shall find that, as force is always on the side of the governed, the governors have nothing to support them but opinion. It is, therefore, on opinion only that government is founded, and this maxim extends to the most despotic and most military governments as well as to the most free and most popular. The soldan of Egypt or the emperor of Rome might drive his harmless subjects like brute beasts against their sentiments and inclination. But he must, at least, have led his *mamalukes* or *praetorian bands*, like men, by their opinion.[24]

As Hume points out, there must be at least a core group of agents that believes in the leader. But even they are not necessarily loyal. The problem is that the mamalukes (the Circassian soldiers of the Egyptians), the praetorian band (the bodyguard of the Roman emperor), or the Sikhs troops (the bodyguard of the Indian prime minister), like men, may develop additional motivations and may act on the basis of those motivations. As Hume explained, the governors' means of control over these men may be precarious.

Interestingly, both Machiavelli and the Grand Inquisitor explicitly recognize the principal-agent problem, doubting the motives of mercenaries and Jesuits respectively. The city-state of Florence relied on mercenaries to do its fighting, and Machiavelli scoffed at the idea that these agents, motivated by money, would fight effectively in defense of the city. In *The Brothers Karamazov*, Ivan concedes to Alyosha that the Inquisitor's men may have "filthy motives," but defends his Inquisitor: "suppose that one among all those who desire only material and filthy lucre, that one of them, at least, is like my old Inquisitor . . . who still loved mankind all his life."[25] Government officials or agents bring their own private motivations to the task of implementing repression, and the assumption of the scholars cited earlier that the "the act of repressing itself provides no utility" is unhelpfully unrealistic. Agents may well value the violation itself and may well be out of control. It is also possible that some agents, like some leaders, may balk at the violence. Recall that featured in Schiller's dramatic description of the soldiers seeking Count Tilly's reward during the sack of Magdeburg, there are not just reward seekers and reward givers. There are "horror-struck" officers too. Not all soldiers are motivated by Tilly's reward; some may adhere to a notion of "combat morality." There was the Italian officer who refused to hand over Jews to the Germans and said that it was "incompatible with the honor of the Italian Army."[26] In a more recent situation, some soldiers refused to obey Lieutenant William Calley and protected rather than shot and raped civilians at the village of My Lai in the Vietnam War. While recognizing that agents bring with them their own motivations and that the weight of selfish motivations careers downhill to excessive violence, one must also acknowledge those whose independence may lead to lower levels of violence. The stress and strain of war on the fiber of society likely exposes raw selfishness, yet it also provides instances of the best commitments. There is an honor guard as well as Count Tilly's reward seekers. Both this honor guard and the reward seekers may present challenges to the principal's control.

In trying to understand the use of violence, it is plausible to assume that the degree of political control that leaders exercise over their bureaucracies, including the army and police, will vary across time and political systems. Government intervention, whether it is aimed at people or pollution, presents some common problems of translating intention to implementation. The management practices of principals and the manner in which institutions structure the incentives for the individuals charged with carrying out the policy are all-important in translating the leader's intention into implemented policy.

There are two well-known problems for the principal: the problem of goal variance, where agents have goals independent of those of the principal, and the problem of information asymmetry, where agents have an information advantage over the principal. These problems may lead to the delivery of a product or a service in a manner or in an amount different from what is ordered by the leaders. Conventionally, agents are expected to want to avoid work, or shirk, or even to have a negative impact on productivity through sabotage, and to use their information advantage for these ends.[27] Agents seek what is in their own best interest, which may conflict with what the principal seeks.

Economists have lifted concepts from the insurance industry to clarify the informational difficulties or deficits that the principal faces. The principal is unlikely to know all the actions of the agents, just as an insurance company is unlikely to know all the actions of the insured. The term "moral hazard" is used to refer to the unobserved actions of the agents, and originally to the incautious practices or even arson of those with fire insurance.[28] The term "adverse selection" refers to the character and habits of those who become agents, and originally to the types of individuals who most value health insurance, the bad risks who have knowledge of their poor state of health and their likelihood of needing care and treatment. Lazy or vicious agents seek their own selfish goals by using their superior knowledge of the policy issue and the opportunity to hide actions from the principal. Clearly, the information inequality in the principal-agent relationship is compounded by the number of agents and the number of principals involved. Multiple agents make specific actions more difficult to attribute to individuals. If agents are responsible to more than one principal, lines of control are disputed, and agent discretion likely increases.[29] Multiple principals are more of an issue in the Arab-Israeli conflict than in the English and Russian civil wars in which Cromwell and Lenin asserted control.

I argue that these information problems are likely to be particularly acute in the area of repression, as a consequence of the unique and immediate temptations and rewards, and of the particular difficulty of getting good information about violence. Service in the agencies of repression is likely to be attractive to those with preferences and talents for violence, the "rough and hard of heart." These problems also take on an unusual shape in the administration of violence. With violence, the information problem is compounded by the incentives for cynical manipulation by principals and the high cost of auditing or monitoring repressive agencies. In general, principals are expected to want more information, but in the administration of violence they may find ignorance concerning the actions of their agents convenient. In general, agents may be expected to shirk, but in the administration of violence they may be tempted to overwork for the fun of it.

Irrespective of the goals of the principal, police or security forces may use the authority and means of violence that goes with their offices for private reward. They may use repression to satisfy their own desires for revenge or gratification. A squad of British troops handed four Jewish Haganah soldiers to an Arab lynch mob in February 1948, in revenge for the murder of some of their mates by Jewish irregulars.[30] Agents may have private, entrepreneurial, or even corrupt motivations for repression that can be at variance with the leader's goals. When there is low esprit de corps, when "zealots" ascetically committed to the cause do not run the bureau, and when pay is poor, agents may be tempted to use their positions for personal gain. For example, the problem of corruption is endemic in India's "awful prisons." While India faces significant opposition threat, particularly in the northern border states, police corruption tends to be a very significant factor in the overall level of government violence. The threat of brutality and torture is used on those in custody to extort bribes: "as with many other Indian officials they feel driven to supplement their incomes. The detainees themselves, or their families, are threatened with torture if they do not bribe the police—a threat that can only work if those who do not pay, or cannot pay, are in fact tortured."[31] The ubiquity of the temptation of corruption in bureaucracies is illustrated by its appearance even where one would least expect to find it. The Inquisition in Spain, where one would expect superior levels of zealotry, encountered the problem of corruption. Two inquisitors in Cordoba were removed in succession for extortion at the turn of the sixteenth century. In contrast, Tomás de Torquemada, the first inquisitor general and confessor to Ferdinand and Isabella, who is estimated to have burnt some 2,000 heretics, is described as an "austere Dominican friar."[32] While we know, thanks to the political philosopher Isaiah Berlin, that all good things do not go together,[33] it may be that many bad things do; and that high levels of corruption in a country likely extends to police and security agencies, whose employees will use the authority and means of violence that go with their offices for private reward, and in doing so visit their own additional share of suffering and pain on the citizens they supposedly protect.

These self-interested agents are difficult to control because of the direct temptations that they face, and because they will attempt to preserve their information advantages over the principal. Officials will know more than their leaders about the repression, and they exploit this information advantage in order to realize their own goals. They may exaggerate the dimensions of the security problem that the principal faces, and they may disguise the amount of violence that they are using.

In contrast to other bureaucracies in which the private motivation of agents is to shirk and is clearly an opposing goal to that of the principal, in the area of political violence the principal may also derive additional benefits from the "extra work" put in by reward-seeking agents. Their self-indulgent acts may have positive externalities for the principal; there may be beneficial political, tactical, or even justice consequences stemming from the agents' killing and looting. There are layers of incentives at work. The visible outer layer is the agents' vengeful, monetary, or sexual incentives. Underneath lies the inner layer of the "won't control principal's" tactical incentive to avoid responsibility for otherwise useful violence, to reward and encourage the troops, and to terrorize, expel, or annihilate the opposition.

In some circumstances, politically astute principals will not want to know of the violence, will prefer and will even manufacture distance between themselves and their agents—as did Cesare Borgia with his Spanish minister, or, more subtly, as did Henry II, who dispatched his twelfth-century death squad to Canterbury Cathedral by obliquely posing a question, "Who will rid me of this meddlesome priest?" rather than by issuing a direct command. Thomas Becket, once Henry had appointed him archbishop of Canterbury, put his loyalty to the church before his friendship and loyalty to the king. Henry's initiative-taking four French knights delivered their response to the threat to the monarch's power, the "meddlesome priest," and then bore the ignominy of their murderous act. This political technique of the principal, in which he knows but finds it convenient to conceal his knowledge, in which he is in control but pretends not to be, might be called artificial information asymmetry.

This artificial asymmetry may be achieved organizationally by manipulating motivated paramilitaries or death squads. Here the leader is off the line of accountability and passively refuses to assert control and close down these apparently independent agents, at least as long as their self-interested activities serve his strategic goals. In other circumstances, leaders may, like Count Tilly, ignore information in order to reward the troops or be simply indifferent to the excesses and corruption associated with this sort of government intervention. Lenin was generally a leader of this type, indifferent to the personally motivated excesses committed along the way as long as the organizations achieved his goals, and often he was not too concerned about disguising his indifference.

Looting and killing may be attractive to both agent and principal. Loot may be divided, even with the commander, according to more or less institutionalized systems of distributing prize money, and it may be used to support the soldiers in the field. Most immediately, killing captives may sate revenge, provide enjoyment, and remove a security threat or a strain on resources. At Agincourt, Shakespeare's Henry V offers a tactical concern about a fresh French charge for his having ordered the slaughter of prisoners. At Nanking, a tactical explanation offered for the recreational killing of Chinese prisoners of war was food shortages.[34] Deeper still than the tactical incentives of deniability, resources, troop motivation, and terror, both killing and looting may be deemed proportionate penalties and even fitted with some crude conception of reprisal and punishment. Shakespeare's Henry V also offers reprisal for the French killing of the boys with the baggage train as rationale for his own brutal decision.

Rape is the most indefensibly private and indivisibly agent-enjoyed of Count Tilly's rewards, yet even in this act we may glimpse an underlying layer of tactical benefits. It may be used as a way of motivating troops, and it carries the tactical externalities associated with a fearful reputation. Avoiding rape may encourage capitulation, as at Harfleur, although there is likely a crosscutting effect to the degree that it is thought inevitable or likely because it then may motivate stiffer resistance. This activity is least likely to be rooted in the innermost justice-enhancing layer of incentives. While killing and property penalties may have some notional relationship to punishment, rape is generally inflicted on those who never were combatants and contaminates the pain of punishment with the lust of the punisher. Even the early philosophers and legal theorists of war separate rape from other actions, observing its selfish, nonstrategic, and singularly dishonorable characteristics. Albenco Gentili (1552-1608) states that "to violate the honour of women will always be held to be unjust."[35] Hugo Grotius (1583-1645), in the *Law of War and Peace*, argues that rapists should be punished for moral and practical considerations, explicitly noting the enjoyment for the agent as well as the pain of the victim, and that rape neither enhances security nor represents punishment: "not only the injury but the unrestrained lust of the act; also, the fact that such acts do not contribute to safety or to punishment, and should consequently not go unpunished in war any more than in peace."[36] History's Henry V forbade rape, and Shakespeare's Henry V is morally aware, to say the least, of what he is threatening. He blames the "hot and forcing violation" on his wicked soldiers with "conscience wide as hell," as well as on the town's defiance. Of Count Tilly's rewards, the incidence of rape represents an important measure of the severity of the principal-agent problem. While Grotius underestimates the "safety-enhancing" calculations of commanders using rape as a reward, and Red Army men may have had some finely balanced scale of justice in mind as they forced themselves on the women of Berlin, rape is somewhat less easily linked to the inner layers of incentives. When three U.S. nuns and a lay worker were raped and killed by Salvadoran soldiers in 1980, the truth commission that investigated this incident reported the killing but not the rape of the women, separating the actions of agents from principals. They did not doubt that rape had occurred, but "since there was no evidence that the rapes resulted from orders from above, and it was assumed that the rapes were the initiative of the soldiers, they were not considered to be politically motivated acts and were therefore left out of the report."[37] War, conflict, or just a uniform provide an opportunity for perpetrators to commit and get away with this more private crime. Of Count Tilly's rewards, looting is less serious; confusion and the anxious fingers of soldiers and security forces may sometimes contribute to the deaths of prisoners and civilians; but rape is not done by mistake. So we can fit rape to principal-agent logic, use it as an indicator of the principal-agent problem in security forces, and read it as follows: while the presence of rape may result from either a principal who won't control or a principal who can't control, the absence of rape reveals a principal in control.

Principal-agent problems are general to organizations. The principal's key response to control problems is to overcome the information gap with recruitment procedures that expose the "bad risks" and offset adverse selection, and by setting up auditing or monitoring mechanisms to reduce the likelihood of moral hazard. But the repressive principal may have particular reasons for not wanting to know too much and actually facilitate adverse selection and the consequent moral hazard. In any case, security forces are particularly hard to monitor. Because of the general public sensitivity to the use of political violence and human rights violations, and the understandable disinclination of leaders or principals to audit security agencies (fearing that what they uncover might inconveniently reflect on them), problems of information asymmetry may be particularly severe in this policy area. Not only do agents tend to exploit their information advantages, principals may exploit the advantage of ignorance. Further, if, as scholars have pointed out, the cost of auditing varies across policy areas,[38] then it is likely to be highest with respect to violence.

Generally, the establishment and activity of government agencies stimulates the reactive formation of advocacy and interest groups, which can help to oversee the work of the agencies. The costs of auditing can be reduced or transferred when private organizations assume monitoring roles. It is important to apply these insights to government use of violence. Even assuming a "sincere" principal, agents have particular advantages over principals in this policy area and are particularly prone to being out of control. There may be higher costs to establishing even private auditing mechanisms over agencies engaged in human rights violations. The organized groups or interests that are important to reducing the costs of monitoring and political control may be absent in the area of human rights violations. Those that care most about the use of violence may encounter an intimidating environment and severe problems in organizing collective action and gathering information about repression. Think of the specific targeting of human rights workers and journalists by repressive regimes and the rare and heroic example of the mothers and grandmothers of the disappeared in Argentina, who under the military regimes of the late 1970s and early 1980s publicly stood up for their missing children. In turn, repressive agencies can claim to be working for the most vital interest of the state, national security and survival, which makes those who raise questions concerning these agencies' activities highly vulnerable to counterquestions about their own loyalties.

Democratic societies, which by definition include rights to free organization and association and a free and critical media, are most likely to develop self-regulating mechanisms for auditing the bureaucracies of repression. This invisible hand for the political marketplace provides a causal foundation for the standard explanation's finding of a correlation between lower human rights violations and democracies. An example of this sort of organization would be B'Tselem, the major human rights organization in Israel that monitors government use of violence. In some cases, established democracies and transitional democracies have formed specific and relatively independent auditing agencies. There are national human rights commissions in India and Mexico, both of which were set up in the early 1990s and that have developed some reputation for independence—although in the Indian case the commission is specifically designed to receive far better information on police conduct than on the activities of military and paramilitary forces that operate against the separatist organizations on the northern frontiers. In the absence of domestic response and monitoring, transnational groups and international organizations (such as the United Nations) fulfill the monitoring role in this policy area as best they can.

Additionally, under conditions of democracy, even the cynical principal may be forced to know and to correct the information asymmetry. As a result of public outrage, inquiries or commissions may be formed to investigate violence. The very fear of the loss of public support that forces the principal to know tends to bias the inquiry. The principal will view the inquiry as an exercise in "symbolic politics,"[39] with the only significant consequence being its effect on public opinion. The best outcome in Machiavelli's phrase is "a stunned and satisfied public." The principal will attempt to control the appointment and terms of the inquiry within the parameters that maintaining public confidence allows. Lord Chief Justice Widgery's controversial inquiry into Bloody Sunday, 1972, when British troops in Northern Ireland fired on an unarmed crowd and killed 14 people, is an example of such an inquiry. The controversial findings of the Widgery inquiry are now being reexamined by a multinational inquiry, chaired by Lord Saville. Set up by the Blair government as a concession within the peace process, its panel includes an Australian and a Canadian.

Agents are probably more often inert than innovative, and resist efforts to reform. They tend to share a viewpoint that it is wrong to decide policy anew in response to each situation. Past policy responses hang heavily over the present. Set a policy course, and then time will build in expectations on both the agents' and the community's part, contributing to the legitimacy of a policy response and the development of community standards in a policy area. Earlier administrations using similar techniques may provide precedent and authority. The bias of policy precedent applies no less to the area of repression and adds to the difficulties of a leader who attempts to alter direction.

Policy habits, however, may be good as well as bad, leading to restraint in the use of violence. In related work, principal-agent scholars have begun to recognize the importance of "culture" and "softer" instruments of control. Discovering that not all agents make the most of their opportunities to shirk, they even refer to "principled agents" and emphasize the importance of careful recruitment and the inculcation of professional values.[40] Economist Anthony Downs, although focusing on the selfish motives of agents, entertains the possibility that such motives as professional pride and commitment to the public interest are important to some officials.[41] As principals can operate on the basis of commitment, so can agents. Tilly's horror-struck officers belong in this category of agent. And one of the reasons that Oliver Cromwell was able to keep violations low across the battlefields of the British Isles was that he followed a recruitment strategy of finding soldiers of conscience rather than of fortune. By attending to the motives of the agents in addition to those of the principals, and to the effort and intelligence that the principal invests in controlling the agents, it is possible to bring the policy area of repression more in line with the progress made in policy research generally.

MOTIVATED MALIGNANCY:
MACHIAVELLI, THE GRAND INQUISITOR, AND COUNT TILLY

Iago's poisonous actions in Shakespeare's *Othello* were once described as the outcome of a motiveless malignancy. But generally atrocities have motives, even general motives. Without becoming too absorbed in either the personalities of a particular case (such as a Milosovic or Hitler) and the elements that make the case *sui generis* or the environmental context (such as poverty, colonialism, ethnic antagonism in Rwanda, and the lack of democracy), it is possible to use these general motives—that is, selfish reward seeking, the rational pursuit of power, and the logic of an intolerant political argument—to organize this type of violence. Human beings are uninventive when it comes to reasons for atrocity, and, as Dostoevsky points out, even the intolerant political argument is formulaic.

Faced with criminal violence, detectives attempt to isolate means, motive, and opportunity. In civil wars, the means and the opportunity for widespread violence against noncombatants are present, but the levels of atrocity vary dramatically. This variation draws our attention to motives. Leaders use violence to gain support from followers while attacking challengers, or they use violence to destroy those on the wrong side of the ideological argument. Agents take advantage of slack or cynical leadership to seek self-gratification of one sort or another.

This explanation aims at the heart of the dark decisions, rather than at the context captured in the standard explanation of human rights violations. It does, however, provide structure for what we know from that approach. The most consistent statistical findings connect civil and international war with higher propensities to violate human rights, and democratic political arrangements with lower propensities to violate human rights. What is it about democracy that reduces the likelihood of violations? It is not so much the presence of a set of rights written in a constitution. Depending on the circumstances, political leaders in democracies are capable of almost anything. Written guarantees, including international written guarantees and conventions, depend on the good will of the current political leadership. Democracies with competitive elections are, however, generally biased against the more extreme and divisive ideologies. Assuming political parties want to win elections, they tend to moderate their platforms to maximize the political support they receive from increasingly less-committed voters. More active citizens and the growth of private monitoring organizations enhance officials' fear of accountability in democracies. In this way, democratic institutions may sift out the more divisive, intolerant, and cleavage-enhancing ideologies, the Inquisitor's motive, and generally reward moderation rather than extremism with government office.

More commonly, it is Machiavelli's motive that is operating when democracies engage in violence and atrocity. But the public, when not convinced that government violence is appropriate to the threat, may well restrain democratic leaders (by demonstrating, forming monitoring associations, and demanding judicial inquiries), or the leader may have some notion of community's standards and anticipate the public's reaction and exercise self-restraint. The extremely democratic Weimar Republic, which facilitated the rise of extremist parties, is an obvious and important exception to this process, and even stable democracies fail from time to time to protect the rights of ethnic or racial minorities, or unpopular groups. As democracies include oppositions in the channels of representation, offering the parliamentary as well as the revolutionary road, there is less incentive for the opposition to take more threatening action, and defeated political parties have the hope of future opportunities to regain power.

Warfare increases violations. It puts the principal-agent issue front and center. Machiavelli was acutely aware of the principal and agent problem in warfare, specifically the problem of goal variance. He found risible the efforts of the mercenary armies that Italian princes employed. Mercenaries are a liability when not in the field because they may oppress those they are hired to protect, and they are useless during war. As he said: "they have no other passions or incentives to hold the field, except their desire for a bit of money, and that is not enough to make them die for you."[42] Machiavelli was preoccupied with the threats to government and to national survival posed by war. In addition to leadership without scruple, he wanted a citizen army rather than a mercenary army to face what Rome or France deployed to those Tuscan hills.

In the following discussion of the specific civil wars, the focus is on the bastards involved, the motivations of the leaders and their agents. It is a general argument resting on motivations not bound by any particular period or place; nevertheless particular periods and places provide useful illustrations of the dynamics at work. We start with Israel as an example of Machiavelli's motive. The Russian Civil War belongs to the Inquisitor, and his antithesis, the Tolerator, influences the English Civil War. All three principals are confronted with self-motivated agents. For the Tolerator, these agents present a problem. The Tolerator seeks to control and restrain the behavior of the agents. The Inquisitor puts up with the filthy motives of the agents so long as they contribute to the wider mission. For the Machiavellian principal, these self-motivated agents present an opportunity as much as a problem. He is acutely aware of their selfishness and is alert to the chance to manipulate it for tactical advantage, as the atrocities marking the birth and maturation of the state of Israel illustrate.

THREE

The Arab-Israeli 20,000-Day War

Out of this nettle danger we pluck this flower safety.
—William Shakespeare, *Henry IV, Part 1* Act 2, Scene 3

Israel has a citizen army, as Machiavelli advised, and only in recent years has its motivation become a little ragged. From the beginning, Israel also has had leaders willing to follow Machiavelli's advice to use violence strategically in managing opponents who threaten not just government survival but national survival. Israeli violence and deception may be seen as calibrated to maintain and to hold on to power in a context not entirely dissimilar to Italy in Niccolò Machiavelli's day. Subterfuge, assassination, and atrocity are the order of the day, borders seem easily permeable, and violent conflict may trip external intervention. Machiavelli knew that the field of play for the *virtù* of Cesare, great leader that he was, was circumscribed by the ultramontane strategic ambitions of France and the superpowers of his day. Israel's leaders too have been realists rather than idealists, more or less single-mindedly concerned about threats to national survival and safe borders, while keeping the United States well disposed. Broad agreement on the goal does not mean that leaders' tactics are interchangeable in responding to internal and external threats to those borders. They are not equally unencumbered in their willingness to use force.

MACHIAVELLI IN THE PROMISED LAND

Machiavelli attributes about half of what happens in the political world to the goddess Fortuna. In Israel and the occupied territories, however, it is tempting to attribute almost all of what happens, going back to the founding of the state and before, to a community of faith in the bitch goddess of retribution, Nemesis. The British general Bernard Montgomery, who was in Palestine in 1939 to provide a military solution to the violent Arab reaction to Jewish settlement, commented that "the Jew murders the Arab and the Arabs murder the Jew. This is what is going on in Palestine now. And it will go on for the next 50 years in all probability."[1] He was right. But in contrast to Fortuna, our sacrifices to Nemesis are potentially within our control. We can calculate the amount of retribution, and it is true to say that the Israeli response has never been mechanically dependent on violently responding to threat. It has mattered which "prince" makes the decisions about how violently to respond to the threat and how well he has controlled the agents.

Israeli leaders divide between activists and moderates, labels for their broad differences of opinion about the use of violence. Activists more readily choose violence and a "nasty" strategy.[2] They believe that a nicer strategy will be seen as weakness, leaving their own forces and people exposed to further attack. Activists are less sensitive to the costs and counterproductive consequences of violence until the violence reaches high levels. Moderates have moral inhibitions about the use of violence and are more sensitive to its costs. Although real politics do not present perfect types, the Israeli moderates, while fixed on the goal of securing power, feel the gravitational pull of the Tolerator to bring down the level of violence (see fig. 2.1). In defending their position to activists in the cabinet, moderates are less likely to emphasize their moral inhibitions and more likely to emphasize the prudential or cost side of the argument, as this is the language activists will understand. In recent years, the division between activists and moderates has been represented in the competition among political parties in Israel, especially between the more moderate Labor Party and the more activist Likud Party. For the earlier period, the moderate-activist divide was the most serious internal rift in the governing Mapai Party. Prior to that, during the British Mandate (the name for the colonial administration that replaced the Ottoman Empire after the First World War), the division took organizational form in various defense and paramilitary forces. The hyperactivist paramilitary forces were to provide future Likud leaders, including prime ministers Begin and Shamir. Ariel Sharon had a somewhat more orthodox military background.

Yaacov Bar-Siman-Tov describes the differences between activists and moderates in a classic account of the contrasting positions of Prime Minister David Ben-Gurion and Foreign Minister Moshe Sharett in the 1950s: "Ben-Gurion espoused a hawkish and activist approach to the Arab-Israeli conflict, while minimizing the prominence of external constraints . . . Sharett represented a doveish and more restrained line of conflict management, attributing great importance to foreign powers, the United Nations and international public opinion."[3] Bar-Siman-Tov nicely points outs the way the differences between the domestic political leaders filter the influence of even the international elements of the political world.

David Ben-Gurion, a Polish Jew who landed in the Palestine of the Ottoman Empire in 1906, whose political roots lay in the Jewish labor movement of the British Mandate, was Israel's first prime minister and the dominant politician of the postindependence period. He had a brutally realist commitment to establishing the new state and a willingness to make what are by ordinary standards immoral choices for the sake of national security. His activist views, seared in his political consciousness by the experience of European Jews in the Holocaust, guided his choices and actions throughout his period in government.

As the pogroms in Eastern Europe had given impetus to earlier settlement of Palestine, the Holocaust gave urgency to the formation of a Jewish state, and it provides insight into Ben-Gurion's thinking. The fundamental lesson he drew from this disaster was the overriding importance of the national security goal. These are Ben Gurion's words: "it was the final injunction of the inarticulate six million, the victims of Nazism whose very murder was a ringing cry for Israel to rise, to be strong and prosperous, to safeguard her peace and security, and to prevent such a disaster from ever again overwhelming the

Jewish people."[4] Ben-Gurion put the safety of the nascent state above all else; over the need to help potential victims of the Holocaust and, as philosopher Hannah Arendt suggested in her account of Adolf Eichmann's trial, even over justice for the perpetrators of the Holocaust. After *Kristallnacht* in 1938, when the Nazis openly attacked German Jews, their businesses, and their places of worship, Ben-Gurion posed himself a hypothetical choice: "If I knew that it was possible to save all the children in Germany by transporting them to England, but only half of them by transporting them to Palestine, I would choose the second—because we face not only the reckoning of those children, but the historical reckoning of the Jewish people."[5] Ben-Gurion's choice is hypothetical, but his clarity of thought about the priority of national security is as shocking as an episode from *The Prince.*

Ben-Gurion's government caught, tried, and hanged Adolf Eichmann, the Nazi official who arranged the transportation of Jews to the death camps. According to Arendt, the purpose of the trial was to instruct young Israelis and other Jews about the importance of Israel: "The trial was supposed to show them what it meant to live among non-Jews, to convince them that only in Israel could a Jew be safe and live an honorable life . . . the difference between Israeli heroism and Jewish submissive meekness."[6] It was a grand educational event and remains so thanks to Arendt's commentary. The irony, which she points to with her memorable phrase "the banality of evil," is that the trial gave an unworthy little figure few rights as an accused but, at the same time, a place in history.

Years before the Holocaust, Ben-Gurion understood the importance of organizing a Jewish military and had himself enlisted in the Jewish Legion, a unit of the British army established toward the end of the First World War. He had little compunction about the use of violence in order to enhance security, and he viewed the Arab opposition as simply out to destroy the Jews.[7] He anticipated the worst from his opponents and thought restraint or delay in the use of violence suggested weak, sheeplike behavior. His contemporaries, the great soldier Moshe Dayan among them, observed his *virtù:* "determination, activism, leadership, concentrating on the main issue, and proceeding fearlessly, even if many risks and difficulties were involved."[8] In 1936, Ben-Gurion argued that "Arabs respect force . . . these days it is not right but might which prevails. It is more important to have force than justice on one's side . . . the powers that be become hard of hearing, and respond only to the roar of cannons."[9] He was, as Machiavelli recommended, both a lion and a fox and was quite willing to use deception and violence, sometimes both together: "Ben-Gurion believed that under certain circumstances, it was permissible to lie for the good of the state. But Moshe Sharett was astounded by his behavior."[10] Willingness to tell lies as well as to use force divides activists from moderates.

An important theme of this Israeli narrative is how Moshe Sharett, on both moral and pragmatic grounds, struggled to contain his activist cabinet colleagues' willingness to authorize reprisal and, equally important, to limit the agents' independent contributions to the level of aggression and violence. Sharett, who was foreign minister and then briefly spelled Ben-Gurion as prime minister in the mid-1950s, is a complicated and compelling figure in Israeli politics; a thoughtful policy maker who combined a sophisticated appreciation of the strategic goal of security with moral commitment, he struggled to keep control of the security agents.[11] He moves in the space between Machiavelli and the Tolerator (see fig. 2.1). What put him at odds with cabinet colleagues, the Ministry of Defense, the Israel Defense Forces, and the intelligence services, was not just an appreciation that the core issue was two communities, Israeli and Palestinian, both claiming the same nonnegotiable resource. This was also recognized by the activists, as when Moshe Dayan, chief of staff for the army, showed empathy for the situation of the Arabs during the obsequies for a kibbutznik killed by the Egyptians:

> Let us not today cast blame on the murderers. What can we say against their terrible hatred of us? For eight years now, they have sat in the refugee camps of Gaza, and have watched how, before their very eyes, we have turned their lands and villages, where they and their forefathers previously dwelled, into our home . . . Beyond the border surges a sea of hatred . . . This is our choice—to be ready and armed, tough and harsh—or to let the sword fall from our hands and our lives be cut short.[12]

For Dayan, then, this understandable Arab hatred made Israel's use of violence necessary and ongoing. Sharett, in contrast, was convinced that military means alone would not be effective and also that even if the Israelis were playing on the sum side of this zero-sum game, winning had its costs. Prior to the establishment of the state of Israel he said, "one community's growth at the expense of the other community would adversely influence its humane disposition for a very long period."[13] He knew that there were no good solutions and that if Israel were to win its existence, the Arabs would lose. Sharett argued for compensation for those Arabs who left and generosity to those who stayed. Once they had left, however, there was no coming home again as far as Sharett was concerned. There was no good solution to this formative game, no adequate way to fairly compensate the loser, and Sharett understood that it was a formative game with lasting implications for the new nation's innocence—even if the Israelis could pluck safety, they would likely get stung in the process.

Throughout the short history of Israel, from the 1948 massacre at Deir Yassin to the 1982 massacre at the Lebanese refugee camps of Sabra and Shatila, and up to the more contemporary refusenik resistance to military service in the West Bank, leaders faced or appeared to face the issue of controlling the agents of repression. The principal-agent problem provides further definition to the distinction between activists and moderates. Activists have capitalized on the strategic benefits of the murder and mayhem committed by their agents. For moderates who prefer a nicer over a nastier strategy, who might wish to postpone retribution for a period of time, these selfish motivations of the agents, far from an opportunity to be realized, present a problem of political control, which at times has risen to the level of international embarrassment. Sharett constantly struggled to rein in the Israel Defense Force and, notably, Ariel Sharon's special units and paratroopers. In March 1954, after a Palestinian attack on a bus, he said, "a retaliatory operation in reaction to such a blood bath would only diminish the terrible impact of the murder, and put us on the same level as the murderers."[14] He opposed retaliation for both moral and policy-effectiveness reasons.

Underlying the distinction between Israeli leaders, the juxtaposition of the principals who "won't control" to those who "can't control" sorts activists from moderates. Activists from Ben-Gurion to Sharon have discovered the advantages of artificial information asymmetry and have distanced themselves and their governments from the useful violence of their agents, whether the Lebanese Phalange or, in the early days, out-of-uniform Israeli soldiers or out-of-control Irgun and LHI irregulars. Logically, the rarer occurrence of agents resisting control on the grounds of commitment to a concept of "combat morality" has presented more of a problem for activists than for moderates, notably in recent decades. The moral conscience of these agents has meant that they were unwilling to supply the amount violence wanted by the activist principal, who then looked for substitutes: settlers, special units, or irregulars.

Compounding the problems of political control, Sharett was up against a rival principal. Ben-Gurion even when not in office commanded a level of respect from the agents that Sharett could never attain. Eventually Sharett resigned as prime minister over the retaliation policy.[15] While Ben-Gurion at times was contemptuous ("Sharett is cultivating a nation of cowards"[16]), he could also be generous in his estimation of Sharett ("he was honest—and there was a great nobility about him"), and other Israeli leaders described Sharett as the moral or public conscience of the country.[17] Sharett's term left a mark on Israeli politics. No hero, handicapped in the company that he kept, he did have the fortitude to take on the great men of a martial nation and to try to break the habit of reprisal. Beset by problems of political control to which he was unable to successfully adapt, his term suggested that if commitment could be combined with authority over agents, such a combination could substantially reduce the level of violence.

The motor driving the Israeli use of violence runs on the selfishness of agents and the rationality of principals, not the fumes of ancient enmity and the fuel of cultural identity. *New York Times* columnist and veteran Middle East reporter Thomas Friedman sees politics and the use of violence in this part of the world differently. He describes the sudden and brutal way in which Syrian leader Hafez al-Assad crushed his internal Sunni Muslim opposition in February 1982 in the city of Hama with the hideous torture and killing of thousands. Friedman says that Ariel Sharon is a mirror image of Assad.[18] He argues that "the reason one can still find such tribe-like conflicts at work in the Middle East today is that most peoples in this part of the world, including Israeli Jews, have not fully broken from their primordial identities."[19] These leaders' ready use of violence stems from Middle Eastern tribalism and the imperative of Bedouin desert lore: an insufficient response to a slight injury signals weakness and encourages gross injury.

> So the Bedouin called his sons together and said, "Boys, we are in great danger now . . . My turkey's been stolen" . . . but the sons ignored him and forgot about the turkey. A few weeks later, the old man's camel was stolen. His sons came and said, "Father, your camel's been stolen, what should we do?" And the old man said, "Find my turkey." A few weeks later, the old man's horse was stolen . . . the sons came and said, ". . . what should we do?" He said, "Find my turkey." Finally, a few weeks later, someone raped his daughter. The father . . . said, "It is all because of the turkey. When they saw that they could take my turkey, we lost everything."[20]

With this tale of turkey theft turning into a sister's rape, Middle Easterners are cautioned to never give an inch, a finger, a palm, or a cubit. This folk wisdom covers Machiavellian principals and agents in some local color. More generally, the Israeli use of violence and reprisal is aimed at safeguarding national power and security, which are means and ends that we find as firmly lodged in stationary cultures as in nomadic ones. Furthermore, the local color obscures the leadership tension created by the moderates over how to manage strategic interactions with Arab opponents, the international community, and even their own agents.

A SYNOPSIS OF THE CONFLICT

Although we conventionally see Israel's history as peace interrupted by episodic and discretely labeled wars, more accurately its history is war interrupted by limited peaceful episodes. The Israeli war of independence usually refers to the fighting between Jews and Arabs in those months from November 1947, when the United Nations approved partitioning the land between the two communities, until May 1948, when the British withdrew and David Ben-Gurion, Moshe Shertok (Sharett), Golda Myerson (Meir), and others signed the Declaration of the Establishment of the State of Israel. When the British soldiers left, the soldiers of seven Arab countries intervened. By spring 1949, the Israeli forces had defeated or stalled these armies and added about 20 percent more territory to the Israel envisaged by UN partition. Israel decisively defeated its neighbors again in 1956, 1967, and 1973, and then invaded Lebanon in 1982.

Israel has a population of about 6 million, with Israeli Arabs making up approximately one-fifth of the total. There are around 200,000 Israeli settlers living in the occupied territories (the West Bank and Gaza), seized during the 1967 war respectively from Jordan and Egypt, amid more than three million Palestinians. The resounding military triumph of 1967 brought the people along with the territory and created a buffer zone, itself prickling with hostility. A northern buffer zone was the immediate goal of the Israeli invasion of Lebanon in 1982. Again, territorial successes failed to bring security. Over the years there has been a shifting balance of danger between the enemy columns threatening the borders and the Arabs remaining within Israel and the occupied territories. But the reason for conflict and the symmetry of strike and reprisal go back to the 1940s and before.

If we ignore the flight of civilians caused by the violence, there is nothing particularly remarkable about the overall numbers of victims of the violence in this conflict. The most notorious atrocity of 1948 saw a hundred civilian deaths. The worst of all the massacres claimed somewhere between 700 and 2,500 lives in two days on the outskirts of Beirut in 1982, and the nasty year of 2002 saw about 1,000 Palestinian deaths and half that number of Israeli deaths. Remarkable in this history are both the longevity of the pattern of violence and the grim determination of this democracy to adhere to Machiavelli's dictum not to be "good." The present pattern of violence, the pressure of past policies, the underlying problem of reconciling Jewish and Palestinian claims to the same finite territory, and even some of the personalities bridge the whole time span, as do the motives of principals and agents.

PRIMITIVE CHESS

In 2002, Israeli forces were in the midst of violent conflict with their Palestinian opposition. Taking a longer look at the fatalities as a measure of the way the Israeli government and the Palestinian opposition interact, figure 3.1 shows the synchronized moves of tit-for-tat retaliation.[21] As opposition threat rises and falls as measured by the Israeli dead, so does the severity of the government action as measured by the Palestinian dead. The correlation between the deaths inflicted by the Palestinians and the deaths inflicted by the Israelis is remarkably high.

Figure 3.1 catches the tail end of the first Intifada, the Palestinian uprising in the occupied territories during the late 1980s and early 1990s. In this uprising, the Palestinians opted not for nonviolence but for less lethal violence, given the Israeli advantage in firepower. This decision left the Israeli government with a problem of how to respond to this type of opposition threat; their response was a clear example of the ratchet approach to repression. Sociologist James Ron uses the term "savage restraint" for how Israeli troops on the ground worked out their informal procedures to repress the uprising.[22] As historian Benny Morris describes it, the government tried rubber bullets and plastic bullets (used by the British in Northern Ireland), shooting to injure, shooting to kill, beatings, torture, mass arrests, and economic sanctions, but they could not use the methods that would work, as a senior Israeli military official pointed out: "transfer, starvation, and genocide . . . but none of these methods is acceptable to the State of Israel."[23] The Israeli government was constrained by the less lethal tactics of the Palestinians, the high public and international visibility of the conflict, and a democratic framework that had recently revealed serious tensions among Israelis themselves over the 1982 Lebanese invasion, and that reflected substantial popular revulsion with atrocities. According to Morris, then Defense Minister Yitzhak Rabin understood very early on that there would have to be a negotiated political solution, and so the policy became one of containing the violence.[24] The 1993 Oslo agreement that seemed to promise a Palestinian state helped diffuse the situation.

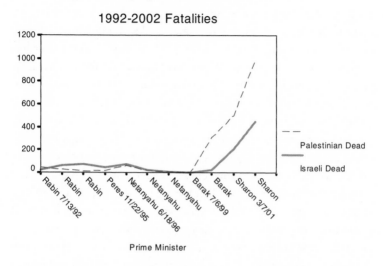

Fig. 3.1. Playing Primitive Chess:

1992-2002 Fatalities

In keeping with my general argument, I mark the passage of time in figure 3.1 by the alternation in Israeli leaders. After noticing the tightness of the violent relationship between government and opposition, the second observation I make from this chart is that leadership seems to shift the intensity of the violence. In figure 3.1 Ariel Sharon's impact is seen before his time as prime minister, coinciding with his September 2000 visit to the most sacred Muslim site in East Jerusalem in the company of hundreds of riot police.[25] There is a small spike in fatalities, most noticeably for Palestinians, with the election of the other Likud leader, Benjamin Netanyahu. Commenting on Netanyahu's election victory, sociologist Baruch Kimmerling and political scientist Joel Migdal noted "the hostile tone of the new government toward the Palestinians" and the opening of a Western Wall tunnel that provoked riots among Palestinians.[26] Not evident in figure 3.1, and perhaps more in keeping with Lucretia Borgia (the sister who kept poison powder in her ring) than Cesare, was Netanyahu's embarrassing effort to put poison in the ear of a Hamas leader in Amman, Jordan. The episode ended with the capture of the Mossad men, who had impersonated Canadians unsuccessfully, and with Israel having to send a doctor with the antidote.[27] This action was reprisal for the wounding of Israel embassy guards in Amman.

Consistent with the distinction between activists and moderates, the type of leader who plays the game makes a difference: without incorporating leaders and their different beliefs on the use of violence, a simple tit-for-tat account only gets us as far as the embrace, and does not extend to the intensity level of the embrace. One violent move met by another violent move suggests, as Moshe Sharett observed, a game of chess: "too often we pursue tactics designed only for the very short run, which are not calculated for the long run. We usually make our moves on the chessboard without considering our opponent's move. That is, we play very primitive chess."[28] Israeli leaders probably did consider the next move of their opponents, and perhaps Sharett should have said, "we usually make our moves on the chessboard *always expecting the most aggressive possible move from our opponent*." We understand Sharett's point, but chess may not be the best analogy for these repeated interactions. Chess implies total conflict and always assuming the "most feared move" from your opponent.[29] This is not necessarily a useful way of representing politics. It is possible that both sides may improve their security situation through mutual cooperation. But the chess analogy probably fits hyperactivist Sharon as closely as any leader, who assumes the worst of the Palestinians, subscribes to the activist belief that force is all that they understand, and believes that a nicer strategy signals weakness.

Israeli leaders consider the potential imposition of external costs on the government for its repression. Throughout the 1990s there was a very active effort by the administration of U.S. president Bill Clinton to promote negotiation, which may have suppressed violence on both sides. The George W. Bush administration deliberately pulled back and disengaged in 2001. While the escalated level of violence took off prior to the shift to a less-interested and less-active U.S. administration and while activists such as Sharon are in any case less sensitive to potential international criticism, this external condition and then the post–September 11 international environment plausibly facilitated Sharon's decision to increase the violence, contingent on Palestinian actions. In late July 2002, an Israeli F-16 dropped a bomb on a Hamas leader in Gaza, killing 14 including 9 children. Despite activist prime minister

Sharon's claim of a "big success," which showed his relative insensitivity to external constraints, President Bush described the action as "heavy handed," and the less-activist Israeli foreign minister Simon Peres promised to release some money to the Palestinians and to alleviate the curfew. Within days a Palestinian bomb exploded at Hebrew University, relieving U.S. pressure on the Israeli government.

In the Barak and particularly the Sharon years, one sees a clear shift in the relationship of Israeli dead to Palestinian dead. The more or less one-for-one exchange of the earlier years became sharply unfavorable for the Palestinians. But while the lethal exchange rate has changed, what we are struck by is the continued and undeterred swapping of dead. Simple tit for tat has created a cycle of violence. But, from this failure to deter the opposition's use of violence, it would be dangerous to draw the general conclusion that violence and terror does not work. In the 1980s the Americans left Lebanon when hit by Islamic terror, and in the 1940s the British eventually abandoned their mandate when targeted by Jewish terror. And we must be sure we know the strategic goal of the violence before we try to evaluate whether or not it works. Despite the statistically tight embrace, the parties may not be simply responding to yesterday's outrage. Derailing the peace process may be the underlying goal of Hamas suicide bombing, as political scientists Andrew Kydd and Barbara Walter have argued.[30] Further, the Israeli imposed curfews, air raids, assassinations, occupations, and demolitions may not be meant simply to deter Palestinian terror. The Israeli actions may be timed by Palestinian terror in order to lower international criticism, but may in fact be calculated to degrade living conditions to the point that more Palestinians consider leaving voluntarily—it is estimated that in the two years following September 2000, 100,000 left for Jordan—and thereby effect Sharon's "lifelong commitment to preventing the emergence of a viable Palestinian state."[31] A Palestinian state and Arabs within Israel threaten Israeli security. Imputing goals is risky analysis, yet it makes sense of the shift in the relationship of Palestinian dead to Israeli dead over the last three years. And, it does not seem so far-fetched to overlay the tit-for-tat response on a broader strategic aim when we consider the earlier periods of the conflict, the strategic goals and consequences of that violence, and Sharon's personal links to that period.

"HAVEN IN SUNNY PALESTINE"[32]

From the beginning of the Zionist movement into Palestine, there has been conflict and violence; as Ben-Gurion put it in the 1930s: "We and they want the same thing. We both want Palestine. And that is the fundamental conflict."[33] The Zionist movement began in the late nineteenth century, with pogroms in Eastern Europe exercising a push factor on the willingness of Jews to emigrate. The bright green light for Jewish settlement of Palestine was the Balfour Declaration of November 1917, in which the British government promised to help achieve the Zionist goal while pretending that it was not a zero-sum game for the Jews and the Arabs, that improving the position of one community was not at the expense of the other. After the First World War, the League of Nations responded to Zionist pressure and defined the British colonial relationship with Palestine as a "mandate," giving Britain the obligation to establish a "Jewish national home" in Palestine while acting as a trustee for "non-Jewish" interests. The British thus assumed charge of two irreconcilable communities for a quarter of a century.

From the beginning, internal violence prompted increasingly heavy security measures. Any concessions to the Arabs generated strong reactions from Jewish organizations, and concessions to the Jews similarly provoked the Arabs. While the British were the initial targets of the Arabs,[34] the rebellions and riots of the 1920s and 1930s prompted Jewish countermeasures and the formation of the organizational forerunners of the Israel Defense Force. With David Ben-Gurion as its secretary general, the Jewish trade union movement established the Haganah, the Jewish defense force, in 1921. Its purpose was to provide security for Jewish settlements, which the British were unable to do on a consistent basis. The British cooperated in setting up the Haganah and armed the units guarding the settlements.[35] Twenty years after its founding, the Haganah set up an elite unit. The Palmach, or "strike companies," were set up again with the cooperation of the British and with the purpose of carrying the war to the enemy, including to the Germans and Italians if they defeated the British. Under the command of the experienced soldier Yitzchak Sadeh, a veteran of the Red Army, which had also been founded for the purpose of fighting a brutal civil war, the Palmach recruited from the kibbutzim and developed a strong esprit de corps.[36]

There were also two rival and more extreme paramilitary organizations. As the Haganah was associated with the labor movement and its political party, the Mapai, these more extreme organizations were associated with the opposition Revisionist Party, which considered itself more vehemently patriotic and committed to accelerating the formation of the new state of Israel. The Irgun Zvai Leumi (IZL, National Military Organization) was formed in 1936, and its first action was the reprisal killing of some Arab workers after three Jews were killed on a bus.[37] It valued the quick and indiscriminate use of violence to deter and terrorize opponents. The other important paramilitary organization was Avraham Stern's Lohamei Herut Israel (LHI, Fighters for the Freedom of Israel), otherwise known as the Stern Gang. It was not the use of terror but the targets of the terror that divided these organizations. When Britain declared war on Germany in 1939 and had to accommodate Arab demands, the Irgun supported Britain's war effort. In contrast, the LHI was militantly opposed to Britain even during the war against Hitler. A little like Neville Chamberlain, Stern imagined that he could make deals with the Axis powers, even to secure a Jewish state when Britain was defeated.[38] Menachem Begin's Irgun restrained its activities against Britain and British accommodation with Arab demands on Jewish immigration until 1944, when Hitler's defeat was clearer.

Indicating the rivalry between the Jewish military organizations, when the British hanged an Irgun member for shooting up an Arab bus in 1938 (in response to the killing of four Jews in a car), Ben-Gurion commented that "I am not shocked that a Jew was hanged in Palestine. I am ashamed of the deed that led to the hanging."[39] The Irgun specialized in setting off bombs in buses and town centers, such as the TNT- and shrapnel-filled milk urn that killed 21 in Haifa in 1938. Benny Morris says that this tactic worsened the security problem for the British and that "this innovation soon found Arab imitators and became something of a tradition."[40] Despite Ben-Gurion's shame for the Irgun, the Haganah itself was quickly drawn into this type of violence. It adopted terror tactics and retribution, setting up a "revenge" unit in 1939 to strike the Arabs and the British. With this unit, the principals indulged the agents' selfish motives. Echoing the regrettably immortal Count Tilly, the official *Haganah History Book* explained: "pressure from the ranks forced the chief commanders to find an outlet for the anger and vengeance that filled their men's hearts."[41] But after a night shooting of some Arab villagers and the wounding of two children, there was public criticism from labor leader Berl Katznelson, who advocated the doctrine of "purity of arms" and the idea that there were moral limits on the use of violence.[42] Moshe Shertok (later Sharett) compared Arab and Jewish terror: "The filth that rules the Arab population has gotten into certain groups in the Jewish population."[43] Occasional protests aside, the retaliatory policy became a standard procedure early in the conflict.

In response to the assassinations and terror from both the Arab and Jewish sides, the British sharply escalated the deployment of soldiers and police to Palestine, many of whom had served in Ireland and had experience with guerrilla war and embattled communities. The British detained thousands without trial, used torture and executions, and punished relatives with curfews as well as with the destruction of Arab houses, which anticipated the current and widely condemned Israeli practice. Between 1936 and 1940 the mandate authorities demolished approximately 2,000 Arab houses.[44] Even the idea of expulsion or forced transfer was in the policy discourse of the British. In proposals at the British Labour Party conference in 1944, the partition of Palestine was recommended with the corollary of the forced transfer of those Arabs who remained on the wrong side of the line.[45] Perhaps at that time and in the immediate postwar years, with much of Europe on the move, transfer could be discussed more blithely. The fact that transfer was a legitimate topic of policy debate in other democracies gave it legitimacy for the Israelis, and when the state of Israel was formed, Israeli leaders used the examples of other population transfers to justify what happened to the Palestinian Arabs.

A significant number of Arab casualties during the 1930s were the result of the activities of Captain Orde Wingate, a British officer leading a unit of 50 British and 150 Jewish troops. He organized these soldiers into Special Night Squads to take the war to the Arabs and to test the limits of his principals' control. Ultimately, he took it too far and was sent home in 1939 with a personnel file that stated: "A good soldier but a poor security risk. Not to be trusted. The interests of the Jews are more important to him than those of his own country. He must not be allowed to return to Palestine."[46] Wingate's activities created a combination of commando romance and nastiness concentrated in a special unit; it was a potent example for those who later set up the Israel Defense Force. Wingate used summary executions and other punishments as retribution for Arab terror against women, children, and the old, although he apparently regretted his lapses of restraint.[47] He was most famous for his organization of a guerrilla campaign against the Japanese in Burma and died in an American B-25 that crashed there in 1944. Many leading Israeli soldiers knew and fought with Wingate, and his emphasis on aggression, the usefulness of special organizations to take the fight to the enemy, and perhaps his willingness to freelance endured. It is important to note that Wingate's operations included attacks on villages across the borders in Syria and Lebanon.[48] The British policies and the men who implemented the policies left a legacy. Israel "retains many security-related regulations from the period of the British Mandate," according to a United States Department of State report on Israeli human rights practices.[49] Major elements of Israeli repression and the habit of retaliation are as "ancient" and culturally freighted as the mandate, which is to say that they are not particularly Middle Eastern.

The outbreak of the Second World War in 1939 rebalanced threats and priorities. Once victory over Nazi Germany was beyond doubt, the Irgun resumed a campaign against the British that culminated in the bombing of the King David Hotel in Jerusalem in 1946, possibly with some level of Haganah involvement.[50] The Irgun then continued its bombing *after* the British announced that they were giving up their mandate, blowing up the British Officers' Club in Jerusalem and killing fourteen officers in March 1947.[51] Terror worked on the British. For them, the strategic reasons for being in the Holy Land had never been compelling, and the Holocaust had made it morally impossible to police the Jews effectively. While Jewish individuals were punished, their organizations were not undermined. As Tom Segev points out, the British treatment of the Arabs was significantly worse than the treatment of the Jews.[52] In addition to the use of torture and execution, the British punished

Arabs collectively and aggressively took the offensive against Arab "gangs" and their communities.

Having long overstayed their welcome, the British left Palestine by handing the League of Nations' mandate back to the international community, now housed in the United Nations. But the Jewish national home was built and peopled, complete with roads, ports, a judicial system, a Jewish civil society and political leadership, and, in the home's darker recesses a trained and hardened police and security force. And then the Jews violently repossessed the home and converted it into a Jewish state. According to Tom Segev, "The British kept their promise to the Zionists. They opened up the country to mass Jewish immigration; by 1948, the Jewish population had increased by more than tenfold. The Jews were permitted to purchase land, develop agriculture . . . set up hundreds of new settlements . . . they created an army; they had a political leadership and elected institutions; and with the help of all these they in the end defeated the Arabs, all under British sponsorship, all in the wake of that promise of 1917."[53] The results for the British: the shambles of departure, an inability to respond to Jewish terror effectively, wasted lives without hope of preventing war, shame from the efforts to limit the immigration of Holocaust survivors, and hatred from the Arabs for facilitating Jewish settlement.

The United Nations approved partition in November 1947. Partition did not part Arabs and Jews, as Arabs made up approximately 45 percent of the population (1.1 million) in the area designated for Israel. The Arabs calculated that, once the British had gone, with the help of the neighboring Arab countries they could reclaim the land by force. As Sir John Glubb, the British commander of the Arab Legion of Transjordan, observed: "The Arab governments did immense harm to the cause of the Palestinian Arabs, because they encouraged them to be defiant, and when it came to violence, they failed."[54] After the partition, the Palestinian Arabs took the offensive with some help from volunteers and then from the neighboring Arab countries. While the resources of the Arab countries were intimidating, with the exception of the Jordanian Arab Legion, which had the most limited strategic aims of the Arab forces, the professionalism of the armies was generally poor. The Arab Liberation Army, supported by various Arab countries, seemed in it for the loot as much as for any strategic end,[55] and the Arab leaders did not achieve a coordinated campaign.

For the most part the 1947-1948 war was a war of villages and cities and the roads between them. The most well-known atrocity of this war was in April 1948 at Deir Yassin. What happened in this village crystallizes Israel's use of violence. Agents, principals, strategy, and victims came together here and then down through the decades. The killing was indiscriminate, but as it was localized to this place and limited to a short duration, it appeared an aberration, an episode of going too far rather than anything more calculated and systematic. The agents were irregulars with a known proclivity for atrocity, formally outside the chain of command. Here the murky, changeable relationship between the Haganah and the more extreme paramilitary organizations made it possible for the Haganah to cloud its share of responsibility for the massacre, and afterward the Haganah leaders condemned the killing of civilians, and in subsequent decades tried to hide its role.[56] Despite the principals' denials, the atrocity fits a strategic and security rationale.

The 130 fighters of the IZL and LHI attacked the village, with the approval of the Haganah. Some Palmach and Haganah fighters participated in the action at Deir Yassin. The attacking forces killed approximately 100 civilians and committed rape, mutilation, and looting. One report states: "LHI members tell of the barbaric behavior of the IZL toward the prisoners and the dead. They also related that the IZL men raped a number of Arab girls and murdered them afterward (we don't know if this is true)."[57] Elsewhere, Haganah troops sought Count Tilly's reward. A month after Deir Yassin, a kibbutz leader, speaking of the destruction of the Arab village of Abu Shusha that neighbored his kibbutz and echoing the "purity of arms" doctrine advocated earlier by Katznelson, protested the Haganah's "killing, robbery, rape." He said, "I don't think our army should be like every army."[58] Aside from the agents' private interests, which all armies share but some manage to control, was there a strategic motive for violence at Deir Yassin as well?

At Deir Yassin an immediate goal of the LHI and IZL was to expel the inhabitants of the village, and in the meeting to plan the attack there were explicit LHI proposals to kill villagers and prisoners in order to panic Arabs elsewhere. These proposals were not approved at the meeting.[59] But they were implemented on the ground. Arab reprisal and flight were consequences of the massacre. Four days later, Arabs slaughtered some 70 medical and academic staff on their way to the isolated Hebrew University campus in Jerusalem, with the British only belatedly intervening. Aside from revenge, the events at Deir Yassin triggered an Arab exodus. A favorable demography has been at the heart of Jewish conceptions of security since the mandate. It could have been achieved by the mandate experience of moving Jews in, or by the wartime development of moving Arabs out. Expulsion as well as immigration could contribute to a more favorable demography. As to the issue of strategy, Deir Yassin fits a pattern of Israeli attacks on Arab civilians that occurred both before and after April 1948.

The activist IZL and LHI had already used indiscriminate violence to spur flight from the cities. In December 1947 and January 1948, the IZL's and LHI's campaign included setting off bombs in the major civilian centers of Haifa, Jerusalem, Tel Aviv, and Jaffa, resulting in a death toll in the hundreds.[60] They wanted land, not Arabs. The LHI summarized their goals in attacking the cities:

A strong attack on the centers of the Arab population will intensify the movement of refugees and all the roads in the direction of Transjordan and the neighbouring countries will be filled with panic-stricken masses and [this] will hamper the [enemy's] military movement . . . A great opportunity has been given us, let us not waste it . . . The whole of this land will be ours . . .[61]

The Haganah bombed the Semiramis Hotel in Jerusalem on January 5, 1948, aiming at some Arab paramilitaries but killing civilians. And it carried out reprisals, killing 60 Arab villagers on December 31, 1947, near Haifa.[62] Nathaniel Lorch describes this action as a "punitive sortie" following the killing of Jewish workers in Haifa.[63] But the IZL and LHI bombing campaign had far broader goals than punishment; they wanted to drive out the Arabs.

The British commander John Glubb uses the term "calculated massacre" for Deir Yassin, attributes the term to a Jewish Mandate official, and argues that massacres were a factor in the refugee crisis.[64]

Deir Yassin is the most notorious atrocity; however, similar massacres continued after Israel achieved its statehood in May 1948, and even without the involvement of the IZL and LHI. In July 1948, Glubb decided not to deploy the Arab Legion to defend the towns of Lod/ Lydda and Ramle. It was a military decision, but he was accused of treachery, and outraged Palestinians in Ramallah stoned some of his men. The Palmach took the towns, killed some prisoners and about 250 of the residents, and were ordered by Ben-Gurion to expel or "drive out" the rest. Sharett opposed this expulsion and others registered their unease: "the military planners speak of how it is possible and permissible to take women, children, and old men and to fill the roads with them because such is the imperative of strategy. I am appalled."[65] Gilbert quotes a passage from Yitzhak Rabin's memoirs that was ultimately deleted by censors:

> "Driving out" is a term with a harsh ring. Psychologically, this was one of the most difficult actions we undertook. The population of Lod did not leave willingly. There was no way of avoiding the use of force and warning shots in order to make the inhabitants march the ten or fifteen miles to the point where they met the [Jordanian] Legion. The inhabitants of Ramle watched and learned the lesson. Their leaders agreed to be evacuated voluntarily.[66]

If not before Deir Yassin, certainly afterward Israeli leaders knew that force and massacres, amplified by Arab propaganda, could panic the Arab civilian population, and the massacres continued into the fall of 1948. This is how Glubb characterized the Israeli strategy:

> The Israelis were now deliberately driving out all Arabs, a process assisted now and again by the usual "calculated massacre." On October 31st, United Nations observers reported that the Israelis had killed thirty women and children at Dawaima, west of Hebron. It would be an exaggeration to claim that great numbers were massacred. But just enough were killed, or roughly handled, to make sure that all the civilian population took flight . . . These particular villages west of Hebron were to remain vacant and their lands uncultivated for eight years. When I left Jordan in 1956, plans for

Jewish settlement in the area were, for the first time, beginning to take shape.[67]

At about the same time in northern Israel, Israeli troops committed "at least nine massacres of Palestinian civilians and prisoners of war."[68] These massacres were part of Operation Hiram against the Arab Liberation Army in Galilee and parts of southern Lebanon.

The 1947-48 conflict produced more than 700,000 Arab refugees. These refugees resulted from a complicated mix of factors that operated in successive stages, Morris argues. Some middle-class Arabs left voluntarily, and some were encouraged to leave by the Arab commanders, although by May 1948 the Arab states were trying to stem the flows. Similar to Glubb's notion of "calculated massacre," Morris describes the "atrocity factor" that was "reinforced periodically during the months of fighting by other Jewish massacres."[69] He discusses a declassified Israeli intelligence estimate that stated: "It is possible to say that at least 55 per cent of the total of the exodus was caused by our (Haganah/IDF) operations and by their influence."[70] Both activist Ben-Gurion and moderate Sharett supported the general idea of transfer, and once the Arabs became refugees, both men adamantly opposed the return of the refugees. They differed over their willingness to use violence to attain the strategic goal of a more favorable demography, but once the Arabs had left, both emphasized the danger of allowing them to return.

The principal line of argument that the new state adopted with the United Nations, which was urging Israel to relent, was that the refugees constituted a potential "fifth column"—a suspect population within the walls of the new state. Israeli officials carefully attended to public feelings concerning the legitimacy of the policy and gathered material on transfers of populations elsewhere: "let us hope that we will be able to give every respectable nation its list of crimes in this sphere."[71] Beyond the you-did-it-too claim, bastard theory suggests another course of action to protect principals from the adverse consequences of strategic atrocities on their political support. It suggests we look for out-of-control agents, Spanish ministers, and artificial information asymmetry.

There are both organizational lines and hierarchical layers to confuse accountability, and for a while these were used to conceal Haganah participation at Deir Yassin. We know that the filthy motives of the perpetrators played a part, but we know that the series of atrocities had a strategic rationale and effect on the 1947-48 conflict. The irregular organizations and their atrocities continued as long as they served the strategic purposes of the Israeli leadership. It was not until September 1948 that Ben-Gurion and the new Israeli state took control of the irregular forces, the Irgun and the LHI, after their activities had helped produce Arab flight. It was not Deir Yassin, or the terror bombing of Arabs in the cities by Irgun and LHI, but the assassination of a representative of the international community that galvanized the new state into closing down the irregular forces. This suggests that up to that point the benefits of the atrocities committed against the Arab population outweighed the costs. Once Israel was established, the new state did begin to assert its monopoly of violence, forbidding "any other armed force outside the IDF" in May 1948. There was a violent dispute between Irgun and Haganah forces over an Irgun arms shipment, but it was the assassination of the United Nations' mediator, Count Bernadotte, and his French associate by the LHI on September 17, 1948, that led to the state taking control of these organizations. After the assassination, Ben-Gurion ordered the arrest of LHI members, and the Irgun was given an ultimatum to disband. Menachem Begin agreed and Irgun members joined the Israel Defense Force.[72] The Palmach was also integrated within the IDF in September 1948.

Individual members of the cabinet were well aware of the singular opportunity that the war presented to deal with the threat to Israel's survival that the Arabs represented. In his letter of August 1948 to Chaim Weizmann, Sharett described the situation:

> As for the future, we are equally determined—to explore all possibilities of getting rid, once and for all, of the huge Arab minority which originally threatened us. What can be achieved in this period of storm and stress will be quite unattainable once conditions get stabilised. A group of people among our senior officials has already

started working on the study of resettlement possibilities in other lands and of the finances necessary.[73]

By the summer of 1948, even this moderate member of the cabinet was enthusiastically alive to the fleeting nature of the "storm and stress" policy window, and atrocities continued into the fall. While Morris says "there was still no systematic expulsion policy; it was never, as far as we know, discussed or decided upon at Cabinet or IDF general staff meetings," he also suggests that there was a deliberate effort to distance the cabinet from the highly controversial policy, leaving it to more localized initiative, rather than to have direct responsibility.[74] It may not be possible to firmly establish the level at which the strategic cause was calculated in the Israeli political and military hierarchy. It is significant that the atrocities were sustained over a period of time, both irregular and regular forces participated, largely without disgrace or punishment, and in the postindependence period direct attacks on Arab civilians continued to be used to reinforce the security of the new state's borders. A principal's nod and wink to French knights or Jewish "gangs" fits a Machiavellian approach.

THREATS ON THE BORDERS

Between 1948 and 1956 violence primarily occurred on or about the borders. Palestinians crossed the border, sometimes just to return to their land. The Israelis responded to these crossings by shooting infiltrators and with reprisal raids. The irony of this situation was not lost on Israelis: "Oh, you Knesset members, you former passport forgers, you infiltrators, grandchildren of infiltrators, how quickly you have learned the new morality of militarism!"[75] Calibrating the response became an issue at the highest levels of the Israeli government and divided the government between activists led by Ben-Gurion and the minority moderates led by Sharett. Things came to an international crisis point in a Jordanian village.

On October 14, 1953, Unit 101, following the IDF's order to do "maximum killing," entered the village of Qibya. The members of the special unit, dressed in civilian clothes, shot or blew up over 60 men, women, and children, and returned without loss to the unit. The provocation had been a grenade attack that had killed an Israeli woman and her children. Unit 101 was a specialized force formed to carry out reprisals, made up of volunteers commanded by Arik Scheinerman (Ben-Gurion later selected the commander's Hebrew name of Ariel Sharon). Because of their willingness to kill civilians, some thought the members of the special unit were former members of the Irgun and LHI, but that was not the case.[76] In an earlier action against a refugee camp in Gaza, Unit 101 killed 20 Palestinians, including 12 women and children. The government denied that it was responsible. One member of the unit recorded his reaction: "Is this screaming, whimpering multitude the enemy?"[77] The Qibya strategy was to embarrass the Jordanians into controlling their borders. It embarrassed the Israeli government too.

Prime Minister Ben-Gurion, in an effort to lower the costs of international condemnation of the attack on Qibya, denied IDF involvement in the massacre.[78] Foreign minister Sharett instructed his ministry not to repeat the falsehood, fearing ridicule. He advocated a public apology instead, and he recorded his opposition to the reprisal: "When initially I opposed the reprisal it did not occur to me that there would be such a blood bath. I thought about a reprisal in the previous style that became the norm, and even opposed it. If I had suspected so much killing, I would have raised hell."[79] Qibya represented an escalation in the violence and Sharett claimed information asymmetry, that he did not know of the extent of the killing planned by the IDF and Sharon. Sharett's friend, the Israeli ambassador to Burma, wrote to him wanting reassurance that he was not part of it and describing Qibya as "this Dir Yassin under the auspices of our government, under its full responsibility, and executed by the IDF."[80] Here is an Israeli government official recognizing that in this case, as an IDF operation, there is no shirking responsibility, no Irgun or LHI agents for the principals to blame as at Deir Yassin, although the soldiers themselves were not in uniform and Ben-Gurion himself did try to blame it on settlers.

This operation raises both the problems and the cynical conveniences of the principal-agent relationship. The advocates of the operation—the defense minister and the IDF—had outmaneuvered

Sharett and had kept information about the bloody extent of the operation from him. The operation had the tacit approval of Prime Minister Ben-Gurion. Concealing the identity of the agents and claiming ignorance of their activities is the principal's recognition of the convenience of the principal-agent relationship in the use of violence. Only Sharett could make a reasonable claim at genuine information asymmetry. Shortly after Qibya, the special unit was merged into the paratroopers. But Ariel Sharon, with powerful sponsors in Moshe Dayan and Ben-Gurion, was no easier to control as a paratrooper. The Qibya massacre illustrated the division between activists, including David Ben-Gurion (a man of the left and the labor movement), the defense ministry, the army, and the intelligence services, and the moderates in the foreign ministry represented by Sharett.

When Sharett became prime minister in 1954, he had difficulty imposing his core beliefs on Israeli policy. Sharett's biographer describes him as a "beleaguered" prime minister.[81] He was beleaguered by goal variance and the bias of policy precedent and was constrained in making an effective response by information asymmetry and auditing problems. Public support was on the side of the activists, as was the influence of past policy patterns in limiting policy options: "Sharett himself acknowledged that to some degree activism reduced terrorist infiltration, for a time in a given area. And, more important, he found that the weight of past tradition, the power of the military establishment, the opinions of his own Mapai Party colleagues, and pressure from a revenge-bent public narrowed his room for maneuver."[82] The "revenge-bent public" and the "primitive chess" mindset of the activists in the military bureaucracy presented Prime Minister Sharett with genuine problems of control. Preoccupying this principal was not agents shirking but agents working too hard.

Sharett faced difficulties in monitoring and auditing the security services. Genuine information asymmetry characterized the biggest policy debacle known as the Lavon Affair. This was the effort by Israeli intelligence agents to terror bomb some western targets in Egypt and frame Egyptian groups, all without informing the prime minister. The plan was exposed and the agents caught: "Prime Minister Sharett expressed outrage at the despicable slanders designed to harass the

Jews in Egypt—until he was discreetly alerted to the facts by Israeli army intelligence."[83] In 1960 he wrote to Ben-Gurion: "For many years now, I have been bothered by the realization that there have been periods during which our military elite has been affected by three sins—adventurism, false reporting, and cover-ups of unlawful actions."[84] Before he became prime minister, his previous governmental experience had been as foreign minister, not as defense minister, which meant that his influence on defense matters was more limited, and ministers in the coalition government had considerable autonomy.[85] Making matters worse, the IDF chief of staff, Moshe Dayan, was not sharing information with Defense Minister Pinhas Lavon. At one stage Sharett threatened to make things public if the unauthorized retaliatory raids and inaccurate reports he received did not cease.[86] This tactic of publicity, revealing one's own administrative inefficacy, is a tactic of last resort for a principal.

He did stop a planned retaliatory raid in 1955 after some sheep had been stolen from a kibbutz. He annoyed Moshe Dayan who advocated retaliation. Sharett visualized the world press headlines concerning retribution on women and children for sheep, revealing in this instance a cost sensitivity rather than moral sensitivity to violence.[87] Further, Sharett argued that the activists assumed that force was all Arabs understood, and asked, is it "really proven that retaliatory actions solve the security problem?"[88] He might have added with Machiavelli that prolonged cruelty means that you have to live with your knife in your hand.

Sharett was deeply concerned about the reprisal policy and Ariel Sharon's approach; he wrote: "without noting, we have removed all psychological and moral brakes preventing this burning urge to hurt—which is inherent in the human psyche—and permitted a paratroopers' brigade to alleviate revenge and turn it into a moral matter."[89] Sharett's statement suggests that violent reprisal was not simply a tactical means to respond to opposition threat; it was also indulging the desire for revenge, like that earlier unit the Haganah had established during the mandate or like the squad of British soldiers who had turned the Jews over to the lynch mob. The statement also indicates that as principal he was unable to effectively transmit his moral commitments to his agents although he recognized that these commitments were critical to lowering the violence. Worried about the ambitions and growth tendencies of the reprisal bureaucracy, he also "denigrated the idea that Ariel Sharon's paratroopers should serve as contractors for all reprisal and revenge operations, since it demands more operations."[90] In return, Ariel Sharon had a low opinion of Sharett and shared that opinion with his men.[91]

SUEZ TO SABRA AND SHATILA

In the 1956 Suez war, Colonel Ariel Sharon's paratroopers took the heavily defended Mitla Pass in the Sinai. He had stretched if not disobeyed his orders and his men suffered heavy casualties in taking the pass.[92] Critics argued that the operation was strategically pointless, and Sharon's superior, Moshe Dayan, thought that Sharon had tricked him.[93] During the Suez campaign, IDF troops killed prisoners and civilians. According to historian Benny Morris, there was "a great deal of unwarranted killing," including the shooting of Egyptian prisoners and about 500 civilians in the Gaza Strip in massacres on November 3 and November 12. In addition, 43 Israeli Arab villagers from Kafr Kasim, a village close to the Jordanian border, were shot by an Israeli patrol enforcing a curfew on October 29, 1956. As a result of press outrage, the government was "forced to know" of the activities of its agents, despite its efforts to hush up the incident, and trials and courts-martial followed. Apparently the villagers were returning from the day's work in the fields and had not known of the curfew.[94] As expected with domestic investigations of agents, the symbolic drama of the judicial proceedings did not produce substantial penalties.

Principals were eventually forced to know about the activities of agents after public outrage burst over events in the Lebanese war, most notably the massacre of Palestinian refugees in their camps in West Beirut in mid-September 1982. The killing and raping in these camps were not committed by the ordinary citizen soldiers of the IDF. Nor was it Jewish paramilitaries, nor a specially led and selected unit as at Qibya. Here it was Lebanese Christian irregulars who made the civilian population scream. While senior Israeli officers and Israeli government ministers orchestrated the Christian Phalange fighters' entry and final exit from the camps, and then decided to turn deaf ears and blind eyes to the suffering, some among the audience of Israeli citizen soldiers were horror struck and attempted, without success, to rouse their commanders from their murderous passivity. Had these soldiers been the ones to go into the camps, their enthusiasm for seeking Count Tilly's reward, even if they had been urged to do so, may reasonably be doubted. The Phalange, on the other hand, was primed to "clean out" the camps as Sharon put it. Before following the disturbing sequence of events that took place in the camps, to understand Sharon's choice of agents at Sabra and Shatila, it is important to take a look at the information available to him and the signals he was getting from those to whom he could delegate the violence. His alternatives were to use the IDF or to use the Phalange.

In the summer of 1982, at the urging and instigation of then defense minister Ariel Sharon, Prime Minister Menachem Begin's cabinet authorized the invasion of Lebanon. The decision to invade was precipitated by the shooting of the Israeli ambassador in London, and the initial, limited strategic aim was to stop border terror by establishing a buffer zone—hence, Operation Peace for Galilee. True to form with Sharon-led operations, the invasion grew well beyond the announced aims. The IDF finally stopped in Beirut. For the first time in Israel's history there was significant political and public division over the choice of war. From the beginning, the invasion generated controversy among the soldiers who participated, among the Israel public, among Israeli politicians, and within the cabinet. During the course of the war it was difficult for the Labor party to register opposition without raising questions about loyalty, but protest groups formed and demonstrated. Peace Now organized a large demonstration in Tel Aviv, and in early July 86 officers and soldiers petitioned not to serve in Lebanon. In August another group of reserve soldiers, Soldiers Against Silence, registered their opposition to fighting in Beirut.[95] The public and the citizen soldier protests were mutually reinforcing, and there were even instances of front-line soldiers standing up to their commanders. Colonel Eli Geva, who commanded an armored brigade, protested the planned capture of Beirut to the IDF chief of staff, Rafael Eitan, mentioning the "price it's going to cost us and the civilians here."[96] In an act of conscience, Geva offered his resignation but wanted to continue in uniform as a tank commander. Instead, the defense minister and even the prime minister personally tried to pressure him into cooperating. But he believed that "going into Beirut means killing whole families." Geva was dismissed.[97] The attention that Geva's principled resistance received from the highest government leaders indicates how seriously they took this soldier's alarming and possibly exemplary dissent.

As an alternative to sending the IDF into the camps in Beirut, Sharon could delegate the violence to the Phalange. The Maronite Christian Phalange was one of the Lebanese Christian factions that had participated in the civil war prior to the Israeli invasion. The Maronites had a long-term relationship with the Israelis and a well-established record of murder and atrocity. The relationship went back to the 1950s and earlier. A previous plan to invade Lebanon, devised by Dayan and Ben-Gurion, hinged on an invasion invitation to be procured from the Maronites. Prime Minister Sharett's prescient diary entry read, "We'll get bogged down in a mad adventure that will only bring us disgrace."[98] The potential consequences of adventures with the Phalange for Israel's reputation did not deter Sharon. The Christian Phalange were trained and equipped by the Israelis and led by Bashir Gemayel. Gemayel's followers had disposed of one rival Christian faction by killing the leader, family, and household help. They had surprised another Christian group at the Safra Hotel in Beirut. They defenestrated Danny Chamoun's Tigers and then shot them on the way down for good measure.[99] This is what they did to their fellow Christians. In 1976 the Phalange had demonstrated a willingness to kill civilians by massacring thousands of Palestinians in the Tel Zaatar refugee camp in Beirut. There were reports of Phalange atrocities in captured Druze villages in the 1982 war: "these reports reinforced the feeling among certain people—and especially among experienced intelligence officers—that in the event that the Phalangists had an opportunity to massacre Palestinians, they would take advantage of it."[100] If their record left any doubt about what would happen if this force was placed among Palestinian civilians, then it was removed by the statements of Phalange officers. An Israeli journalist met with Phalangist liaison officer Jesse Soker, who invited him to accompany the Phalangists into West Beirut. Soker said, "It's time you learned how to use a knife properly . . . but note no rape of girls under the age of twelve is allowed . . . This isn't Switzerland or Denmark, you know." It is reported that at a meeting with the senior Israeli commanders in West Beirut, the Phalange leaders said, in Arabic, that they would carry out "a cutting or chopping action" in the camps.[101] The chief intelligence officer of the Phalange, Elias Hobeika, "was in daily contact with Israeli officers and made no secret of his belief that the only way out of the Lebanese imbroglio was through a cathartic bloodbath."[102] It was Hobeika's unit that went into Sabra and Shatila.

On September 14, 1982, Hobeika's friend Bashir Gemayel, the Phalange leader and since August 23 the president-elect of Lebanon, was assassinated. With revenge on their minds, the Maronites were ordered into the camps two days later. Cabinet ministers and IDF officers, as well as Israeli journalists, were well aware of the high probability of slaughter if the Phalange went in. In his legal analysis, Weston Burnett says of IDF chief of staff Eitan: "Eitan, possessed the requisite command and control over the Phalangist militia and West Beirut and an awareness, beforehand, of the risk of Phalange war crimes and later, of Phalange-committed war crimes, his failure to intervene to prevent or repress those crimes rendered him criminally liable under the customary international law concept of command responsibility."[103] The Israeli officers and ministers did not explicitly order a massacre, but they could have harbored few illusions about their agents, and during the massacre they had chances to intervene to stop the killing and rape of civilians but did not do so. So why would Defense Minister Sharon put men like this among Palestinian civilians?

In preparing the Phalange, Sharon instructed, "I don't want a single one of the terrorists left."[104] The immediate security goal was to kill Palestinian Liberation Organization (PLO) fighters who might be in the camps. Sharon's alternative was to send in Israeli troops. It was argued that the Phalange could identify PLO fighters, and IDF casualties would be avoided. Of course, the IDF had experience identifying and fighting the PLO, the Phalange actually killed Lebanese Shia civilians in addition to the Palestinians, and the Phalange casualties were very low. Yet, given the principled dissent already exhibited within the IDF and Israeli society, and the record and statements of the Phalange on the other hand, soldiers of the IDF could not be expected to behave with the ruthlessness of the Phalange. The tactical motive that can be ascribed to Sharon is that the terrorists, down to the last one, would be "cleaned out."[105] But a wider strategic motive is possible. According to one Sharon biographer, "Phalange leaders were of the opinion that the massacre in the two camps would result in a mass exodus of Palestinians from all parts of Lebanon," which coincided with Sharon wanting to "encourage" the Palestinians to move to Jordan, destabilize King Hussein, and make that their state.[106] Either way, the activist principal made use of the filthy motives of his agents and sought the political cover that the principal-agent logic provides.

Sharon's agents, the Phalange fighters, had his approval to enter the refugee camps on the Thursday evening, and one of his generals ordered their exit on the Saturday morning. The 150 Phalange fighters took 36 hours to do their raping, murdering, and mutilating in the Shatila and Sabra camps.[107] Among the victims were Palestinian doctors and nurses from the Gaza Hospital located in the camp and the Akka Hospital just outside.[108] The foreign doctors and nurses in these hospitals were spared. Just one hour into the massacre, alarming reports about the killing of women and children began to reach high-ranking Israeli officers. Two hours after entering the camps, Soker, the Phalangist liaison officer, reported 300 killed, including civilians: "He stated this in the presence of many IDF officers who were there, including Brigadier General Yaron."[109] Yaron was the senior Israeli officer in West Beirut. He took no measures to independently verify what was happening on the ground. No Israeli officer was dispatched to the camps, no efforts were made to ensure compliance or to take control of the agents. At about the same time, the defense minister and the IDF chief of staff Rafael Eitan briefed the prime minister and the cabinet about the operation. This was the first the prime minister and the cabinet knew of the Phalangists' entry into the camps. Eitan related to the cabinet his instructions to the Phalange commanders to go into the camps "with their own methods," and about how the IDF would not let them fail. He informed the cabinet of the Phalangist thirst for revenge: "now they have just one thing left to do, and that is revenge; and it will be terrible."[110] The lone word of caution at the cabinet meeting came from Deputy Prime Minister David Levy: "we could come out with no credibility when I hear that the Phalangists are already entering a certain neighborhood—and I know what the meaning of revenge is for them, what kind of slaughter."[111] Apparently no one in the cabinet reacted to Levy's words.

During the first night of the massacre, four different IDF headquarters received some communication concerning atrocities in the camps.[112] In the course of the massacre, the IDF provided logistical support for the Phalange, including lighting from mortars and planes for their night work and a bulldozer with its IDF markings removed. The civilians were buried by bulldozer. The IDF allowed fresh Phalange fighters to move into the camps on the Friday, with the original fighters electing to stay. Early on Friday morning, a journalist, Ze'ev Schiff, informed Minister of Communications Mordechai Zippori of the slaughter, who in turn alerted Foreign Minister Yitzhak Shamir. Shamir later testified to the Israeli commission of inquiry that, as he recalled his conversation with Zippori, he was not informed of a massacre or slaughter and did not act. The journalist corroborated Zippori's version.[113] On Friday afternoon, another journalist, Israel Television's military correspondent, was told of the "havoc" in the camps by an IDF officer. The journalist followed up by making inquiries of a Phalange unit: "the officers and men of that force told us candidly that, in coordination with the IDF, they were on their way in to drive the terrorists out of the refugee camps. Some of the soldiers made it quite clear to the other journalists and myself that they intended to kill the inhabitants of the camps without mercy."[114] Later on Friday evening, the journalist was approached in his apartment by a group of IDF officers who informed him of atrocities in the camps. He phoned Sharon that night and told him "that something must be done to stop it, that IDF officers know about it, and we'll be in a terrible fix." Sharon "hardly responded."[115] Despite the information from some IDF officers and journalists, the IDF commanders did not order the Phalange fighters to leave the camps until 8 A.M. on Saturday morning. The lowest estimate is that they had killed 700 or 800 people.[116]

Prime Minister Begin heard about the massacre on the radio on Saturday evening. As word got out about the massacre and public outrage mounted at home and abroad, the principals responded predictably. The IDF and the Foreign Ministry initially denied that the IDF knew of the Phalange fighters going into the camps, which again fits the artificial information asymmetry or convenient ignorance pattern of Qibya and Deir Yassin. The Israeli government even went so far as to announce their innocence in advertisements in the *New York Times* and *Washington Post*.[117] Defense Minister Sharon and Chief of Staff Eitan afterward suggested Henry V's "vain command" option and claimed that the Phalange commanders had lost control of their men.

The Israeli public was not satisfied with this explanation. A protest demonstration in Tel Aviv a week after the massacres drew 400,000 participants, about 10 percent of the population of Israel.[118] Prime Minister Begin conceded to the public pressure and set up a commission of inquiry. The appointment of the Kahan (President of the Israeli Supreme Court) Commission illustrates that democratic pressures may not allow the principal to exploit claims of ignorance about agents' actions. While it might be suggested that democratic governments adhere to legal norms,[119] the decision to set up an inquiry tends to be as much about placating public criticism and about symbolic politics as it is about delivering justice. Whether or not it delivered justice, the Kahan Commission report is a valuable source of information on the events, arguably more compelling than the results of similar commissions investigating their own troops' conduct in other democracies.

The commission report uses the word "pogrom," suggesting that the IDF had played the same role as Russian authorities in not preventing massacres of Jews. But while its report did not recall the earlier atrocities, the commission had closer references in Israel's own revenge units, the undercover special unit at Qibya, and more specifically in the earlier use of irregulars and the supporting role for Haganah units at Deir Yassin, and in the principals' efforts at artificial information asymmetry. The 1982 Israeli cabinet was an extraordinary collection of veterans of these earlier atrocities with Prime Minister Menachem Begin formerly of the Irgun, Foreign Minister Yitzhak Shamir of the Stern Gang, and Ariel Sharon of Unit 101. As Thomas Friedman says in describing what he characterizes as the "blind tribal rage" of the Phalangists, "the Israelis knew just what they were doing when they let the Phalangists into those camps."[120] The phrase adverse selection seems to understate this recruitment procedure and, in fact, carries a connotation of too passive a principal. Adverse selection occurs when bad risks present themselves to the principal in greater numbers than good risks. Here, the principal sought out the bad risks—perverse selection is the more accurate term from an ethical perspective.

Monitoring is a tool that a principal can use to address the hidden actions of agents. The IDF set up the operation in such a way that its officers could not properly audit and monitor the activities of the Phalange and could not receive a detailed and reliable flow of information. No IDF liaison officer accompanied the Phalange fighters, and the IDF command post did not give a direct view of what was happening.

In 1983 the commission found Sharon "indirectly responsible" for the massacres. The commission was puzzled that the defense minister had not informed the prime minister of his decision to allow the Phalange into the camps, and it held Sharon accountable for ignoring the dangers of vengeance and for not taking steps to minimize the risk of massacre.[121] The commission's notion of indirect responsibility amounts to not having physically carried out the atrocity, and thus it provided protection for the principal. But in reality Sharon and the IDF senior officers knew the methods that the Phalange would use and took no reasonable measures to monitor the conduct of the fighters and prevent the atrocity. And once the slaughter had begun, they took no measures to respond to the informal flow of information about atrocities from the Phalange themselves, from IDF soldiers and officers on the outskirts of the camps, and even from journalists. Instead, the IDF actually facilitated the night action by the Phalange and permitted more Phalangists to enter the camps after at least some senior officers had had reports of the killing of women and children.

The Kahan Commission inquiry into this violence wound up with an explicitly anti-Machiavellian aphorism: "the end never justifies the means, and basic ethical and human values must be maintained in the use of arms."[122] The commission's words remind us of Prime Minister Sharett, of the kibbutznik in 1948, and Katznelson in 1939, who all subscribed to the idea that the Israeli military should follow a moral code. Failing the intervention of moral commitment, external pressures from other countries and international organizations are the costs that are ordinarily thought to restrain leaders' use of violence. In the Israeli case, internal restraints in the form of public pressure and citizen soldier protest, and perhaps the anticipation by leaders of greater citizen soldier protest, are also salient. The clear motivational advantages of citizen soldiers over mercenaries formed Machiavelli's preference for the former. Unlike mercenaries motivated by a little bit of money, citizen soldiers would be committed enough to Florence or to Italy to risk death. But citizen soldiers may come with other commitments, a notion of combat morality. Machiavelli was very concerned about the prince's moral inhibitions, perhaps forgetting that his agents may be equally complex.

In democracies, leaders adjust policies and even respond with inquiries and investigations to obtain public quiescence when government violence begins to jeopardize rather than to contribute to public support. In the wake of the report, Sharon was removed as defense minister, not as Borgia's Spanish minister was to the public square to leave the public "stunned and satisfied," but to the brief of minister without portfolio. True to activist form, Sharon likely underestimated the domestic and international costs of the atrocity, and to anyone who cares to look closely, the political cover provided by his Phalange agents was threadbare by the end. But he survived and ultimately prospered politically. In March 2001, with Israeli voters responding to the second Intifada's sharp escalation in violence, Sharon helped create and then seize the "Machiavellian moment" for leadership.

Sharon got off lightly with the findings of the domestic inquiry. International legal proceedings now use the doctrines of "joint criminal conspiracy" and "exercising effective control or substantial influence" to involve the principals as well as the agents who physically perpetrate atrocities, as in the indictment holding President Slobodan Milosovic responsible for the actions of the Serbian paramilitary group known as Arkan's Tigers. The International Criminal Tribunal for the Former Yugoslavia copes with the problem of information asymmetry, using the argument that the principal "knew or had reason to know" and failed to prevent the atrocity or to punish the agents. The new International Criminal Court's statute, in article 28, lays out the doctrine of command responsibility. The article states that the superior is responsible where the "superior knew, or consciously disregarded information which clearly indicated, that the subordinates were committing or about to commit such crimes." Israel, along with the United States, has not ratified the treaty setting up this new court.

Balancing the strategic ledger for the violence of Operation Peace for Galilee is not straightforward. The Palestinian Liberation Organization (PLO) was forced out of Beirut, but to Tunisia and without the destabilization of King Hussein in Jordan. Approximately 6,000 PLO fighters were killed and 368 IDF soldiers lost along with two Phalange fighters in Sabra and Shatila.[123] But border security was not enhanced. The threat reorganized as Islamic fundamentalist groups, and by the late 1980s the internal challenge of the first Intifada taxed the repressive machinery of the Israeli government in new ways. The cost of international outrage at the atrocity, which was not successfully deflected by using the Lebanese Phalange as agents, was less long-term than the divisive effect of the war on Israeli politics and public support. A few years later, Ze'ev Schiff, the journalist who had tipped off Minister Zippori to the massacre, assessed the impact of the Lebanese war:

> From the sobering consequences of Operation Peace for Galilee one may be forced to conclude that a country can be victorious on the battlefield but lose a war strategically; that a small nation whose leaders fail to appreciate the limits of military power is doomed to pay dearly for their arrogance; and that a democracy like Israel, whose defence is based on a militia army, cannot possibly win a war that lacks not only broad public support but even the slimmest national consensus regarding its very necessity.[124]

Machiavelli's argument for citizen soldiers over mercenaries was his solution to the problem of goal variance between principal and agent: mercenaries would not take the necessary risks in exchange for a little money. But Machiavelli's solution was only partial. Citizen soldiers may also have reasons for deviating from the principal and raise control problems of their own. To return to Hume, citizen soldiers, more than any other sort of soldier, require leading "like men, by their opinion."

ACTIVISTS WON'T CONTROL, MODERATES CAN'T CONTROL

From the leaders' perspective, one general motive dominates these fifty years of violence, and we should not confuse Jenin, or Deir Yassin, with Dachau. Israel's use of violence belongs to Machiavelli rather than the Inquisitor. The rational use of violence and atrocity to protect power requires the leader to assess the threat and the costs of violence. Primitive chess players or activists repeatedly opted for nastier strategies, and they assumed a supportive domestic public and a relatively indifferent or impotent international system. The moderates' nicer strategies were predicated on moral inhibitions and enhanced sensitivity to the potential costs of violence.

Scholars generally distinguish between moderates and activists by the nastiness of the tactics that they are willing to use, their relative sensitivity to the costs of using violence, by their "caution" and "courage," and by their commitments to internationalism (the United Nations) or to unilateralism.[125] We can distinguish them by the kind of principal-agent problem that they face. Nastier tactics make the control issue arising from the delegation of violence a convenience rather than a problem. Activists in the Israeli cabinet repeatedly avoided too much knowledge of the activities of their agents and sought to deny or to avoid formal and public involvement, as Machiavelli advised. Irregulars, local Haganah commanders, and special units willingly carried out the cruelty, and their cruelty served a strategic end. Menachem Begin's 1952 memoir has a statement, left out of later editions, that links atrocity and strategy: "without Deir Yassin there wouldn't have been an Israel, and that after it the Zionist forces could advance like a hot knife through butter."[126] On the other hand, actual rather than artificial information asymmetry is usually the problem confounding moderates in the cabinet. Moderates in the cabinet have been particularly likely to be victims of deflated estimates of proposed violence and of the false reporting and cover-ups that Sharett complained of during his term. This contrast in leadership brings us back to Schiller's Tilly and Shakespeare's Henry V: activists won't control, moderates can't control.

The implication of this analysis is that the relationship between principal and agent is dynamic and that the largest single factor explaining the Israeli violence is the ascendance of activist principals, who are willing to extract strategic benefits from even the reward- or revenge-motivated agents and willing to close down these agents when their activities no longer deliver strategic benefits. Agents' truly independent contributions to the overall violence are likely to be largest when moderates are in control.

Finally, there is the concussive effect of 50 years or more of battle in what is clearly a well-blasted land and the hangover from the British Mandate of some of the methods and savagery. Yet, there remains Sharett's prospect of playing different kinds of chess, of breaking with the legacy of the past, of consistent control of the agents of repression, including irregulars and settlers, and paradoxically of the citizen soldiers themselves cooperating to monitor and restrain each other and even their leaders.

FOUR

The Russian Civil War

This inevitable tragedy does not disturb Lenin, the slave of dogma.

—Maxim Gorky[1]

The Russian Civil War shows how Machiavelli's motive can leave too much of the violence unexplained. In Russia the blood flowed from the devastating consequences of the logic of an intolerant political argument and from the slack given the agents of repression. The convictions of the leader and his management practices created the pattern of violence and atrocity. Vladimir Lenin's world was inhabited by friends and enemies of the revolution. He had little interest in monitoring and correcting his agents as the gravitational force of their selfishness and reward seeking plus his commitment to the violent elimination of enemies of the revolution moved policy down the same tragic path.

The Russian Civil War is "one of the forgotten holocausts of modern history."[2] Yet, the use of violations was not a necessary outcome of the civil war. It was not a function of fighting autocratic monarchies or of the contagious effect of bloody international war. It was not simply a tit-for-tat response to what the opposition did. It was beyond the threat entailed and continued after the opposing White armies had been beaten from the field. Arguably, the inefficient and imprudently disproportionate violations actually increased the threat to Lenin's government.[3] We must look instead to the motivations of leaders and led. Beyond the fact that his agents killed all these people, what is the independent evidence of Lenin's intolerant beliefs and policy agenda?

COMRADE INQUISITOR

Lenin's political argument drew on Marxist theories, and sought authoritative and exculpatory references and examples from history, in particular from the French Revolution. He categorized the enemies of the revolution by beliefs, membership in organizations, occupations, and even geography. His concern was not simply to contribute to his personal power. A night shooting of a czar in a cellar and dodging responsibility is the choice of an opportunist, but shooting prostitutes, peasants, and priests added little to the security of his position. Lenin, at times tactically astute, is a sincere Inquisitor. One of his biographers describes his subject:

> He was also a secular "believer." His vision of a future for mankind when all exploitation and oppression would disappear was sincere. This surely is the central point about his life. The danger posed by the Lenins is not that they are simply power-crazed. It is that they combine a thirst for power with an ideological intolerance that casts down all in their path. Lenin was dignified and thoughtful, a decent man in his personal relations.[4]

No less would be said of the Grand Inquisitor: a sincere man, given to personal acts of generosity and mercy, not in it for himself but dedicated to the public interest.

For Lenin, tomorrow belonged to the workers of the world, and was to be reached through violent class conflict. He had no tolerance for those he saw as left behind in yesterday's groups. Lenin's government certainly valued its own survival sufficiently to repress the opposition, and it used techniques that the czar had used. Beyond that, however, Lenin's government ideologically selected or neglected categories of the population to accelerate what history had in store for them. As Lenin said in November 1917, "the state is an instrument of coercion . . . we want to organize violence in the name of the interests of the workers."[5] The propertied classes or bourgeoisie, the czarist officers or Whites, the clergy, the rich peasants or kulaks, and other political groupings, including anarchists and socialist parties, were the enemies of the revolution and therefore were to be silenced or eliminated. The day after the revolution the new government started closing down ideologically suspect newspapers.[6] Prudently, the Moscow Art Theater was prohibited from putting on a stage version of *The Brothers Karamazov*, as well as Friedrich Schiller's *Mary Stuart*, among other plays.[7] These plays contained material dangerous for a regime that killed its own royalty and was uncompromising in its authority and beliefs.

Concerns about justice and individuals get in the way of class struggle. The *Red Sword* of August 18, 1919, described this line of reasoning: "Ours is a new morality. Our humanism is absolute, for it has as its basis the desire for the abolition of all oppression and tyranny. To us everything is permitted, for we are the first in the world to raise the sword not for the purpose of enslavement and oppression but in the name of liberty and emancipation from slavery. We do not wage war against individuals. We seek to destroy the bourgeoisie as a class."[8] Individuals do not count, and there is no place in this argument for tolerance. On the contrary, until communism eventually "solves the riddle of history," humans are irreconcilably grouped against each other and necessarily oppressive toward each other.

On the eve of the revolution, Lenin, in "The Russian Revolution and Civil War," ominously described the Cossacks:

> As to the Cossacks, they are a section of the population consisting of rich, small or medium landed proprietors . . . in one of those outlying regions of Russia that have retained many medieval traits in their way of life, their economy, and their customs. We can regard this as the socio-economic basis for a Russian Vendée.[9]

The Vendée was suppressed by revolutionary terror. It was a bloody revolt in western France triggered by the introduction of national conscription for the army. The Alsatian commander,

François-Joseph Westermann, reported to the Committee of Public Safety, "There is no more Vendée . . . I have crushed children under the feet of horses, massacred women who at least . . . will engender no more brigands. I have no prisoners with which to reproach myself."[10] The Red Army took a similar approach to the Russian Vendée. In the war with the Cossacks, the party's Central Committee resolution of January 24, 1919, stated:

> In view of the experience of the civil war against the Cossacks, it is necessary to recognize the unique correctness of the most merciless struggle against the upper strata of the Cossacks by their extermination to a man. No compromises and no half-measures would do. Therefore it is necessary to conduct mass terror against rich Cossacks by exterminating them to the last man.[11]

One expects calls for genocide, "acts committed with intent to destroy, in whole or in part, a national, ethnical, racial or religious group" (Article II, Genocide Convention), to be more circumspect.

Lenin had absorbed the violent and polarizing lessons of the French Revolution. That revolution had had its "white" counterrevolutionaries (they wore white cockades), its revolutionary tribunals, and its enemies of the people. But if the Cossacks were the Vendée, Lenin was Marat (the Friend of the People), the French revolutionary "who believed the only solution to scarcity was to guillotine hoarders and speculators."[12] There are other obvious parallels between the revolutions, not least the self-destruction of the revolutionary leadership: revolutionary justice claimed Trotsky, Bukharin, Danton, and Robespierre. But most interestingly, in neither case does the use of terror correspond to the level of threat to the regime. Threats to the new French republic were highest in the spring and summer of 1793, with the occurrence of urban as well as rural revolts and foreign intervention: "yet these dire months did not coincide with the height of the Terror. On the contrary, the number of death sentences increased sharply that fall when the situation had significantly improved. And, in the spring of 1794, when domestic insurrections had successfully been quelled and the armies of France had taken the offensive at the borders, the Terror reached its apogee."[13] Historian Susan Dunn argues that violations in the French Revolution derived from the values of the Jacobins and from their notion of an indivisible French community counterposed to an "anticommunity of oppressors and enemies."[14] There were terrible consequences to the narcissistic group experiments of the French Revolution: Do you prefer Klee to Kandinsky, David to Francis Boucher, the French court painter?

Lenin's violence was integral to his vision of social progress, not simply a response to what an opponent was doing: "violence is *always* the midwife of the old society" [my emphasis].[15] His political position prior to his seizing power was that a really good revolution required a really violent civil war. In September 1917 he wrote that "a revolution, a real, profound, a 'people's' revolution to use Marx's expression, is the incredibly complicated and painful process of the death of the old and birth of the new social order, of the mode of life of tens of millions of people. Revolution is a most intense, furious, desperate class struggle and civil war. Not a single great revolution in history has taken place without civil war."[16] Lenin's radical view of violence as essential to the revolution, as an end in itself and not just an instrument to hold on to power, was clear to others. A leader of the Left Socialist Revolutionary Party and participant in the early Bolshevik-led government said that it was this attitude to violence that distinguished the Bolsheviks: "It was soon evident that the Bolshevik leaders—Lenin, Trotsky, Zinoviev, Bukharin and others—wanted to intensify the violence of events . . . absence of violence would prove that the upheaval was not sufficiently revolutionary."[17] Lenin's lethal syllogism took the form:

Premise I: Revolutionaries are violent.
Premise II: Bolsheviks are revolutionaries.
Conclusion: Bolsheviks are violent.

Lenin's practice followed this political argument, he moved relentlessly from premise to conclusion, and he delivered a very violent civil war. What is shocking is that an abstract mental performance, whether by the Grand Inquisitor or Comrade Inquisitor, then leads to such a dire outcome for so many people.

Lenin directed his agents against the Cossacks, kulaks, White Guards, prostitutes, and priests. In 1918 he was urging his agents to, "apply mass terror immediately to execute and exterminate hundreds of prostitutes, drunken soldiers, former officers, etc."[18] And he was arguing that, "we need tens of thousands of advanced and steeled proletarians . . . resolute enough to ruthlessly cast out of their midst and shoot all who allow themselves to be 'tempted' . . . we need proletarians steadfast enough and devoted enough to the revolution to bear in an organized way all the hardships of the *crusade* [my emphasis] . . ."[19] Selecting for execution such a wide variety of people—drunks and the well off, prostitutes and priests, as well as the incompetent—had real consequences, as Lenin's position in the new government was unassailable and as he took such a detailed interest in the application of terror: "I'm sure the crushing of the Kazan Czechs and White Guards, as well as the kulak-bloodsuckers who support them, will be carried out with an exemplary lack of mercy."[20] Lenin's repeated calls for terror and firing squads bring to mind Alice's Queen of Hearts and her off-with-his-head obsession. Beyond the obsessive concern with execution and the exhortation to his officials to embrace slaughter, what also emerges in the documentary record is Lenin's cynical propensity for opportunism and manipulation. In a 1920 memo to a colleague he wrote: "A beautiful plan. Finish it off together with Dzerzhynski. Disguised as 'Greens' (and we'll pin this on them subsequently), we'll advance for 10-20 versts and hang the kulaks, priests, and landowners. The prize: 100,000 rubles for every man hanged."[21] The Greens were deserters and peasants, opposed to both Whites and Reds in the civil war, who took to the forests. Lenin was willing to use the Greens as Stalin later used the Wehrmacht for his massacre of the thousands of Polish officers in Katyn Forest in 1940. The abusive and manipulative father of the revolution left the predictable legacy of a state apparatus unhinged from any ethical support.

Sometimes Lenin showed cleverness on issues of language. In January 1918, his Left Socialist Revolutionary coalition partner I. N. Steinberg asked him: "why do we bother with a Commissariat of Justice? Let's call it frankly the Commissariat for Social Extermination and be done with it!" Lenin replied: "Well put . . . that's exactly what it should be . . . but we can't say that."[22] Joseph Stalin and Adolf Hitler faced the same issue of "defending the indefensible," as George Orwell put it, and they generally opted for euphemisms.

Euphemism may have been employed to make their own actions more acceptable, yet Lenin and the Communists at the same time used a pestilential vocabulary to make enemies truly unacceptable. He did not rely solely on the arcane language of class struggle to identify and isolate class enemies. Lenin refers to the kulaks as "spiders," "leeches," and "vampires."[23] In December 1917, in "How to Organize Competition," he wanted to rid Russia "of all vermin, of fleas—the rogues, of bugs—the rich, and so on and so forth."[24] This artful language serves as a lubricant for the action of violence. Language clearly differentiates the victims as separate from and inferior to the perpetrators, and it provides principals and their agents with the psychological preparation to do what is, by ordinary standards, evil. For example, the Nazis would frame their actions as racial hygiene and a final solution, and Japanese soldiers would claim they fought "beasts"; they referred to the Chinese as "pigs" and slaughtered them at Nanking and elsewhere.[25] Language magnifies the minor differences.

In trying to explain to foreign supporters what he was doing, Lenin argued that the terror of the Russian Civil War just followed the pattern set by earlier civil wars. He referred to the English, French, and American civil wars in justifying his actions. Lenin invited American workers to compare his use of terror with bourgeois terror: "The British bourgeoisie have forgotten their 1649, the French bourgeoisie have forgotten their 1793. Terror was just and legitimate when the bourgeoisie resorted to it."[26] But one historian of the Russian Revolution, William Chamberlin, makes an explicit comparison between these wars: "the fiercest episodes of the British Civil War of the seventeenth century or of the American Civil War seem mild compared with the regular practice of the contending sides in Russia."[27] Neither of those wars had a principal in the grip of Inquisitorial logic, and neither permitted agents the latitude that they enjoyed in Russia.

Lenin's repeated and rebarbative commitment to terror directed at whole categories of the Russian people meant that if his agents did not implement high levels of human rights violations, it would be through no lack of incitement from the principal. His enthusiasm for mass terror, his championing of the agencies of terror even when others pointed out excessive violations, and his dominant position within the new government gave a carte blanche to reward-seeking agents. He was undeterred by initial resistance to the use of terror from other political parties and groups that supported the Bolsheviks. The Left Socialist Revolutionaries (LSRs) opposed repression and broke with the Bolsheviks over the decision to make peace with Germany, while the Kronstadt sailors' newspaper in November 1917 editorialized for the purity of the revolution:

> The bloody shadows of Robespierre and Marat must not darken our revolution. We must set an example of humanism, for we fight for the peace of nations. We stand against bloodshed in general and needless bloodshed in particular. Let every soldier remember that we are not the gendarmes of Nicholas the Bloody! Let no drop of wantonly shed blood torment our consciences![28]

Both the LSRs and the Kronstadters became victims of the Bolsheviks. Within the small group of leading Bolsheviks, Lenin faced down internal resistance to his use of terror. Lev Kamenev argued for compromise with the other socialist parties and tighter control of the secret police.[29] Kamenev's merciful intervention saved some priests in 1922.[30] But nobody intervened for him in 1936, when he was shot, with the revolution now under Lenin's bloody shadow.

A SYNOPSIS OF THE CONFLICT

Most immediately, the civil war followed from the czar's abdication in February 1917 in the face of strikes, riots, and mutinous soldiers and in the midst of Russia's disastrous participation in the First World War; from the German stratagem to entrain a revolutionary at their enemy's rear; and from that revolutionary's decision to seize and stay in power in order to transform Russia. In October 1917, the Bolsheviks and their supporters stormed St. Petersburg's Winter Palace and wrested power from the provisional government that had replaced the czar. Sailors from Kronstadt, the island fortress in the Gulf of Finland off St. Petersburg, who had welcomed Lenin off the exile's express at the city's Finland Station, provided support for the coup by training the battleship Aurora's guns on the palace and by helping to fill the ranks of those who stormed the palace and arrested members of the provisional government.[31] While the new Bolshevik government wanted to make peace with Germany, its seizure of power provoked peasant wars, further foreign intervention, military opposition from czarist White generals, and armed resistance from former comrades and supporters. In the Urals and Siberia, the Red Army fought the Czech legion and the Socialist Revolutionaries and then the Whites under Admiral Alexander Kolchak. In the south, they fought White armies led by Generals Anton Deniken and Peter Wrangel. Leon Trotsky in his armed train and the Red Army stopped General Nikolai Yudenich before Petrograd. The Red Army invaded Poland, only to be repulsed by the Poles. They fought peasants who organized the Green resistance in the countryside and Black anarchists, as well as the mutineers at Kronstadt. Under Lenin's direction, the Bolshevik response to the enemy—whether Kolchak, Deniken, the peasant leader Nestor Makhno, or the mutinous sailors—was inelastically merciless.

It is difficult to date the start and end of the civil war with precision. The year 1917 saw bitter fighting and casualties. Nevertheless, many waited for Red Army combat with the peripatetic Czech legion in the summer of 1918. These soldiers, deserters and prisoners of war from the Austrian and German armies who had fought for the Russians and who carried British hopes of a reignited Eastern Front, were en route to France via Siberia. Their movements inadvertently hastened the Communist decision on the fate of Czar Nicholas and his family, prisoners in the city of Ekaterinburg. The Communist leaders, heavily dependent on Latvian riflemen to protect their revolution, were anxious to ensure peace with Germany. The Germans objected to the Czech legion as an "allied military force in neutral Russia."[32] On May 25, 1918, the commissar for military affairs, Leon Trotsky, ordered the legion disarmed. The legion rejected Trotsky's order and resisted Red Army efforts to implement the order. They allied with the Socialist Revolutionaries, the party that was particularly strong in rural Russia and that had most popular support.[33] With these allies, the legion took the city of Samara on the River Volga, and by the end of August 1918 it was running the Trans-Siberian Railway to the eastern end of the line in Vladivostok.[34] But the Red Army, with units redeployed from the German front, mounted a successful offensive. The German threat to the Bolsheviks had diminished after August 8, when British and French tanks smashed the German lines at Amiens. The Socialist Revolutionaries were caught between the Red Army and the Siberian White forces under Admiral Kolchak, and the Czechs became increasingly disinterested in Russian affairs and anxious to get out.

Red on red conflict might also mark the end of the Civil War. The end is sometimes dated to late 1920 by the defeat of the White armies, which were handicapped with their poor discipline, repression, and authoritarian old regime connections. Yet, significant combat continued after the defeat of the major White armies. In the spring of 1921, 50,000 Red Army troops led by the top Red Army commander, Mikhail Tukhachevskii, defeated the 15,000 defenders of the naval fortress on Kronstadt and treated the survivors with no mercy.[35] The sailors' revolutionary pedigree and socialist demands provided no protection from Communist propaganda labeling them White, counterrevolutionary, and condemned.

RED TERROR: "SENTENCE FIRST—VERDICT AFTERWARDS"[36]

The toll in the Russian Civil War from disease, famine, combat, and in particular from the government's routine execution and killing of noncombatants was on a different scale from either the English war that came before or the Israeli war that came after. All three civil wars are cases of extreme military threat to government, yet this constant threat is accompanied by a puzzling variability in violence.

It is not unreasonable to include deaths from famine and so bring into the reckoning the catastrophic impact of Lenin's economic policies. In 1921 the New Economic Policy to induce trade in agricultural production replaced the forced confiscation of War Communism, which had effectively destroyed the peasants' incentive to cultivate food for any but themselves. The savagery of the forces sent to requisition food precipitated peasant revolts in the provinces and resulted in urban hunger. Compounding the problem was the difficulty of transporting the food that was available. The civil war cut lines of communication and supply to the major cities. Urbanization actually reversed during the civil war period, as Russians, like Dr. Zhivago, abandoned cities to survive. Petrograd lost about two-thirds of its population between 1917 and 1920 and Moscow's population declined by half, which was by about one million people.[37] Prostitution, including child prostitution, also increased as a way for the hungry and out-of-work to cope, as did the incidence of venereal disease.[38] Historians arrive at a total mortality of around 10 million for the Russian Civil War, including deaths from famine and disease.[39] The international bill of human rights, adopted after the Second World War, extends to economic rights including adequate nutrition. But our central issue is the killings of prisoners and civilians by Lenin's government forces, not famine deaths.

From 1917 to 1921 Russia was a slaughterhouse. One's fate depended on one's side in the political argument, as signaled by a system of categorizing and color-coding. Even prior revolutionary service and proletarian credentials provided no guarantee that you would be on the safe side of the argument, as Reds could be rebranded Whites. There was little recourse for the individual marked for execution. Mute in the chute as a White, a Black, or a Green, there was no opportunity to turn around.

This civil war ranks among the worst of the blood baths of the twentieth century, or of any century, and serves as a proving ground for the repressive techniques of the 1930s and 1940s. This ranking may be shocking, particularly for those on the left who isolate the single dark factor in this massive social experiment as Joseph Stalin. But it was Lenin, a revolutionary "blown in from abroad, raised on" the shoulders of drunken soldiers and mutinous sailors whom he had bought with promises of bread and peace and then had shot, who made and betrayed the revolution.[40] The agents who carried out the repression were organized in the Red Army and the security police, the Cheka. The Cheka or Vecheka, the acronym for the All-Russian Extraordinary Commission for Combating Counter-Revolution, Sabotage, and Speculation, which had both a central organization and regional and local units, was the special agency set up in December 1917 by the new government to repress those who belonged to various criminal, economic, and political categories.

Like most official accounts of human rights violations, Soviet accounts of general numbers killed or of particular executions are unreliable. The most notorious execution occurred on the night of July 16, 1918, when Cheka agents and Latvian riflemen fetched Czar Nicholas, his wife, his son, his four daughters, his doctor, servants, and the chambermaid to the cellar of a house in the city of Ekaterinburg and then shot them. They burnt and buried the bodies: no remnant for counterrevolution. It seems most likely, and there is some consensus among historians, that Lenin made the decision. It was too important a decision, and Lenin was too actively engaged in the details of making and implementing the policy of repression, for him not to have made it. A leading Bolshevik was later quoted as saying: "We decided it here. Ilyich believed that we shouldn't leave the Whites a live banner to rally around . . ."[41] Yet, the official Soviet account ran: "the Ural Territorial Soviet decided to shoot Nicholas Romanov . . . the wife and son of Nicholas Romanov were sent to a safe place." On July 17, other members of the Romanov family were murdered in a mining town in the Urals, but it was announced that persons unknown had abducted them, and the previous month the czar's brother and his English secretary had been shot.[42] Official accounts lied about Red Terror, from particular cases to its general impact.

Russian and western historians' accounts of all those killed by Red terror provide figures ranging from the hundreds of thousands to over a million. For the Crimea alone, Sergey Melgounov sets the range from 50,000 to 150,000 killed.[43] Melgounov was a Russian historian who was imprisoned and later exiled by the Communists. His account is widely used by historians of the civil war. He describes the details of slaughter in the Crimea:

At first the corpses were disposed of by dumping them into ancient Genoese wells; but in time even these wells became filled up, and the condemned had to be marched out into the country during the daytime (ostensibly to work in the mines) and there made to dig huge graves before daylight should fail, and then be locked into sheds for an hour or two, and, with the fall of dusk, stripped except for the little crosses around their necks, and shot. And as they were shot they fell forward in layers . . . Only when morning came did any victim who seemed to be still breathing have his brains dashed out with a piece of rock. And, for that matter, many were buried alive. At Kertch the Boshevists organised what they called "trips to Kuban," when victims were taken out to sea, and drowned, and their terror-stricken wives and mothers flogged with nagaiki [thick Cossack whips] or, in a few cases, shot along with their sons or husbands.[44]

The leading western historian of Soviet terror, Robert Conquest, describing his estimates as conservative, reports a minimum of 200,000 executed up to 1923, which rises to 500,000 if you include deaths in custody and killings of insurgents. Supporting a figure in Conquest's range for the activities of the Cheka alone is I. N. Steinberg's statement that Felix Dzershinsky, the head of the Cheka, brought "irreparable sorrow to hundreds of thousands, and perhaps more."[45] Within three days of the assassination of the head of the Petrograd Cheka and the attempted assassination of Lenin on August 30, 1918, authorities in that one city had selected 500 individuals and shot them.

With his thorough and detailed analysis of the Cheka's activities, historian George Leggett supports an overall total approximating Conquest's. Leggett also describes post–civil war killings at two northern concentration camps. Those shot or drowned in these Archangel killings were in the "scores of thousands" and perhaps as high as 100,000, and this continued until 1922.[46] They included White Army soldiers and peasant prisoners from Tambov, Siberia, and the Ukraine. For defeated soldiers in this civil war, there was no option to go home or to carry their weapon abroad. Showing a capacity for morbid irony, the Communists sunk in barges some 2,000 sailors who had survived from Kronstadt. It seems an innovative, elaborate means to execute enemies, but its wider use suggests some efficiency. Bolsheviks, Nazis, and French revolutionaries converged on this same sinking technique, which combined execution with disposal. During the French Revolution the suppression of counterrevolution in the Vendée, with a death toll put as high as a quarter of a million, included the submersion ("republican baptism") method of execution. The French revolutionaries used the Loire as the Communists used the River Dvina. They submerged priests and others in holed barges, or *noyades*,[47] producing a ghastly riparian environment downstream to Nantes. And according to the Nuremberg Indictment, the Nazis sank barges to drown over 144,000 people off the Crimean peninsula.

Dmitri Volkogonov has come up with a more recent reckoning for Red terror with better, post–cold war access to official sources of information. Volkogonov was a senior officer in Leonid Brezhnev's Red Army and was appointed director of the Institute of Military History in Moscow in the 1980s. Under Yeltsin he was head of the Russian Archive Declassifying Commission. For just the years 1918-1919, he comes up with an estimate of 1.7 million. This figure is attributed to N. N. Golovin, who was a professor at the Imperial Military Academy, and is for "Bolshevik terror," which presumably includes all organizations, not just the Cheka.[48] Lastly, Taisia Osipova states:

> The total casualties of armed peasant detachments, the Greens, deserters, and other insurgents were 1 million, counting those who were killed or executed or who died in prisons and concentration camps. The casualty rate was even higher among the civilian population in areas of the most serious insurgencies. The civilian casualties of the Red Terror in those areas were estimated at 5 million.[49]

Whites as well as Reds in the Russian Civil War routinely committed atrocities. Admiral Kolchak's White forces executed, raped, and amputated their way across Siberia in response to peasant insurgencies and Soviet action. War on the limbs and digits of civilian populations was practiced before the recent civil war in Sierra Leone. In the south, General Wrangel wrote that, "I had 370 Bolshevik officers and non-commissioned officers shot on the spot."[50] But White agents, out of control, were responsible for a large measure of the killing. The drunk and atrocious behavior of General Deniken's army included widespread pogroms in the Ukraine. Jews were identified with Communists in White propaganda. Interestingly, and eerily similar to accounts of pre-Holocaust Germany and to relations between Serbs and Muslims in the former Yugoslavia, there is testimony to the preexisting neighborly relations between Ukrainians and Jews.[51] The majority of White victims were killed by out-of-control agents: "by far the largest number of persons who met a violent end under the regime of the Whites seem to have come to their death not as a result of any regular trial, or even of a summary verdict by a drumhead court-martial, but were simply slaughtered by more or less irresponsible bands of soldiers whose leaders certainly kept no records of their actions."[52] Approximately 150,000 Cossacks and their families, who had supported the dictatorship of Admiral Kolchak, preferred the long march to China to the prospect of Communist rule, although just 30,000 saw the border.[53] The Cheka shot Kolchak.

Violations typified White conduct, but there was no symmetry of violations. The White armies were spontaneously murderous, yet, other opponents of the Communists behaved and still perished.

The Cheka killed without trial. The different types of revolutionary tribunals, including ordinary, military, and railway tribunals that coexisted with the Cheka, did offer that formality, but there was no appeal and the sentence was carried out immediately. These tribunals executed thousands, "often merely for belonging to the exploiting class." In 1921, which is after the defeat of the major White armies, the statistics reported by the Military Collegium of the Supreme Tribunal recorded the execution of 4,337 soldiers and officers.[54] Two years earlier, tribunals conducted in the region of the River Don gave perfunctory consideration to the individuals who appeared before them.

> Most of the time the tribunals dealt with cases on the basis of lists. Sometimes it took only a few minutes to consider a case. And the sentence was almost always the same: shooting . . . Old Cossacks from various families were shot, officers who had voluntarily laid down their arms were shot. Even Cossack women were shot.[55]

Lenin on occasion advocated hanging, and local Cheka units and others improvised unspeakable deaths for their victims, but the routine method of execution was shooting.

Torture was widespread. Stories of torture appeared in the Communist press. In March 1919 *Pravda* reported that the Cheka had facilities for "pricking prisoners' heels with needles."[56] When the Cheka released a British diplomat, Bruce Lockhart, the Cheka's bulletin published a letter from a provincial Cheka asking, "why didn't you subject this Lockhart to the most refined tortures . . . a dangerous scoundrel has been caught. Extract everything possible from him, and dispatch him to the next world."[57] A German diplomat likened the Cheka to the Spanish Inquisition in the fear that it created.[58] The sailors in Kronstadt spoke up about czarist and Communist torture, before the Cheka came for them:

> The power of the police and the gendarme monarchy passed into the hands of the Communist usurpers, who, instead of giving the people freedom, instilled in them the constant fear of falling into the torture chambers of the Cheka, which in their horrors far exceed the gendarme administration of the czarist regime . . .[59]

These Red horrors far exceeded the czarist regime and any proportionate response to threat.

Lenin and the Communists did not adjust repression to the type of threat posed, and no means of repression or weapon was outside consideration. Trotsky, in the spring of 1919, informed Moscow by telegram that "it is necessary to find a possible way of using asphyxiating gases."[60] A way may have been found in 1921. The ubiquitous Tukhachevskii, assigned to put down insurgent peasants in Tambov province, gave the following order: "The forest where the bandits are hiding must be cleared with poison gas; careful calculations must be made to ensure that the cloud of asphyxiating gas spreads throughout the forest and exterminates everything hiding there . . ."[61] Combatants in the First World War used gas, although at least not deliberately on their own people.

Consistent with Lenin's Inquisitorial mission, his agents in the Cheka dealt with enemies in groups, Romanovs included. The Cheka came first for criminals like Prince Eboli, a common criminal's alias, and Britt, presumably his princess. The Cheka executed these two for extortion on February 26, 1918. Lenin, like Marat, had it in for speculators. In a meeting on January 14, 1918, he said, "We can't expect to get anywhere unless we resort to terrorism: speculators must be shot on the spot."[62] Speculation included going shopping on the black market, which was a matter of survival in the starving cities. Patrols guarded the city limits to stop the exodus to the countryside. Weeks into the revolution, Lenin loosened control of his agents by explicitly encouraging them to decide on and implement executions on the street.

In July 1918 the Cheka came for the Left Socialist Revolutionaries (LSRs), formerly in coalition with the Communist Party. The LSRs even had members in the Cheka, and their opposition to the death penalty is credited with limiting the Cheka's mission and activity in its first months of operation. The LSRs' political position sanctioned individual and selective assassination for political purposes but condemned the systematic use of executions. They opposed appeasing Germany, and in a desperate act, two of their members talked their way into the German embassy using Cheka credentials and then assassinated Count von Mirbach, the German ambassador. Concerned to placate the German invaders, the Communists responded vigorously to the assassination. Their Latvian regiment quickly dealt with LSR resistance, and the Cheka executed 13 of the LSRs on July 7. Maria Spiridonova, one of the leaders of the LSRs, later testified that she had organized the assassination, while vehemently denying that she had conspired with the British or French. As a girl, she assassinated a repressive czarist governor. His soldiers raped her in retaliation, and she spent years in prison. The Communists amnestied this visible revolutionary for her part in the Mirbach assassination, but subsequently arrested her for her consistent condemnation of the Communist use of torture and terror. The Revolutionary Tribunal declared her hysterical, and they considered sending her to an asylum.[63] She escaped and was recaptured.

Members of other socialist parties were treated similarly. In Lenin's words: "In my opinion, we must extend the use of executions (commutable to deportation abroad) . . . to all forms of activity on the part of the Mensheviks, SRs, and so forth; we must find a formulation linking these actions to the international bourgeoisie and its struggle against us."[64] Whatever the action of members of these groups, they were to be defined as a counterrevolutionary threat, and then they were to be killed or driven out. Their activity might vary; the government response would not.

In March 1919 workers in some Petrograd factories went on strike, demanding free speech and a free press. Estimates suggest that the Cheka shot about 200 strikers, including some 15 LSRs whose executions were published in the Communist press. The Bolsheviks extracted from the workers false public confessions admitting the influence of counterrevolutionaries, which, as Vladimir Brovkin points out, presaged the techniques associated with the 1930s.[65] In that same month, workers in Astrakhan on the Volga struck over inadequate food rations and killed some 47 local Communists. The Cheka executed several hundred and the overall toll amounted to between 2,000 and 4,000 killed. Some prisoners kept on barges went overboard with stone ballast. The repression extended to local merchants and their wives.[66] Brovkin's account mentions strikes in other cities at this time with similar outcomes. It is fair to say that the Bolsheviks broke strikes more ruthlessly than any western bourgeois government, though they took the Jesuitical trouble to secure confessions and make the argument that the strikes were a White tactic.

Then they came for the kulaks, the White Guard, the bourgeoisie, the clergy, the Mensheviks, the Socialist Revolutionaries, prostitutes, the families of Red Army officers, the anarchists, and the sailors of Kronstadt. In an August 1918 article, "Civil War in the Villages," Lenin said, "the kulaks are rabid foes of the Soviet government. Either the Kulaks massacre vast numbers of workers, or the workers ruthlessly suppress the uprisings of the predatory kulak minority . . . There can be no middle course."[67] Peasants had never had high standing in Marxist theory, but for Lenin the kulaks were not just bystanders lost to rural idiocy. They were class enemies. While the term was supposed to refer to rich peasants, it was interpreted loosely, and Lenin urged total not exemplary measures: "Proletarian discipline is essential and necessary for us; real proletarian dictatorship, when the firm and iron rule of class-conscious workers is felt in every remote corner of our country, when not a single kulak, not a single rich man, not a single opponent of the grain monopoly remains unpunished . . ."[68]

In some areas, the peasants organized and fought the Bolsheviks, even with pitchforks. In the Ukraine, Nestor Makhno's Green insurgents fought quite successfully for a while against the Chekists, against the requisition detachments, against the Red Army, and against the Whites. The peasants had good grounds for resistance. A delegate to the Communist Party Congress in Moscow expressed concern about the uncontrolled behavior of their agents in the countryside: "we have received such an endless number of horrifying facts on drunkenness, debauchery, bribery, robbery, and reckless actions on the part of many officials that it was simply hair-raising."[69] But there was no effort to exercise control. On the contrary, these local officials could draw legitimacy for the selfish reward-seeking from Lenin's vigorous calls for extreme violence.

As Brovkin argues: "In the atmosphere of class hatred propagated from Moscow it is not surprising that local functionaries defined the words 'merciless struggle' literally."[70] Lenin had the energy to monitor and control his agents, but only when he was worried that they were doing too little rather than too much violence. In a telegram to Stalin in July 1918 he felt it necessary to exhort even this comrade—known to us as the paranoid, narcissistic, archvillain in the history of the Soviet one-party state—to not succumb to any human feelings that he might have: "And so, be merciless against the Left S.R.s and report more frequently."[71] The following month Lenin instructed a local commander, "It is necessary to organize a reinforced guard from specially trustworthy people to carry out a merciless mass terror against the kulaks, the priests and the White Guards; to lock up doubtful types in a concentration camp outside the town. Get an expedition in motion. Telegraph about implementation."[72] All resistance was crushed.

Between 1917 and 1923, 28 bishops and 1,000 priests were executed, according to figures provided by the Russian Orthodox Church and cited in the literature.[73] In addition, 12,000 lay persons were arrested and executed.[74] In 1922 there was a demonstration organized by local clergy in the town of Shuya. Lenin wanted them shot: "The greater the number of representatives of the reactionary clergy and reactionary bourgeoisie we manage to shoot on this basis, the better."[75] He wanted workers who observed religious holidays to be shot, too: "the entire Cheka must be put on the alert to see to it that those who do not show up for work because of 'Nikola' [religious holiday] are shot."[76] Leading church figures died horribly. "The Metropolitan Vladimir of Kiev was mutilated, castrated and shot, and his corpse was left naked for the public to desecrate."[77] Others were crucified, burned, and frozen to death. There is no indication that Lenin ordered specifically gruesome methods be used. His revealed general preferences were for shooting and hanging, so local agents must have improvised freely.

The September 4, 1918, issue of *Pravda* published the "Order for Intensified Red Terror." It stipulated, "all Right Socialist Revolutionaries . . . must be arrested immediately. Considerable numbers of hostages must be taken from among the bourgeoisie and the officers. At the least attempt at resistance or the least movement among the White Guards mass shooting must be inflicted without hesitation." By this time the Socialist Revolutionaries, with the help of the Czechs, had set up a rival government, the Komuch, in the East. Hostage-taking meant holding the women and children of officers serving in the Red Army to ensure their commitment to the revolution. Initially, the Bolsheviks had committed to a democratized and voluntary army, but both officers and conscription were quickly reinstated.[78] They recruited former czarist officers but treated them with suspicion. So according to the Red Cross in Kiev, they executed a group of wives of officers who had deserted to the Whites.[79] Hostage-taking was also Lenin's answer to the agricultural problem. He recommended taking hostages as a general policy in the countryside to ensure the delivery of food supplies and to suppress peasant unrest. According to the *Izvestia* of Tambov province: "On September 5 five villages were burnt to the ground" and "on September 7 over two hundred and fifty peasants were shot."[80] On June 11, 1921, the government announced:

> Antonov's band [in Tambov] has been smashed by the decisive action of our troops . . . In order finally to tear out all the SR-bandit roots . . . The All-Union Executive Committee orders as follows: 1. Citizens who refuse to give their names are to be shot on the spot without trial; 2. The penalty of hostage-taking should be announced and they are to be shot when arms are not surrendered. 3. In the event of concealed arms being found, shoot the eldest worker in the family on the spot and without trial. 4. Any family which harboured a bandit is subject to arrest and deportation from the province, their property to be confiscated and the eldest worker in the family to be shot without trial. 5. The eldest worker of any families hiding members of the family or the property of bandits is to be shot on the spot without trial. 6. If a bandit's family flees, the property is to be

distributed among peasants loyal to the Soviet regime and the abandoned houses burnt or demolished. 7. This order is to be carried out strictly and mercilessly. It is to be read at village meetings.[81]

Concentration camps run by the Cheka, labor camps, and ordinary prisons held tens of thousands from the Communists' list of counterrevolutionaries and criminals. In 1922, 60,000 were interned in forced labor camps, not counting those held in the Ukraine and Kirghiz.[82] For the years 1919 and 1920, Martyn Latsis, the head of the Ukrainian Cheka, admitted to a total of 128,010 arrested—including hostages, inmates of concentration camps and prisons, and laborers in forced labor camps.[83] This total is likely to be an underestimate, as with the official figures for executions.

The Communists themselves regressed to some of the Inquisitor's own categories of victims. After the Red Army defeated General Deniken and his troops, Lenin's policy for the reoccupation of the Ukraine included the stipulation to "treat the Jews and urban inhabitants in the Ukraine with an iron rod, transferring them to the front, not letting them into government agencies."[84] He had adapted to the local custom of antisemitism, not wishing to alienate the Ukrainians.

Finally, in 1921, Lenin set his agents on his comrades. In the fable of the Grand Inquisitor, Jesus comes, works miracles, is recognized, and is arrested by the holy guard of the Grand Inquisitor. The Inquisitor considers that the prospect of free choice and individual moral responsibility that Jesus represents is too much uncertainty for the majority of ordinary people to bear. These ordinary people are mocked by the teachings of Jesus, and they wish for the irrational comfort and the certainties of dogmatic and collective faith. The Inquisitor lies to the people in the public interest, not for the lust of power or for the lucre that he concedes may motivate some of his agents. The Inquisitor says he rules in Jesus's name, while repudiating his teaching and quarantining him from the people. The Inquisitor had informed his captive that he would have the people burn him. Yet he relents, and lets Jesus out quietly into the night, with a warning never to return.

The Communists were more severe. At Kronstadt, the sailors had returned to the original revolutionary message. The sailors argued for democratic freedom for the non-Communist left, with free speech for workers, peasants, anarchists, and left socialist parties, freedom of assembly for trade unions and peasant associations, the release of socialist political prisoners, and equal rations. The sailors demanded an end to the Cheka and the death penalty. Their actions were in solidarity with strikes by hungry workers in Petrograd.

The party authorities lied about this "second coming" of the revolution and isolated the sailors from the people in Petrograd. They redefined the sailors as Whites (similar to labeling Jesus as a heretic). Lenin stated that "we must counter it with rifles, no matter how innocent it may appear."[85] He took this position even though the White armies were defeated, the czar and his family were shot and long buried, and the sailors were committed to the revolution. There was no ratchet, no calibration of repression to threat, no half measures like imprisonment or shooting just the leaders.

In his account of the Russian Revolution and Civil War, Victor Serge, a Belgian revolutionary and writer who died stateless and pesoless in Mexico, but who was part of the Communist administration at the time, expresses his surprised outrage at the party's systematic lies and describes his initial paralysis in the face of "official falsehoods." He does, however, come around to the view that the party's action is in the public interest. Listen to how Serge struggles to reconcile himself to the political argument and consequent policy of lies and repression:

> After many hesitations, and with unutterable anguish, my Communist friends and I finally declared ourselves on the side of the Party. This is why. Kronstadt had right on its side. Kronstadt was the beginning of a fresh, liberating revolution for popular democracy: "The Third Revolution!" it was called by certain anarchists whose heads were stuffed with infantile illusions. However, the country was absolutely exhausted, and production practically at a standstill; there were no reserves of any kind, not even reserves of stamina in the hearts of the masses. The working-class elite that had been moulded in the struggle against the old regime was literally decimated. The Party, swollen by the influx of power-seekers, inspired little confidence. Of the other parties, only minute nuclei existed,

whose character was highly questionable. It seemed clear that these groupings could come back to life in a matter of weeks, but only by incorporating embittered, malcontent and inflammatory elements in their thousands, no longer, as in 1917, enthusiasts for the young revolution. Soviet democracy lacked leadership, institutions and inspiration; at its back there were only masses of starving and desperate men.

The popular counter-revolution translated the demand for freely-elected Soviets into one for "Soviets without Communism." If the Bolshevik dictatorship fell, it was only a short step to chaos . . . The Bolshevik Party is at present the supremely organized, intelligent and stable force which, despite everything, deserves our confidence.[86]

A poor casuist, Serge never really reconciled to the priority of stability. Looking backward to these times, he said that, "the only problem which revolutionary Russia, in all the years from 1917 to 1923, utterly failed to consider was the problem of liberty."[87] I think that Serge's hindsight was faulty, too. Revolutionary Russia considered liberty and considered it a problem in the same way that the Inquisitor saw liberty as a problem.

The structure of the party's argument, the way alternatives are framed, and the ordering of values, follow the Inquisitor's rhetorical scheme. First, privately admit that Jesus is Jesus, that Kronstadt was a liberating revolution. Second, divide society into the elite and the certainty-seeking masses of ordinary people, identifiable by their inability to manage choices and to resist the temptations that come with political freedom. Third, value order, stability, and dogmatic obedience over freedom and honesty. Fourth, identify the necessity of the leader, the Inquisitor, or the party. Fifth, commit violence in the public interest against the enemies of the people, not simply to hold on to power. While admitting that Jesuits or new party members may be power seekers, the authoritarian leadership's motives are the long-term good of the greater part of humanity. But in the Communist version, the heretical sailors are not let off and out into the night with a warning.

The usual foundations for tolerance are sympathy, a belief in reason resolving disagreement, and recognition that human weakness and error are part of the human condition. Lenin's argument was binary and divisive—there are those who are right and those who are wrong—and with stunning processing speed he could switch comrades from one side to the other. Imagine how it must have shaken those Red sailors, who had enthusiastically risked their lives for the revolution, to hear Lenin's characterization of them:

> the Socialist Revolutionaries and the bourgeois counterrevolutionaries in general resorted in Kronstadt to slogans calling for an insurrection against the Soviet Government of Russia ostensibly in the interest of the Soviet power. These facts fully prove that the White Guards strive, and are able, to disguise themselves as Communists, and even as the most left-wing Communists, solely for the purpose of weakening and destroying the bulwark of the proletarian revolution in Russia.[88]

Even after assiduously preparing the political argument, the government still had difficulty marshalling an effective and committed attack force. They took substantial casualties and required several attempts to take the fortress as Red Army regulars at first lacked martial spirit for fighting these former brothers-in-arms.[89] One regiment, the 561st, refused to storm the fortress and some of the soldiers changed sides. According to a Red Army telegram: "The 561st Regiment, after moving one and half versts toward Kronstadt, refused to advance any further. The reason is unknown. Comrade Dybenko ordered a second formation to deploy and open fire on any troops returning to the rear."[90] With springtime coming to the Gulf of Finland, there was some urgency in controlling the honorable motives of the agents and mounting a successful offensive. The Communists relied on party volunteers, some recruited from among the delegates to the Tenth Party Congress that was meeting at the time, and Central Asian forces, "soldiers who knew little about Kronstadt's history and merit,"[91] to brace the attackers. After what the war-hardened Tukhachevskii said was as terrible a slaughter as any that he had witnessed, hundreds of Kronstadt prisoners were summarily executed.[92] The orders sent by telegram from Petrograd stated: "deal harshly with mutineers, shooting them without mercy . . . not to be too particular about taking prisoners."[93] These executions were done even though the Kronstadt sailors, the comrades from the Finland Station and the storming of the Winter Palace, did not themselves execute captured Communists. The sailors treated their prisoners decently: "the worst that befell the imprisoned Communists was the confiscation, on 10th and 12th March, of their boots, sheepskins and great coats for use of the soldiers manning the outer defenses."[94] Incrementally, over succeeding months, the Cheka dispatched hundreds more, and one of the Kronstadt battleships was renamed *Marat.*[95] It may seem an odd choice to name a ship after someone who died in a bath, but it was an unmistakable signal of the course set by the revolution.

SOME TRULY HARD PEOPLE

Throughout the tragic events of the Russian Civil War, Lenin was in command. He ordered the terror and fully supported the institutions and agents that carried it out. The Council of the People's Commissars created the Cheka on December 20, 1917, as a specialized bureaucracy to tackle the enemies of the revolution. Lenin, chair of the Council of the People's Commissars, appointed Felix Dzerzhinsky, a Pole, as head of the Cheka. Dzerzhinsky himself is credited with pushing for the creation of a political police force, but the French Revolution had authenticated the historical role for this sort of institution, and Lenin was fastidious about the parallels: "Surely we shall not fail to find our own Fouquier-Tinville who will be able to tame the encroaching counterrevolution."[96] Fouquier-Tinville was the public prosecutor who secured the conviction of enemies of the people tried by the Revolutionary Tribunal, ultimately an engineer hoist with his own petard. Dzerzhinsky knew the inside of czarist prisons and Siberian exile and was by every account a most zealous revolutionary. To remove temptation from the soldiers, he emptied the imported wine of the Winter Palace into the Neva River. According to George Leggett, Dzerzhinsky was referred to as "the Soviet Savonarola" and the "Grand Inquisitor of Bolshevism."[97]

The Cheka's original task was to carry out investigations, leaving trials and executions to the revolutionary tribunals. But it quickly expanded its mission to include all stages, from investigation to killing, forming its own combat detachment in January 1918. Its budget expanded commensurately. From July 1918 to December 1919 the Cheka's budget increased by 2,000 percent.[98] As the size of a bureau grows, so does the volume of its activity, and so does the task of controlling it.

Killing in the numbers Lenin had in mind required numerous killers. Total Cheka troops and staff numbered about 260,000 in 1921. Cheka personnel included battalions of special troops who were assigned to provincial Chekas, to Red Army units, and to guarding the frontier. According to Leggett's figures there were 137,106 Cheka troops, 94,288 Frontier troops, and 30,000 civilian staff—roughly one Chekist to every ten Red Army soldiers.[99] These police units killed numbers approaching or exceeding front-line units of the Red Army.[100] The Cheka dispatched victims from across the political spectrum, from Black anarchists to White monarchists and republicans, and included criminals and other "undesirable" social categories.

Lenin knew it was important to find agents who could cope psychologically with the task that he had in mind. In August 1918 he issued directions concerning a local insurgency:

> Comrades! The uprising of the five kulak districts should be mercilessly suppressed . . .
>
> Hang (hang without fail, so the people see) no fewer than one hundred known kulaks, rich men, bloodsuckers.
>
> Publish their names.
>
> Take from them all the grain.
>
> Designate hostages—as per yesterday's telegram.
>
> Do it in such a way that for hundreds of versts around, the people will see, tremble, know, shout: they are strangling and will strangle to death the bloodsucker kulaks.
>
> Telegraph receipt and implementation.
>
> Yours, Lenin
>
> *Find some truly hard people* [my emphasis].[101]

There were two likely sources of hard people. There were those who were politically hardened by their commitment to communism and those reward seekers who came already psychologically hardened. The Cheka recruited from among members of the Communist Party, and Cheka personnel were, at least initially, often idealists committed to communism.[102] At the same time, this institution, like the Red Army, attracted individuals who brought with them their own selfish motivations and sought violence, rape, and loot. Victor Serge regarded Dzerzhinsky as sincere but his agents as susceptible to degeneration and perversion.[103] The historian Sergey Melgounov noted a shift from zealots or idealists to those who found personal rewards in the violence: "One of the prime causes of the degeneration of Cheka activity into tyranny and violence was the quality of the Cheka personnel. Political fanaticism alone will not explain the horrors I have described. It is only sadists and madmen, it is only social elements which life has rejected, and greed of gain and lust of power have attracted, that can engage in bloodshed on such a colossal scale. Yet the mentality even of a healthy-minded individual would have broken down amid the atmosphere of orgy . . . ."[104] Melgounov documented the revolting activities of the Kiev, Kharkov, and Odessa Chekas that resulted from this problem of adverse selection:

> In fact, each Cheka seems to have had its speciality in torture. Kharkov, for instance, under Saenko, went in primarily for scalpings and hand flayings; and in Voronezh the person to be tortured was first stripped naked and then thrust into a nail-studded barrel, and rolled about in it, or else branded on the forehead with a five-pointed star, or, if a member of the clergy, crowned with barbed wire. As for the Chekas of Tsaritsin and Kamishin, it was their custom to saw their victims' bones apart, whilst Poltava and Kremenchoug made it their special rule to impale clergy . . . another Kievan method was to thrust the living victim into a rough coffin already containing a decomposing body . . . Similarly, the well-known report of the Kievan Sisters of Mercy mentions the local practice of locking up living prisoners with dead.[105]

Others picked up on the issue of the severity of psychological stress for the agents. The great civil war novelist Mikhail Sholokhov's fictional idealist, Bunchuk, was posted to a revolutionary tribunal. He confesses to the mental toll: "The destruction of human filth is a filthy business. To shoot them down is injurious to the health and the mind, you see. Damn it all . . . For such filthy business volunteer either fools and beasts, or fanatics. We all want to live in a flower garden, but . . . [b]efore the flowers and trees can be planted the dirt must be cleared away."[106] In Russia, the organizational response to psychological stress was, sans imported wine, to increase the vodka ration for Cheka agents.[107] Descriptions of German killing units in the Second World War suggest similar problems. Himmler, like Lenin, looked for "hard" men but eventually constructed death camps that put some distance between the agents and the victims, with victims themselves being used to achieve the killing.[108] Some perpetrators likely pay a psychological price for "too much" of Count Tilly's reward.

Rape does not receive much specific attention in accounts of the Russian Civil War. Its incidence is a direct measure of the principal-agent problem in the bureaucracies of repression. Women deserve separate mention on the list of groups victimized by the Bolsheviks. They were not identified as enemies by the logic of the political argument, but they formed part of the agents' incentive structure and the Inquisitor did not care enough to provide protection. Collecting the testimony of scattered sources suggests that rape was widespread. Melgounov, for example, says, "dozens of cases of rape have taken place in Morshansk."[109] Cheka officials were known to arrest males in order to extort sex from women relatives.[110] Vladimir Brovkin says that rape and murder was the lot of some of the "bourgeois" women of Astrakhan.[111] Red Army soldiers, in fictional accounts like Sholokhov's, seemed to make rape an everyday occurrence. In Isaac Babel's diary of his summer spent with the Red Cavalry (Kuban Cossacks) in Poland, horses, quarters, shooting prisoners, and rape were diurnal notations. An Odessa Jew and protégé of Gorky, Babel was assigned to the Red Cavalry for the Polish campaign. "The Jews look for liberation—and in ride the Kuban Cossacks," was the ironic entry for July 21, 1920.[112] Of the little towns visited by these syphilitic soldiers, he records: "the girls and women, all of them can scarcely walk."[113] On 17 August 1920: "Fighting near the railroad track at Liski. Massacre of prisoners. Spend the night in Zadworze."[114] An indifferent Count Tilly is running this army. As they cross the frontier, our diarist notes an order from the Southwest Army Group to behave, but no further reference is made to this order and no officer attempts to enforce it. Babel suggests that this conduct is just what soldiers do. And the official record on the behavior of the Red Cavalry authenticates Babel's personal account.

Semyon Budyonny led the Red Cavalry and Josef Stalin was his main political sponsor. He had been a noncommissioned officer (NCO) in the Czar's cavalry. In August 1918, because of the shortage of officers, the Bolsheviks had promoted all former NCO's to command positions.[115] Budyonny's Cossacks occupied Rostov in January 1920 and took their reward. According to a Cheka official's communication to Dzerzhinsky (15 January 1920) "instead of pursuing the fleeing army, Budyonny's Army preferred to spend its time in looting and drunkenness in Rostov. Local comrades have spoken of atrocities in the pogroms carried out by Budyonny's men."[116] Rape, plunder, and pogrom were the Red Cavalry's quotidian routine, apparently part of the Cossacks' martial tradition, and a reward the Communist leadership was willing to grant.

Elsewhere, from the Urals to the Ukraine, there is testimony of the mass killings of the bourgeois for being bourgeois and of the women being sent to "wash the barracks,"[117] military slang meaning that they were to be raped. While the Red Army had a disciplinary code, historian D. Fedotov White describes the code as "more in the nature of a blueprint of a building the Soviet authorities expected to erect in the future."[118] But accounts of the Red Army's behavior 20 years later suggest that little progress was made. The very high rates of desertion from the Red Army provide another indication of the state of discipline,[119] and obviously the food shortages encouraged predatory behavior on the part of the soldiers.

Finally, loot or ordinary monetary gain was on the minds of some of the agents: "Letts [Latvians] flock to the Extraordinary Commission of Moscow as folk emigrate to America, and for the same reason—to make their fortune."[120] Chamberlin states: "The Cheka acquired a reputation not only for inhuman cruelty, but also for blackmail and corruption. Its real or self-styled agents not infrequently took bribes from friends or relatives of prisoners . . ."[121] Even senior Cheka officials like Latsis were open about the problem of adverse selection:

"Often unworthy elements, sometimes even counterrevolutionaries, attached themselves to the Vecheka, some for motives of personal gain."[122] So the unchecked selfish motives of agents contributed their own measure of lethal activity to the overall performance of the bureau.

Beyond supplying vodka, how did the principal interact with the agents? The Cheka reported directly to the Council of the People's Commissars chaired by Lenin; it was the top decision-making body in the new government. No other agencies represented a rival to Cheka supremacy. Leonard Schapiro testifies to the preeminent position of the Cheka: "there is no doubt that the Vecheka was a law unto itself, little restrained either by decrees, or by the party, whose executive arm it admittedly was."[123] In 1919 the All-Russian Central Executive Committee passed a decree limiting Cheka powers. But the qualification that it could only summarily execute where there was armed rebellion and where martial law applied meant that the decree had little impact; they moved prisoners to the martial law areas to shoot them. George Leggett, in discussing the position of the Cheka, concludes: "the guardians were to be guarded by none save themselves."[124] The zealot Dzerzhinsky was himself concerned about Cheka officials using their positions for personal gain. As theory predicts, auditing and monitoring bureaus and commissions were established, but their own effectiveness was marred by corrupt personnel.[125] Dzerzhinsky's attempt to get the public to report corruption was not successful, given the reputation of the Cheka and the fear of consequences for informing on Cheka personnel, and his efforts to control the activity of Cheka officials also lacked consistency.[126]

The immense Russian distances added to the problem of controlling local Cheka activity. Dzerzhinsky, despite Lenin's at best indifferent attitude to Cheka excesses, made some effort to limit entrepreneurial repression; but his effectiveness in doing so was limited to Moscow and Petrograd. Historian Lennard Gerson provides a good summary of the control problem and the motives of the agents:

> The situation was apparently not as serious in Moscow and Petrograd, where the supervision of the Vecheka and Communist Party officials was able to prevent excessive abuses. But the farther the

Chekas were from the scrutiny of the central leadership, the fewer the controls and the more dishonorable the Chekists were likely to become. In a moment of candor Latsis wrote that work in the Extraordinary Commissions, conducted "in an atmosphere of physical coercion, attracts corrupt and outright criminal elements who, profiting from their positions as Cheka agents, blackmail and extort, filling their own pockets."[127]

In our terms, Lenin's government faced problems of adverse selection and moral hazard. But while the Bolsheviks knew of these problems, overall, for them, the benefits of the Cheka's activity, as with the Inquisitor's Jesuits, outweighed the cost of lost innocent individuals. Dzerzhinsky argued that, "The Cheka is not a court of justice. It is a defender of the Revolution, just like the Red Army. And just as the Red Army in the civil war cannot stop to see whether it is wronging individuals, and is obliged to pursue a single aim, i.e., the victory of the Revolution over the bourgeoisie—in the same way the Cheka is obliged to defend the Revolution and crush the enemy, even if its sword sometimes chances to strike the heads of innocent people."[128] Lenin provided no support for the effort to control the Cheka. He had a precise interest in the Cheka and how it carried out its mission. He was, however, generally indifferent to agent-initiated suffering. Lenin was the agency's first apologist, as evident from these statements:

> What surprises me in the wailing about the mistakes of the Cheka is the inability to place the question in a larger perspective. Here they are picking on the Cheka's individual mistakes, sobbing and fussing about them.[129]
>
> The Cheka is putting into effect the dictatorship of the proletariat, and in this sense it is of inestimable value.[130]
>
> Yes, the terror and the Cheka are absolutely indispensable . . . our Cheka is magnificently organized.[131]

In rejecting the idea that the Cheka should be subject to external judicial controls, Lenin said: "When I consider the activities of the Cheka and compare them with the attacks on it, I find the latter to be petit bourgeois considerations of no value."[132] For him, Count Tilly's reward was worth paying in exchange for the revolutionary returns that the bureau provided. The same thinking applied to the Red Army. When the Red Army retreated from Poland, diverting itself along the way with its own pogroms, we catch another glimpse of Lenin's leadership style. On October 17, 1920, Jewish members of the Communist Party's Central Committee notified Lenin of the appalling activities of the Red Cavalry who "have been destroying the Jewish population in their path, looting and murdering." Earlier, on 6 July 1920, Central Committee members alerted Lenin to what they described as the systematic extermination of the Jewish population of Gomel and Minsk provinces and Lenin simply files the memorandum.[133] Lenin, like Count Tilly when his officers alerted him, is unmoved.

BEYOND THREAT, COST, AND THE ORIGINAL PRINCIPAL

In examining the estimates of victims attributable to the Bolsheviks in the Russian Civil War, the actions of the revolutionary government exceeded a rational response to "the state of siege," exceeded retaliatory symmetry between government and a vicious opposition, and exceeded the total suggested by a policy path dependent only on authoritarian Russian history. Lenin is sometimes put in the context of nondemocratic Russian traditions, and he himself pointed to that tradition to justify Communist repression. It would, however, have been an improvement had Lenin behaved as badly as his predecessors. The trend line for czarist oppression was far lower than for Leninist oppression, a fraction of the number of executions over a far longer period. There was a czarist secret police that used informers and provocateurs, and the Bolsheviks borrowed the expertise of former czarist officers for the Red Army. At the same time, Lenin set up new institutions and control mechanisms that made the independent activity of these former czarist officers inconsequential to the pattern of violations. They were more likely victims.

Lenin's slavish devotion to his political argument and the very long leash given his dogs of internal and external war led to excessive violations from a rationalist or strategic perspective. It was "logical cruelty," in the apt phrase of an erstwhile comrade.[134] The violations had serious counterproductive consequences in provoking resistance to the government. And there were other costs. There was foreign criticism, and the violations provided good propaganda for western military intervention. Not just foreign governments but foreign socialists such as Karl Kautsky criticized Red Terror. But the regime's response to these costs was counterpropaganda, a show trial for the Socialist Revolutionaries, not ratcheting down the terror. Most importantly, the regime was wasteful of human capital, the talented, energetic, and dedicated Russians who died or went into exile, or those unknown numbers who went into hibernation to survive Lenin's government and the dark times that followed, and from whom nothing was ever heard.

Lenin was dispatching—not just deterring—those without historical roles, and his normative rearrangement made it acceptable to reject ordinary decency as counterrevolutionary or "petit bourgeois." The general characteristics of bureaucracies, the tendency to expand consonant with the selfish motives of the agents, and the control problems all contributed to the toll of the Russian Civil War. The design and control of the institutions responsible for repression contributed additional disproportionate violations. The men of Lenin's security forces did what Count Tilly's Croats and Walloons did at Magdeburg and delivered what Shakespeare's Henry V threatened at Harfleur. At best, Lenin was simply not interested in the filthy motives of his forces as they helped to achieve *revolutionary* levels of violence, and at worst, he encouraged them with his repeated exhortations to be hard and merciless.

For the Soviet period as a whole, former Politburo member Alexander Yakovlev (appointed in 1987) says that "the number of people . . . killed for political motives or who died in prisons and camps . . . totaled 20 to 25 million. And unquestionably one must add those who died of famine—more than 5.5 million during the civil war and more than 5 million during the 1930s." The decades of slaughter raises the question—less politically loaded than it has been in the past yet difficult to ignore—of whether Lenin launched and charted the course for Stalinism. The material from the Russian Civil War period suggests that he did, leaving little for Stalin to discover in the policy of repression. Lenin personally communicated to Stalin his own commitment to killing not just those on his list of undesirable political, social, and economic categories, but on any given day the telephone operator responsible for a bad phone line or the railway man responsible for a train delay. In February 1920 Lenin sent the following telegram to Stalin: "Today I heard you and all the other very clearly, every word. Threaten to shoot the incompetent person in charge of communications who cannot give you a good amplifier and ensure uninterrupted telephone communication with me."[135] We have an eyewitness comparison of Lenin and Stalin from V. M. Molotov, that great political survivor who endured the treacherous inner circles of Communist government from the civil war until the cold war. He said that of the first two communist leaders, Lenin was "more severe" or "harsher."[136] The evidence from the civil war gives one no reason to doubt Molotov's evaluation.

When we think of Stalinism, the images are of rigid authority, a malignant and ubiquitous bureaucracy, individual helplessness, lies, political language in Orwell's sense, purges, show trials, betraying one's comrades, shootings, and the gulag, overshadowed by a toweringly dysfunctional personality. But what should be clear is that Stalinism evolves from the earlier period of "well-adjusted" leadership. Narcissism, paranoia, and the cult of personality (Lenin put up a statue of Robespierre rather than himself in the Kremlin) were not necessary conditions for slaughter. The agents of Lenin's government shot, tortured, raped, and took hostages. They sorted victims collectively, not by individual guilt or innocence. The summary procedures for implementing repression followed from this position, as did the taking and executing of hostages. This hostage policy, which usually brings to mind Nazi behavior in occupied France or Yugoslavia, was ordered at the highest levels and was used to secure the loyalty of key personnel (for example, officers who had served in the czar's army who also served in the Red Army), and to punish. Updating the auto-da-fé, the leaders advocated show trials, or "model trials" in Lenin's words, for the Socialist Revolutionaries, denied the relevance of individual guilt or innocence, purged the Workers' Opposition from the Communist Party, shot Red Army officers, and lied about and shot comrades. False confessions, an Inquisitorial technique thought to be quintessentially Stalinist, were extracted earlier in Russia. Even confining opponents in psychiatric hospitals or asylums is part of the Russian Civil War policy discourse. The terror of the 1930s was targeted at Trotskyites and also at kulaks and White Guards, thereby reverting to the Kronstadt formula for converting comrades into enemies.

It might be argued that the difference between Lenin and Stalin is their victims and the identification and killing of enemies within the party. Stalin used terror at the highest echelons of the Soviet government and the Red Army. Tukhachevskii was named a "German spy" and shot in 1937—a condign punishment, perhaps, for the executioner of the "White" Kronstadt sailors. Victims too were Tukhachevskii's wife, sisters, brother, and mother. Yet, it is a baby step from using lies and then terror on old comrades from the Finland Station to using them on generals and senior party members. At Kronstadt, the Communists crossed a frozen Rubicon. Clearly, Stalin was in a position to make his own choices, but the political argument, the policies, and the specialized bureaucratic heritage of the revolution and the Russian Civil War put forces in motion that made his choices much easier. One could say that he was an unadventurous bastard.

FIVE

The English Civil War

They killed Nicholas II after midnight, in a cellar east of the Urals. They shot his family too. They killed Charles I in the morning, in public, in the capital. They left his family untouched. Captive monarchs, revolutionary mutineers, and peasant resistance presented Vladimir Lenin and Oliver Cromwell with some similar challenges. They dealt with them quite differently.

To reach the scaffold for his own beheading, Charles I stepped out of a window of Banqueting House, a building designed by his father's surveyor of works, but with ceiling panel paintings that he himself had commissioned. Inigo Jones, Rubens, and his own insouciance conspired to give Charles a grand exit on a cold day in January 1649. This was an exit for a man who had marched four nations to war and left 175,000 dead on the battlefield.[1] Small wonder that Shakespeare's exit line for another Scot occurs to biographers: "Nothing in his life became him like the leaving of it."[2] But his leaving did not end the war, which went on for another two years.

The English Civil War actually refers to a series of wars in Britain and Ireland fought by the parliamentary and royalist armies between 1642 and 1651. The combatants fought in three major national theaters in four episodes. The suffering caused by the war was extensive, yet was not the result of the systematic slaughter or atrocities that we associate with civil wars. As historian Charles

Carlton says, "compared to other wars, both ancient and modern, few folk became victim of atrocities."[3] Folk could thank Oliver Cromwell's systematic rejection of the "Borgia option" in his interaction with his opponents, his repudiation of the Grand Inquisitor role, and the discipline he exercised over his agents. Here, the principal's commitment to tolerance and his attention to the effective control of the parliamentary army suppressed violence below the levels expected under conditions of civil war. The two worst and most notorious atrocities attributable to the parliamentary army, at the battle of Naseby in England in 1645 and at Drogheda in Ireland in 1649, fit the principal-agent logic and breakdown in control.

POWER, PRINCIPLES, AND TOLERANCE, HOME AND ABROAD

Just as divisive commitments push atrocities higher in the Grand Inquisitor's case, beyond what is required to secure power, so a different set of commitments can reduce the incidence of atrocities. Oliver Cromwell, though devout, supported an agenda of toleration, as did Thomas Fairfax, another leading parliamentary soldier.[4] Cromwell was a member of parliament at the beginning of the war. By the end of the war he served on the executive body known as the Committee of Both Kingdoms. Political office did not initially preclude military service, and his battlefield successes led to rapid promotion from captain in 1642 to colonel in 1643. In 1644 Cromwell was appointed to the rank of lieutenant general and was second in command to Thomas Fairfax at the decisive battle of Naseby in 1645. At Naseby, Cromwell's tightly disciplined cavalry turned the tide of the battle in which the main royalist army of the first civil war met defeat. Although a politician turned soldier, his political career followed from his military accomplishments. Cromwell's values generally deferred and decreased even the opportunist's optimal demand for violations, presumably making his hold on power less secure.

Independent of the low incidence of atrocities, that Cromwell valued toleration is evident from both documentary evidence recording Cromwell's own views and a consensus among historians on his general tolerance. Across the years, from his time as a soldier serving in the field to his years as a statesman addressing parliaments, he voiced and recorded his commitment to toleration in his private communications and in his public speeches. "I have waited for the day to see union and right understanding between the godly people (Scots, English, Jews, Gentiles, Presbyterians, Independents, Anabaptists and all)."[5] Left off the list are the Irish. Some 40 years later, John Locke, in his celebrated argument *A Letter Concerning Toleration,* came up with a similar list and constructs a similar general argument for toleration, qualified by security concerns.

> Those that are seditious, murderers, thieves, robbers, adulterers, slanderers, etc., of whatsoever church, whether national or not, ought to be punished and suppressed. But those whose doctrine is peaceable, and whose manners are pure and blameless, ought to be upon equal terms with their fellow subjects. Thus if solemn assemblies, observations of festivals, public worship be permitted to any one sort of professors, all these things ought to be permitted to the Presbyterians, Independents, Anabaptists, Arminians, Quakers, and others, with the same liberty . . . neither pagan nor Mahometan nor Jew ought to be excluded from the civil rights of the commonwealth because of his religion.[6]

Locke, like Cromwell, qualifies toleration with fear of incitement, violence, and the undermining of political community. It remains difficult for philosophers to find a way around this problem of tolerating those who, if successful, make toleration impossible.

In responding to complaints from one officer against another, Cromwell counseled his agents: ". . . in some things, we have all human infirmities . . . the State, in choosing men to serve them, takes no notice of their opinions . . . I advised you formerly to bear with men of different minds from yourself . . ."[7] On September 4, 1650, the day after the battle of Dunbar, he penned a remarkable letter to the speaker of the House of Commons that described his victory over the Scots and then went on to suggest a vision of the sort of system for which he fought. He urged Parliament to use its power mercifully and generously.

Relieve the oppressed; hear the groans of poor prisoners in England; be pleased to reform the abuses of all professions; and if there be any one that makes many poor to make a few rich, that suits not a Commonwealth . . . besides the benefit England shall feel thereby, you shall shine forth to other nations, who shall emulate the glory of such a pattern, and through the power of God turn in to the like. These are our desires; and that you may have liberty and opportunity to do these things, and not be hindered, we have been and shall be (by God's assistance) willing to venture our lives."[8]

In making his request that the exercise of power be tied to an agenda that favors the politically and economically oppressed, and in revealing his compellingly naive international idealism, this veteran pointedly reminds the speaker that he and his soldiers are the ones taking the risks. In earlier dispatches, after the battle of Naseby in 1645 for example, Cromwell had reminded Parliament that they were fighting for liberty of conscience. When his attention is on Ireland, it is the landowners, those that fought against Parliament, and the Catholic priesthood suspected of Spanish sympathies, not the laboring class, who are targeted.

Some days after his Dunbar dispatch, Cromwell, before Edinburgh Castle, gets into an exchange of letters about religion, the role of law, and liberty, with the governor of Edinburgh Castle. He, the droll besieger, begins, "because I am at some reasonable good leisure, I cannot let such gross mistakes and inconsequential reasonings pass without some notice taken of them," and continues:

Your pretended fear lest error should step in, is like the man that would keep all the wine out the country lest men should be drunk. It will be found an unjust and unwise jealousy, to deprive a man of his natural liberty upon a supposition he may abuse it. When he doth abuse it, judge. If a man speak foolishly, ye suffer him gladly because ye are wise; if erroneously, the truth more appears by your conviction. Stop such a man's mouth with sound words that cannot be gainsaid; if he speak blasphemously, or to the disturbance of the public peace, let the civil magistrate punish him: if truly, rejoice in the truth."[9]

With the liberal idea of exchange of opinion, whether it is true or in error, speech counters speech and in the process we more confidently appreciate truth. This position becomes John Stuart Mill's claim in *On Liberty* that we gain, "the clearer perception and livelier impression of truth produced by its collision with error."[10] In practice, Cromwell did not make much of blasphemy, and the other limit to speech is the familiar one of when it causes a public disturbance; Mill's prohibition of inflammatory speech: we are not to tell a mob in front of a corn dealer's house that "corn dealers are starvers of the poor."[11] In 1654, speaking to members of Parliament, Cromwell again asserts "Liberty of Conscience is a natural right; and he that would have it ought to give it . . . Indeed, that has been one of the vanities of our Contest. Every Sect saith, Oh! give me liberty. But give it him, and to his power he will not yield it to anybody else . . . Truly, that's a thing ought to be very reciprocal." He argues that liberty of conscience is a constitutional right as well, or in his terms, a "Fundamental."[12] He is warning of the universal drive to dominate the marketplace of ideas and to construct barriers to prevent the entry of competing ideas. Given this drive, it is sensible to institutionalize liberty and remove that fundamental idea from dispute. Liberty is a "natural right" and not to be interfered with by sects or groups. It is also a question of fairness and, as Cromwell suggests, hypocritical to do otherwise—if we have benefited from toleration, then we ought to be willing to extend toleration to others. We end up with the familiar liberal conundrum of whether to tolerate the intolerant.

Thomas Carlyle, introducing Cromwell's letters and speeches, makes some remark about the prose of practical men. Although Cromwell's words might be put together more elegantly, we have here the fabric of modern liberal arguments for tolerance. Loosely woven perhaps, it works in human frailties and weakness and ties liberty to speech. Truth is valued, but he has modest expectations for any one group always getting it right. Therefore, he commits to the process of exchange of opinion, rather than to systematic correction through imprisonment, torture, and killing. These coercive measures are the Inquisitor's techniques for responding to those on the wrong side of the political argument. In the twentieth century, Cromwell's positions constituted a conception referred to by Sir Isaiah Berlin as negative liberty, requiring governments to refrain from action rather than to take it. The default position in public policy is thus set at doing nothing, instead of anticipating wrongdoing. Berlin provided the principal philosophical defense for toleration in the age when massive, comprehensive, and total systems to suppress speech became viable.

Cromwell was no American-style prohibitionist—we can always find examples of antiliberal policy in the liberal heartland—and even Cromwell's anti–Merry England tranche of policies, the prohibitions on animal sports, seem to have rested on a fear of public disturbance, not on a simple antipathy to fun. For Cromwell, punishment must be proportionate. He criticized the overreliance on capital punishment. He wanted it to be reserved for murder and treason: "I have known in my experience abominable murders quitted; and to see men lose their lives for petty matters. This is a thing God will reckon for . . ."[13] As Lord Protector, the title he assumed in 1653, Cromwell objected to the intolerant decisions of Parliament in the case of James Naylor. Naylor was a Quaker charged with blasphemy: he had confused himself with Jesus and mistaken Bristol for Jerusalem. Over the Protector's objections, Parliament asserted the judicial powers of the abolished House of Lords and put Naylor on a via dolorosa of tortures and imprisonment. During the Protectorate, Cromwell claimed that Catholics were being treated with more tolerance than before. In his letter to the French statesman Cardinal Mazarin, dated 26 December 1656, he said that toleration could not at this time be publicly extended to Catholics, but that his government was making things easier for Catholics than previous governments had.[14] The French ambassador thought that the situation for English Catholics was better under Cromwell than under the monarchy.[15]

And it is Cromwell who supported Jews settling openly in England again, 350 years after they had been expelled. In 1655, Cromwell organized a conference to consider a petition from the Dutch Rabbi, Manasseh Ben Israel, and converted Marrano Jews who were actually already resident in London and elsewhere requesting that Jews be officially allowed to settle. There was opposition from the merchants of the City of London, who feared commercial competition, and from the nation generally. According to historian William Abbott, "the general opinion in Council, City and country was against it. The result was widespread agitation . . . It was apparent that the Protector faced an almost united nation; but it was no less apparent that he was as little dismayed by it as he had been by other expressions of disapproval of his course; only in this, unlike his earlier measures, he could not count on the support of the army."[16] But in 1656 Cromwell stood up to elite and public opinion and extended toleration. The first synagogue opened in London in 1657, although there were secret synagogues prior to this time.[17] These themes—tolerance, human weakness, the free exchange of ideas, the power of argument, the truth eventually coming out, disturbance or riot as grounds for limiting speech, and proportioning penalties to abuses rather than acting preemptively through prohibitions or in a Draconian manner—form a more or less seamless pattern for liberal arguments from John Locke to John Stuart Mill. Remember that Locke, who is regarded not only as one of the original liberals but also as one of the original human rights theorists, in his *Letter Concerning Toleration* (1689), did not extend toleration to all. He excluded the intolerant as well as atheists on the practical grounds that the denial of god increased the likelihood of such individuals, unbound by oath, breaking the contracts and promises that make human society. He excluded those whose religious attachments put them in the service of a foreign prince, not for the religious belief itself but for the practical security problem that the political associations of the religious belief created. Cromwell, also a practical man, left out the Irish and Catholics, whom he saw as treasonously in the service of hostile foreign powers.

It is, of course, reasonable to take the position that toleration is only as secure as the political community that achieves the implementation of toleration. The reasoning for negative rights by social contract theorists begins by assuming a situation without government, establishing these rights prior to government, perhaps calling them natural or fundamental to suggest their immutable character, and protecting them from the actions of the government of the day. But a political community is as necessary for providing the security, trust, and public confidence, let alone the educational infrastructure for realizing these negative rights, as it is for providing the material resources for a positive right to shelter or adequate nutrition. To protect tolerance, one needs to protect the community that has developed the practice of tolerance.

Cromwell's position is consistent with what we might term a situational theory of toleration, advanced in the seventeenth century and, with modification, still employed today when we qualify tolerance to deal with threats to the political community or national security. His situational toleration helps us to understand his view of Ireland. Historians have described Cromwell's position on the Irish as a "blind spot" or as racist. Cromwell's own language, rationales, and policies do not support a racist interpretation.

Christopher Hill considers Cromwell a racist where the Irish are concerned. "A great number of civilized Englishmen of the propertied class in the seventeenth century spoke of Irishmen in tones not far removed from those which Nazis used about Slavs, or white South Africans use about the original inhabitants of their country . . . In these matters Cromwell was no better and no worse than the average Englishman of his time and class."[18] An Englishman's dogmatic hatred of the Irish as a people sounds plausible, but the evidence on racism is not compellingly linked to the actions of Cromwell's army. The claim that Cromwell thought the Irish inferior as a race, which is how the term racism is ordinarily understood, is not well substantiated. Relatedly, some Irish historians, questioning the evidence for Cromwellian massacres in Ireland, are now engaged in an effort to revise the self-serving Nationalist and Jesuit histories and the curriculum in Irish schools that portray Cromwell as an "English bastard."[19] There is the danger of the circular argument that violations were higher in Ireland because of English racial hatred as evidenced by the higher violations. If racial hatred were the driving force behind Cromwell's actions in Ireland, like a Nazi's on the Eastern Front, then in all likelihood the violations would have been significantly higher and more widespread than they were. Had racism been strongly in play, Cromwell's soldiers would not have observed the restraints on their behavior to ordinary Irish people (restraints similar to those that they had in Scotland), and the most infamous of the actions of the Irish campaign would not have been the killing of an English commander and his English and Irish soldiers at Drogheda. There is now some inclination among historians to reassess Cromwell's record in Ireland and to "question the uncritical ease with which the allegations of indiscriminate slaughter have been repeated by historians. The statistics and the continuities of life in the communities involved bear this out."[20] Further, there is evidence that Cromwell was not hostile to the people. He distinguished among the Irish based on economic and political status, held the elites responsible, and explicitly protected the "country people" from his soldiers.

We can call on a collection of historians and biographers to testify to Cromwell's commitment to tolerance. Christopher Hill says that, "Cromwell—and it is one of his very great contributions to English history—clung tenaciously to this belief that truth was not certainly possessed by any one sect."[21] Of his treatment of the various dissident political and religious movements and sects, Maurice Ashley says that Cromwell "tried to understand their point of view (Quakers, Fifth Monarchy Men) and to persuade them that if they would be content to preach their gospel in a peaceable manner, his government would leave them alone. Similarly, he attempted to induce John Lilburne, the leader of the Levelers . . . that if he would only promise to refrain from stirring up mutiny in the army, he would be allowed to propagate his views."[22] Antonia Fraser says "the truth was that Cromwell had showed, and would continue to show, lamb-like restraint in his attitude to these demonstrative critics, which does him much credit in comparison with many other practitioners of supreme power." And she asserts that "Cromwell never ceased to emphasize . . . the extent to which freedom of conscience did flourish under the Protectorate—greater than ever before in England, he said, and it has been shown to be a valid claim."[23] Roger Hainsworth concludes:

> When he told an Irish commander that he 'meddled with no man's conscience' but would not permit the Mass, he meant what he said. His forbidding the Mass reflected his determination to stamp out subversive preaching, not the tenets of the Catholic faith. Cromwell was a hero to the Congregationalists of Massachusetts since he not only protected them but protected their co-religionists in Britain. However, they would have shuddered in their meeting houses, those citadels of intolerant conformity, if they had grasped how deep his commitment to toleration lest intolerance unwittingly suppress the truth.[24]

Ashley also notes that "what recent historians do appear to agree about . . . is that Cromwell was fundamentally a tolerant and conciliatory statesman, far removed from the police-state autocrats of modern times."[25] Conceptually, Cromwell's toleration shifted his demand for violations lower than what would have been risked by an opportunist fixated on power.

A SYNOPSIS OF THE CONFLICT

Charles I took the throne following the death of his father, James I of England, who was also James VI of Scotland. As old as the century, he had been king since 1625 and was married to the unpopular Henrietta Maria, French and Catholic. He lacked personal appeal, being devious, impetuous, self-righteous, injudicious in his selection of advisors, uxorious, and saddled with a speech defect. Actually, even the king's mount appears deformed in the court painter Van Dyck's horseback portrait—too small a head or too expansive a chest.[26] A sorry warrior king, Charles I needed little provocation to get into wars that he could not finish and into a mortal conflict with Parliament that he also could not finish.

Constitutional and religious issues divided the combatants in the civil wars. Charles I had adopted a variety of tactics to subdue Parliament and other institutions that acted with autonomy. Between 1629 and 1640 Parliament did not meet, constituting an unprecedented 11 years of "personal rule." To avoid the necessity of calling Parliament, the king collected revenue in innovative ways. He demanded loans from the rich, some of whom refused and were imprisoned, and raised money through fines. He levied "ship money" inland (ship money was a crisis tax usually levied in the ports to provide for their naval protection). The wider reach of this admittedly strange tax (presumably inland inhabitants were free riders on the protection bought from coastal revenue) galvanized the opposition to the king. Only defeat by the Scots in the Bishops' wars, a consequence of Charles's efforts to assert his power as head of the Anglican church and force Scottish conformity, led him to summon Parliament in 1640. The Short Parliament, not in a compliant mood, lasted a matter of weeks before it was dissolved. The Long Parliament, summoned in November 1640, endured through the civil war. In January 1642, in the wake of the Grand Remonstrance that laid out Parliament's complaints against the king and its proposals to give Parliament control of the army, the king went to the House of Commons with 400 soldiers to arrest John Pym and four other members. Knowing the king's plans, Pym and the others escaped while Speaker William Lenthall rebuffed Charles. Following this very visible and unsuccessful escalation and militarization of the conflict with Parliament, the king sent his family to France and he left London. Both sides mobilized and in October they fought their first major battle at Edgehill. The royal army then approached London from the west, before being turned back.

The English Civil War was actually a series of wars that began in the last years of the continental Thirty Years' War, which ended in 1648. The first English civil war extended from 1642 until 1646, with the parliamentary army prevailing. During this first war the Scots, enemies of the king from the earlier Bishops' wars, were in alliance with Parliament. In exchange for their military help, the Scots extracted a promise to establish Scottish Protestantism in England. Reinforcing the Scots' religious agenda was "a hard-headed desire for Scottish security" that religious unity with England was calculated to bring.[27] The Scots contributed importantly to the victory at Marston Moor in 1644 but not to the parliamentary victory at the final major battle of Naseby in 1645. That battle was the notable success of the Parliament's newly reorganized New Model Army, and as a result Scottish influence over Parliament diminished.[28] In the second and third civil wars the Scots took their religious and political agenda to the royalists. The second war, when the imprisoned Charles I negotiated the invasion of England by a Scottish army, lasted for several months in 1648. The king had briefly escaped, was recaptured and held on the Isle of Wight, where he renewed hostilities by reaching a secret agreement with the Scots for them to restore him to the throne by invading England in return for establishing Scottish Protestantism in England for three years. Outnumbered, Cromwell's forces intercepted, pursued, and destroyed the invaders and accompanying English royalists at Preston in the north of England. In 1649, after the execution of Charles I, Cromwell led his army on a successful campaign against Catholic and royalist forces in Ireland. By the time Cromwell landed in Ireland, Colonel Michael Jones's parliamentary forces had already defeated the numerically superior royalist army at the battle of Rathmines, and Cromwell's entire campaign came down to sieges. The violations in the Irish campaign stemmed from siege warfare producing greater opportunities for violations and because of a notable breakdown in control of the agents.

Cromwell later said of his men and his selection methods: "I raised such men as had the fear of God before them, as made some conscience of what they did. And from that day forward I must say to you, they were never beaten . . ."[29] Cromwell's men were never beaten, and the Scots never learned. The Scots again fought for the royalist cause in the third civil war. At the battle of Dunbar in 1650, they suffered a shattering defeat by Cromwell's men, who successfully attacked from the low ground and in inferior numbers and surprised the Scots. The following year Cromwell caught and defeated the Scots again at the final major battle of Worcester, but failed to capture the heir to the throne, Charles II. If Charles I's political strategy was to subordinate autonomous institutions, secular and religious, Oliver Cromwell's was to oppose personal rule and foreign threats to English national security, and to advocate religious toleration. With predictable historical irony, and by default as much as by design, he himself ended his career as a personal ruler.

At the beginning of the first English civil war, the parliamentarians remained in session and went to war to defend the role of Parliament in the existing constitutional structure. They left the king a way out, holding accountable the king's "evil councilors," and they fought for the "preservation of the safety of His Majesty's person, the peace of the Kingdom and the defense of Parliament."[30] But, according to one source, Cromwell told his soldiers that if he met the king in battle "he would as soon discharge his pistol upon him as at any other private person."[31] For the second civil war, there were no councilors left between the king and the blame. After the king's execution, the new regime abolished the monarchy and the House of Lords. Constitutional experimentation with veto power held by Cromwell and his soldiers characterized the period until the restoration of the monarchy when Charles II assumed the English throne in 1660. The military and its leader dictated the composition and duration of the interregnum parliaments, and the military eventually restored the monarchy. Cromwell was the first chairman of the Council of State of the new republic, or Commonwealth. It endured until Cromwell and his soldiers dissolved the "rump parliament" in 1653. He took the title Lord Protector, refused enthronement, and true to his political origins continued to try to find a way to constitute and work with Parliament. At his death in 1658, his son Richard briefly and unsuccessfully assumed power. Finally, the restoration of the monarchy was itself engineered by the parliamentary general George Monck.

Some balance of reconciliation and punishment is the familiar aftermath of civil wars. The victor's justice, sharpened by filial emotion, was immediate. Charles II's agents tracked down ten of those involved in executing his father, and they were hanged, drawn, and quartered as traitors. Some managed to escape abroad, but the dead remained within reach. Cromwell's remains were dug up, hung at Tyburn, and his head put on a pole elsewhere. Yet Cromwell's remaining family members survived. Parliament, taking an entirely different approach to the modern era's postwar practice of setting up a truth commission, passed the Act of Oblivion and Indemnity, and that was that.

Despite some Restoration nastiness and quasi-judicial executions, the consensus among historians is that the English civil war was "unusually benign,"[32] and perhaps that is why the Restoration decision makers could choose oblivion as the civil war victors had done before. The more widely reported atrocities committed by the parliamentary army are the focus of this chapter. Whether compared to the contemporaneous Thirty Years' War or to later civil wars, these atrocities were small scale and intermittent. The Thirty Years' War, in which Count Tilly commanded when he chose to command, saw horrors on a different order of magnitude. Ireland had the worst of the English Civil War, and siege warfare, not open battle, generally led to the worst incidents. Combatants killed civilians and prisoners at Leicester and Bolton, at Basing House, and at Drogheda, although nothing in England or Ireland compared to the savagery seen at Magdeburg.

THE PUZZLE OF THE ENGLISH CIVIL WAR

The relatively low level of atrocities in the English Civil War is a puzzle. In trying to understand human rights violations, we generally focus on extreme cases like the Rape of Nanking or the Holocaust by asking, "Why the level of violence?" But the English Civil War allows us to ask the no-less-diagnostic question "Why exercise restraint?" With the means of violence, the soldier's temptation to the short-term opportunism of a high-risk occupation, the fear of losing and being subject to victor's justice, and with expectations of the collapse of formal and informal rules of behavior, we may ask "Why behave?" Civil wars are intense conflicts. The combatants have no exit and are struggling for governmental power and the administration of the postwar settlement of scores. Institutional uncertainty or even meltdown, the high stakes, and a society mobilized for violence increase the probability of human rights violations. What happened to the Bolshevik law of civil war? Why did they not slaughter all the wounded?

My argument connects the principles of the leader and the way he controlled his agents to the low level of atrocities, but it is important to consider other possible explanations. Instead of an internal adherence to combat morality and attention to the management of violence, some argue that external factors are all that restrain violence and human rights violations. Pressure from the international community or the domestic economic elite may reduce atrocities.[33] The leader will settle on a lower level of violence than threat alone would suggest—unless presumably the government can hide its high levels of violations in order to avoid additional costs of the policy of repression. It is worth noting that hiding violations and the artificial information asymmetry between principal and agent are common features of human rights violations and imply that governments anticipate some sort of externally imposed cost. But these sorts of factors are unlikely causes of restraint in this case from the seventeenth century. The direct influence of the international system to suppress human rights violations does not precede efforts to suppress the slave trade at the end of the eighteenth century, and that was largely a bilateral activity.

As far as the English Civil War is a theater of the Thirty Years' War, the impact of international forces is as likely to encourage violations as suppress them. The wars the English Parliament fought began late in the Thirty Years' War, and many of the combatants in these northern wars had been to the epicenter, had earned their martial apprenticeship in Count Tilly's war. Soldiers on both sides in the British and Irish wars had direct experience of the conduct of the continental war between Catholic and Protestant. Among parliamentary officers, Fairfax, the Earl of Essex, Monck, Skippon, and Balfour had fought in the Dutch army, and Crawford and Ramsay had fought in the Swedish army.[34] In 1626, an English soldier in the army of Ernst Von Mansfeld, one of the generals in the Thirty Years' War, describes the stop in Weiss Kirchen, Moravia: "we entered killing man, woman and child: the execution continued the space of two hours, the pillaging two days."[35] A year later the troops of Count Tilly burned villages, slaughtered cattle, plundered graveyards, killed peasants, and amputated the hands and feet of the Protestant pastor and placed the rest of him on the altar of his church.[36] Tilly had yet to reward his soldiers with the men, women, and children of Magdeburg. According to military historian Charles Carlton, perhaps as many as 15,000 Englishmen fought abroad, a similar number of Irish, and about 25,000 Scots.[37] These soldiers fought for all the European armies. They returned valuing field guns, cavalry tactics, but not systematic savagery.

We can also eliminate the domestic economic elite as a primary source of restraint on the parliamentary army. The economic elite, the cream of England's commercial society drawn from the large London market, had strong parliamentary sympathies and thought that parliamentary victory would lead to prosperity.[38] This elite was likely to be more accepting of repressive measures by parliamentary forces, an acceptance reinforced by their immobility. Specialized commercial farming, located next to navigable waterways in the east and southeast of England and supplying London, drove the English economy. Navigable waterways rather than roads were essential for economic specialization. Only waterways provided the means to efficiently transport the large quantities of goods necessary to serve the London market. In the middle of the seventeenth century, London had a population approaching half a million. These economically interdependent areas, the east and southeast of England, provided strong support for the parliamentary cause. Examining the political affiliations of members of the Long Parliament, 80 percent of the members from the east (Cambridgeshire, Essex, Hertfordshire, Huntingdonshire, Lincolnshire, Norfolk, and Suffolk) and 68 percent from the southeast (Hampshire, Kent, Middlesex, Surrey, Sussex, Cinque Ports) supported Parliament's cause against the king.[39] In contrast, support for Parliament dropped to 31 percent of members from the west and Wales. The east provided soldiers to fight the cause as well as politicians to argue it. It was the men of Cromwell's Eastern Association that formed the core of what became Parliament's New Model Army.

Let us suppose that the economic elite that supported the parliamentary cause disagreed with Parliament's methods; what options did they have? Given a continent at war, the London market, and perishable agricultural goods, there were no obvious exit options for investment. The commercial elite had no good alternatives to a parliamentary England. Finally, consistent with these interests, we would need evidence that members of this elite were concerned about the good treatment of royalist soldiers, the Scots, the Irish, or west-country peasants and attempted to actively suppress violations. Far from exercising a restraining influence, leaders of public opinion in the form of the London newspapers at times encouraged violations. In January 1644, 120 Irish camp followers had been captured at Nantwich. The papers wanted them "put to the sword." Instead, the parliamentary commander, Thomas Fairfax, "sent them home."[40] Neither international nor domestic forces sent a clear material signal for good behavior to the parliamentary leadership. There is no evidence of external pressures from the international system or the economic elite placing a price on bad behavior by the parliamentary troops. With the exception of the execution of the king, there is no evidence that either the international system or the domestic economic elite even cared much about their behavior. The relative restraint of the parliamentary soldiers is curious.

It was a commitment to toleration and self-restraint that extended to the control of the agents, not external restraints, that explains the generally low level of violence. When self-restraint broke down, atrocities happened. They were infrequent, unexpected, commented on at the time, and attributable to temporary breakdowns in control of the agents. Royal and royalist heads rolled on convictions about appropriate punishment for untrustworthy opponents, rather than on calculations about how best to manage threats to parliamentary power and to maximize political support.

ATROCITIES IN THE ENGLISH CIVIL WAR

Siege warfare, which put soldiers in direct contact with civilians, was most likely to present the opportunity for atrocity. Yet, the battle of Naseby in June 1645, which decided the first war for Parliament, was the occasion of a well-publicized slaughter. It was a victory for the newly reorganized parliamentary New Model Army and for Cromwell, whose cavalry first routed the opposing cavalry of Sir Marmaduke Langdale and then, still under control, reformed and set on the royalist infantry. The famous royalist cavalry commander Prince Rupert of the Rhine had successfully charged the more numerous parliamentary cavalry on the other flank, but his men then removed themselves from the battlefield by continuing the chase to the parliamentary baggage train. At Naseby over 4,000 royalists were taken prisoner, but in the aftermath of the battle parliamentary soldiers killed about 100 women with the royalist baggage train.

It is possible that their killers considered these women whores and Irish, and felt threatened as the women carried knives. Apparently they were Welsh and spoke Welsh, which may have been mistaken for Irish, and the knives were cooking implements. It is likely that the perpetrators, who were not held to account for what they had done, were infantry rather than the more disciplined cavalry under Cromwell's command.[41] The historian C. V. Wedgwood reports this story and argues that "the likeliest answer" to this "indelible blot" on the New Model Army is that "the women, finding themselves surrounded by the enemy . . . fought with what weapons they had to protect their belongings, and the soldiers, angry at resistance when the battle was over, beat them down with their swords."[42] There was no discernable strategic benefit from the slaughter and no report of Fairfax or Cromwell refusing to control these agents. Historians regard this atrocity as exceptional and point out that, as such, it was widely reported in the London newspapers. These newspapers offered no restraint: "There is no palliating this outrage, which at least ten London newspapers reported without a hint of shame or apology."[43] Public opinion, as far as these newspapers represent a gauge of it, and assuming that parliamentarians rather than royalists were more responsive to public opinion, does not exercise a restraining or civilizing influence on the conduct of the war.

Some civilians also died when Cromwell's men stormed Basing House, a fortress that was a center of English Catholic resistance. The attackers shouted, "down with the Papists," and had been worked up by an attending preacher for whom the royalists were "open enemies of god . . . bloody Papists . . . vermin."[44] They killed about 100 in the assault and took 300 prisoners. One account mentions one woman and six priests among those killed.[45] And when eight or nine women tried to escape, they "were entertained by the common soldiers somewhat coarsely, yet not uncivilly . . . they left them with some clothes upon them."[46] This is more than can be said for the unfortunate Inigo Jones, architect and Royal Surveyor of Works, who was stripped naked and left the house wrapped in a blanket.[47] He was later pardoned and remained professionally active.

In Ireland Cromwell has the reputation of an "English bastard." His troops sacked the port city of Wexford. As far as the English were concerned, this city was a lair for pirates with associations with the Catholic forces financed by the Vatican and led by the papal legate Cardinal Rinucinni. Somewhere between 1,500 and 2,000 soldiers, priests, and civilians died in the assault.[48] Governor Sinnott of Wexford did not surrender immediately. As he negotiated with Cromwell, he received reinforcements into the town. Cromwell offered to spare civilians and officers and allow the soldiers to return to their homes if they promised not to fight again. Before this offer could be presented to the governor, some of the castle defenders under Captain Stafford abandoned their posts. Cromwell's soldiers, apparently on their own initiative, took immediate advantage and stormed the town, while Cromwell was planning to use the city for winter quarters. Soldiers and civilians were killed or perished trying to flee. Two boats, overloaded with those trying to escape, sank, drowning 300. Other civilians were killed at Market Cross. The Irish historian Tom Reilly says, "civilians were killed, but the evidence will show that the majority were likely to have been fully armed and engaged in the conflict"[49]—so they were not really civilians. Cromwell's men did take 3,000 prisoners, and another historian, Nicholas Canny, states that "unarmed civilians were also killed in the taking of Wexford, although this was because they were caught in the cross-fire rather than because slaying non-combatants was part of Cromwell's policy . . . whenever he [Cromwell] was forced by military circumstances to grant terms to besieged garrisons—notably at Clonmel—he observed the terms of the surrender to the letter."[50] According to historian Roger Hainsworth, "the report that Cromwell slew every man, woman and child in Wexford is another fantasy."[51] There seems some consensus that the worst at Wexford was what we now refer to as collateral damage.

There was no policy of extermination, although that was the accusation of the Catholic priests in Ireland who had their own political agenda. Cromwell responded angrily to this charge, recalling the 1641 massacre of some thousands of Protestants in Ireland, and asking whether the Catholic clergy's loyalty was with the French, Spanish, or Scottish monarch. He said he would prohibit Catholic ceremony, but that he had no control over the peoples' thoughts and would not kill noncombatants, who would be "protected equally with Englishmen." Cromwell said that it was the Catholic religion that used the "fire and sword" to convert people. He claimed that: "the Word of God . . . is able to convert . . . together with humanity, good life, equal and honest dealing with men of a different opinion, which we desire to exercise towards this poor people . . ."[52] In this sense, he did not see nor did he conduct his military campaign in Ireland as a crusade.

Catholic priests in Ireland were very much at risk, some "treated more or less as officers in a hostile army, and put to death in circumstances in which officers were executed, but there were also instances of their lives being spared, and Cromwell was more merciful than the old Protestants such as Broghill and Coote."[53] Parliamentary forces regarded the priests as agents of rival foreign powers, notably of Catholic Spain, and responsible for a 1641 killing of Protestants in Ireland.

English policy toward Ireland sought reprisal for the 1641 "massacre" of the Protestants. The toll from the 1641 killings was vastly exaggerated in England. Cromwell, in a speech to Parliament, attributed the killings to the influence of Spain.[54] Careful estimates suggest around 4,000 Protestant settlers were murdered and another 8,000 died of starvation and the cold.[55] Others have argued that it is "futile" to try to estimate the numbers killed, and that a better understanding of the events comes from examining the nastiness of the attacks. Historian Nicholas Canny argues that priests gave the killing of Protestants some legitimacy: "Thus, what would have remained an orgy of looting and killing became a movement with which some people could proudly identify."[56] Off the battlefield, parliamentary oppression took an economic form with the confiscation of the estates or parts of the estates of those who fought against the English— "Ringleaders, the rebellious Landlords, and Papist Aristocracy" and those who could not demonstrate their "constant good affection" for Parliament; the land was parceled off to soldiers in lieu of pay. The policy of confiscating the property of opponents had been applied in England since 1642 and was used to support the parliamentary army.[57] After the second war, the parliamentarians confiscated the estates of leading royalists and imposed fines from a tenth to a third of their estates on others.[58] Ordinary people—"husbandmen, ploughmen, labourers, artificers and others of the meaner sort"—were "exempt from punishment and question."[59] Judicial action led to some being charged with murder. One Irish royalist commander was convicted and condemned to death, "but he might well have saved his life had he not continued to deny that he had received a commission to take arms from Charles I," and others like the Catholic vicar general of Dublin were condemned to death but were actually exiled.[60]

Parliamentary troops sacked no English cities. Royalist forces behaved differently. To explain royalist behavior, historians draw contrasts between the convictions of parliamentary and royalist commanders, as well as between the discipline that they enforced over their men. According to historian John Morrill, "the royalists, unlike the parliamentarians, had commanders who believed in terror, believed in the efficacy of looting to instill obedience or at least acquiescence from the country."[61] The royalists sacked the cities of Bolton, where 700 civilians were killed,[62] and Leicester, where according to the contemporary royalist historian, "the conquerors pursued their advantage with the usual license of rapine and plunder, and miserably sacked the whole town, without any distinction of persons or places; churches and hospitals as well as other house, [were] made prey to the enraged and greedy soldier, to the exceeding regret of the king."[63] To offset the regret about the actions of his greedy agents, sacking Leicester "gave the king's army great reputation, and made a wonderful impression of terror upon the hearts of those at Westminster."[64] But any strategic advantage taken from this city was insufficient to counter parliamentary supremacy on the battlefield of Naseby shortly afterward.

For a brief period of time in rural England localized and spontaneous antiwar groups formed, armed themselves, and resisted the combatants. The Clubmen unrest of 1645 shook the royalist west and then spread south. Clubmen Associations—the name communicates the state of armament and discipline—formed spontaneously to provide self-defense for the locals in their conflicts with plundering soldiers or tax collectors. They mobilized thousands. With clergy and local gentry sometimes providing the leadership, they developed articles of association that stipulated a watch and warning system against plundering soldiers, a hierarchy, and the turning out of armed men to deal with the threat. They appeared in the counties of Shropshire, Worcestershire, and Herefordshire from January until March 1645, then spread to Wiltshire, Dorset, and Somerset from May to September, and finally to Berkshire, Sussex, and Hampshire, as well as the Welsh border by November.[65] The Clubmen foreshadowed the Greens in the Russian Civil War,[66] when in some regions of that country, Russian peasants with pitchforks also managed to coordinate resistance and to adopt a position of armed neutrality. They were annihilated. While the English Clubmen presented a parallel opportunity for massacre, they were tolerated within limits. Cromwell referred to them as "poor silly creatures" and asked Fairfax's permission to send home the 300 he had taken prisoner, provided they promised to behave. He even allowed them to continue in their mission: "the Clubmen were to have the liberty to defend themselves against plundering."[67]

Taking prisoners, no less than contact with civilians, presents the opportunity for violations. How did the parliamentary army treat the prisoners that it took? In October 1644, a parliamentary ordinance stipulated: "no quarter shall henceforth be given to any Irishman, or papist born in Ireland."[68] A similar ordinance was passed by the Scottish parliament the following year. Retribution seems the most obvious reason for this decision to selectively kill Irish prisoners; it represented reprisal for the slaughter of Protestant settlers in Ireland in 1641. But such treatment, publicly announced, might also serve to deter third-party involvement in the English Civil War, and intervention on the royalist side by other nationalities, while Parliament secured help from the Scots. The king's own correspondence, captured at the battle of Naseby, revealed that Charles sought military assistance from foreign countries and the Catholic Irish Confederacy. Some Irish soldiers heading for England were captured and drowned at sea, which worked as a deterrent: "The drownings were highly effective, making Irish soldiers, admitted the Marquis of Ormonde, loath to sail to fight in England."[69] After the capture of Shrewsbury in February 1645, parliamentary forces under the Earl of Essex took fifty Irish prisoners and chose by lot thirteen to hang. The earl saw this action as reprisal for 1641 and the atrocities against "harmless British protestants . . . without distinction of age or sex."[70] In return, Prince Rupert hanged thirteen parliamentary soldiers. After this episode Parliament stepped back from the policy and, as Ian Gentles claims, "a descent into barbarism was only narrowly averted."[71]

But captivity had its perils and could result in transportation to the West Indies, where prisoner fatalities resulted from disease and work. In 1648 Scottish volunteer soldiers were transported after Cromwell's victory at Preston. Parliament recommended that Scottish conscripts, with their word that they would not invade again, should be allowed to go home.[72] Cromwell, in his battlefield report to the speaker of the House of Commons, appealed for help in dealing with the prisoners. He said that ten soldiers could guard a thousand prisoners, as the prisoners were most afraid of the local people, and that they would not be able to get home without protection.[73] The defeated Duke of Hamilton later testified to Cromwell's responsible and humane behavior at Preston: "Indeed he was so very courteous and so very civil as he performed more than he promised, and I must acknowledge in his favour to those poor wounded gentlemen that I left behind, that were by him taken care of, and truly he performed more than he did capitulate for."[74] After the battle of Dunbar in 1650, Cromwell took 10,000 Scottish prisoners. Cromwell instructed that "humanity be exercised towards them." He released 5,000, mostly wounded. But others fell ill and died, some escaped, some with skills stayed in Newcastle, and some went to the New World or to fight in Ireland.[75] After Worcester in 1651, some prisoners were permitted to go abroad to fight, some were transported, some were sent to work on draining the fens, and some went home to Scotland with money and a clothing allowance.[76] English prisoners were transported after the siege of Colchester, and in 1649 survivors of the bloody storming of Drogheda in Ireland were sent to Barbados. Other prisoners were given the option of going abroad: "On surrender, the Irish soldiers were normally allowed to go abroad. As war was to continue between France and Spain until 1659, these countries were willing to absorb the many Irish swordsmen . . . others left less willingly, being transported to English plantations in America."[77] With the exception of Drogheda, the majority of prisoners in England, Ireland, and Scotland were not subjected to the Bolshevik law of civil war.

The slaughter of the prisoners at Drogheda in 1649 was the most terrible action of the Cromwellian army. A mix of Irish and English soldiers defended the town. The besieged commander was Sir Arthur Aston, a veteran of the Thirty Years' War who had served in Russia and Poland. As governor of Oxford in the first civil war, Aston was noted for hanging those merely suspected of being sympathetic to Parliament.[78] Aston and most of his senior officers were English. The defenders, some 2,221 infantry and 319 cavalry, sheltered behind the formidable defenses of a 20-foot-high wall with 29 guard towers and refused to surrender the town. On the evening of September 11, 1649, the heavy parliamentary artillery breached the walls. The "forlorn hope," the first soldiers into the breach, failed on the initial attempts and their leader, Colonel James Castle, was killed. The town fell on the third assault, with Cromwell personally leading his troops.[79] Under the rules of war at the time, to take by storm after the defenders had refused to surrender meant that the attackers could refuse "quarter" or to take any prisoners. That is what Cromwell did. His troops trapped Aston and some of his men, and Cromwell immediately ordered that they be put to death: "it appears that the English van granted the Irish quarter, but Cromwell . . . countermanded that no prisoners be taken."[80] They clubbed Aston to death with his leg, which was wooden and said to hold the wearer's gold.

Cromwell explained himself to Speaker William Lenthall, of the House of Commons, in his letter of September 17, 1649. He wrote, "being in the heat of action, I forbade them to spare any that were in arms in the town, and, I think, that night they put to the sword 2,000 men."[81] Cromwell's men saved some of the defenders. Cromwell estimated that he lost about 100 men. The following day, when the last defenders gave up, the royalist officers were killed and Cromwell's troops shot every tenth man of those captured from one tower; the remainder he had transported to Barbados. Despite reports to the contrary, Cromwell did not order the killing of civilians, did not kill all the armed defenders, and the evidence suggests that his army did not kill noncombatants at Drogheda.[82] Cromwell, then, offers "the heat of action," as the immediate explanation for his decision to execute the prisoners. Antonia Fraser puts it this way: "The conclusion cannot be escaped that Cromwell lost his self-control at Drogheda, literally saw red—the red of his comrades' blood—after the failure of the first assaults . . . The slaughter itself stood quite outside his usual record of careful mercy."[83] Participating in rather than delegating the violence, he lost control of himself and sought the reward of vengeance. Most of those defenders surrendering on the following day, when the action was "cooler," survived.

Later in his September 17 letter to Speaker Lenthall, Cromwell says that it is the judgment of God "upon these barbarous wretches, who have imbrued their hands in so much innocent blood; and that it will tend to prevent the effusion of blood for the future, which are satisfactory grounds to such actions, which otherwise cannot but work remorse and regret." The innocent blood that he mentions is that of the Protestant settlers killed just before the beginning of the civil war in 1641. Cromwell recognized Spanish influence at work in Ireland and had an inflated view of the numbers of Protestants killed in 1641. Years later Cromwell noted the influence of the hostile superpower and stated that: "through [Spanish] power and instigation, twenty-thousand Protestants were massacred in Ireland. We thought, being denied just things, we thought it our duty to get that by the sword which we could not otherwise do. And this hath been the spirit of Englishmen."[84] The number of Protestants actually murdered is estimated to be between 4,000 and 5,000, with more dying of starvation and mistreatment.[85] Toleration did not extend to treason, and the sword brought "justice." Despite Cromwell's view, the Drogheda defenders were never linked to the killings of Protestants in 1641, so no ordinary conception of justice was served. Historian William Abbott points out that Cromwell held the whole country responsible for the 1641 massacres though "there can have been few— if any—at Drogheda who had taken part in them; certainly not the officers, certainly not the English soldiers, and almost certainly not Ormond's own regiment . . ."[86] Cromwell's third justification is strategic efficiency and the prevention of future bloodshed: with the fear-inspiring effect of Drogheda, future sieges would be unnecessary. Cromwell wanted his reputation alone to breach a city's walls, and to some extent this happened, for as the campaign unfolded some towns did yield without fighting. Yet, if strategic efficiency were more than an additional rationalization to the "heat of the action," he likely would have used this approach elsewhere.

No other sieges compared to the brutality of Drogheda. Even at Clonmel, where Hugh O'Neill's brilliant defensive tactics inflicted very significant losses on Cromwell's army, the town's inhabitants were spared although they were party to the escape of the defending force. The defenders, instead of throwing themselves at the breach, constructed a defensive cul-de-sac in from the breach, and Cromwell committed more and more troops to the enfiladed dead end. O'Neill, born in the Spanish Netherlands and trained in the Spanish Army, was finally captured the following year at Limerick. He survived imprisonment in the Tower of London and with the king of Spain coming to his aid he was permitted to end his days in Spain.[87] Arguably, this Irishman or Spaniard came closest to claiming to have beaten Cromwell.

Generally, Cromwell's New Model Army acted with restraint wherever it fought, and unlike other Protestant forces in Ireland it did not harm civilians.[88] Even after Wexford and Drogheda, Cromwell explicitly denied killing any unarmed civilians. He challenged the priests: "give us an instance of one man, since my coming into Ireland, not in arms, massacred, destroyed or banished."[89] After Wexford, Cromwell, mentioning the starving and drowning of Protestants and piracy, recited a similar formula of "just judgment" and seemed to have no personal sense of responsibility for the events that followed the opportunistic storming, which was an "unexpected providence" of God.[90] The divine actions of his storm troopers at Wexford is an unlikely and certainly unworthy rationale, not that of "our chief of men," but also not racism. In terms of the specific events at Drogheda, it is unnecessary to assume racism when we have a simpler explanation. The simplest and most selfish explanation, the one Cromwell offers first, is consistent with the principal-agent argument, although unexpectedly it is the principal-turned-agent who takes this reward. Then the principal volunteers strategic incentives as if to mitigate his selfish act.

In addition to summary executions, some prisoners went to trial. The king, Parliament's most prominent prisoner, was executed following a trial that could not be described as fair. With the second war, the parliamentary forces initiated quasi-judicial executions of some leading English royalist officers. Three royalists, one of whom had broken his parole given two years earlier, were sentenced to death after the siege of Colchester. One got off for the "surprising touristic reason that as he was Florentine by birth, his killers or their descendants might find themselves subject to persecution during future visits to Italy."[91] They contrived some leniency even in the harsher second war.

Notable English royalists tended to be treated more harshly than the Scots. The Scottish commanders captured after the battle of Worcester in 1651 went to the Tower, gaining freedom with the Restoration, but the Earl of Derby was executed despite Cromwell's objection.[92] Unless there is reason to believe that execution works to deter the English but not the Scots, commitments, not calculation, account for these decisions, and the English royalists were committing treason. Betrayal of their word and their country, not the level of threat posed to government survival, was what differentiated the defeated in the second civil war.

Like Lenin, Oliver Cromwell also faced dissension within his own ranks. The Levellers were a radically democratic political movement that shook the parliamentary New Model Army. They advocated manhood suffrage and a republic, freedom of religion, and economic reform.

More radical elements advocated free schools and welfare policies, and made common cause with the ordinary people of Ireland. Cromwell and Fairfax, with regiments not swept up by the Levellers' demands, suppressed the mutinous soldiers in the spring of 1649. They captured about 400 mutineers and locked them overnight in Burford Church, Oxfordshire. In the morning, and with the prisoners watching, Cromwell had three mutineers shot in the churchyard; he pardoned a fourth. Among those shot was a Corporal Perkins who thought "it a great mercy that he was to die for this quarrel."[93] Without mitigating this sad episode, it was not Kronstadt in the Cotswolds. Lenin, faced with mutinously democratic sailors, opted for comprehensive rather than exemplary executions. The parallel challenges of king and czar, Clubmen and Greens, Leveller soldiers and Kronstadt sailors elicited uniformly different sets of responses from the two leaders.

The English Civil War contrasts with the Russian Civil War and is an anomaly in the standard explanation of human rights violations. The standard explanation points to the institutional, economic, cultural, and demographic environment rather than to the leaders and agents who commit the violations. The standard explanation finds primarily that warfare and the absence of democracy are associated with systematically high levels of human rights violations. This explanation does not prepare us for the treatment of civilians and prisoners during the English Civil War. Violations occurred in the war-torn and nondemocratic environment of seventeenth-century Britain and Ireland, but they were intermittent and relatively few. Cromwell's principles help us understand why he did not choose more prudential nasty strategies and did not deal with the king and his family, the Levellers, and the Clubmen more ruthlessly. But with the opportunities that armed force and the fog of war present, why did Cromwell's agents not routinely seek vengeance and the other selfish rewards as their counterparts were doing on the continent?

PRINCIPAL AND AGENT: COUNT TILLY'S REWARD DENIED

Leaders' commitments are only part of the explanation. We also need to understand a leader's relationship to those who implement the violence, and how a leader effectively signals commitments and intentions to the agents. There is a story about Prince Rupert of the Rhine visiting an inn in Shropshire. He drank the local brew and paid, and encouraged his soldiers to do the same. Once Rupert had left, his soldiers drank the lot and did not pay.[94] It is hard to imagine Cromwell taking his men to the pub, but harder still to imagine them ignoring him in order to satisfy themselves. The role of leaders and their followers is at the heart of my argument. (I should add parenthetically that while no one so far seems to consider him a roué, Cromwell's reputation as puritanical is being revised by historians.[95] They point out that he drank, smoked, danced, and indulged in practical jokes on occasion.)

We need to understand why we would not expect Cromwell's men to drink the pub dry like Prince Rupert's men (and why Cromwell, but not Rupert, could reform his horsemen for a second charge at the crucial battle of Naseby). The critical difference is the signals the principal sends to the agents. The agents of repression, in this case soldiers of the parliamentary army, like soldiers in any other army, follow their own interests all the way to the baggage train if they think they can get away with it. An oversupply of violations results from principals not having the information or not being willing to exercise control over their agents. In examining the use of violence, scholars have ignored the principal-agent logic that characterizes policy implementation generally, where the agent has, in this case, the opportunity for revenge or for monetary, sexual, and sadistic benefits.

Excepting Naseby and Drogheda, how did the principal prevent the agents committing violations for their own sake? Why did not the victorious parliamentary soldiers routinely exact Count Tilly's reward? The temptations were great and intensified by the risks that the soldiers endured, as Count Tilly observed. Soldiers everywhere and in every era take this reward. But there are solutions to the problems of control that the agents' independent goals and informational advantages create for the principal. The solution to the problem of moral hazard, of the self-serving, hidden actions of the agents, lies in clear signaling of the rules and effective monitoring and enforcement mechanisms that compensate for the information asymmetry, as the real Henry V discovered centuries before Cromwell. The solution to adversely selecting those already predisposed to exact Count Tilly's reward, those with a particular taste for violence, is to take care in the recruitment of agents and to find and encourage agents of conscience.

In Schiller's account it was Count Tilly's discretion to decide whether to exercise command responsibility immediately, in two hours, or in three days. More routinely, the principal does not manage the bureaucracy from event to event, moment to moment, but relies on rules and standard procedures. The articles of war for the parliamentary army, entitled "Lawes and Ordinances of WARRE, Established for the better Conduct of the ARMY,"[96] organized the regulations applying to parliamentary soldiers among several "duties." And, most important, Cromwell had the will to see that his soldiers knew and carried out these duties.

Soldiers had duties to God and to superior officers, general duties, moral duties, marching duties, camp and garrison duties, and duties in action. General duties included prohibitions on treason, yielding "without the utmost necessity," and negligence. Duties to superiors laid out the importance of discipline and observing the chain of command. Capital punishment applied to a range of transgressions. Under "Of Duties Morrall," it stated, "Rapes, Ravishments, unnatural abuses, shall be punished with death." The Hague Convention, in Article XLV, provides a much vaguer prohibition: "family honour . . . must be respected." As legal scholar Theodor Meron points out in his discussion of Henry V's prohibition of rape by his soldiers, extraordinary as it may seem in international law, rape was only specifically prohibited by name in the fourth Geneva Convention of 1949.[97] In contrast to the Nuremberg charges, the statute of the International Criminal Tribunal for the former Yugoslavia at The Hague explicitly includes rape as a crime against humanity.

The parliamentary articles of war provided that murder "shall be expiated with the death of the Murtherer," and theft and robbery over a certain amount (twelve pence) were also capital offences. Under marching duties, taking "a Horse out of the Plough, or to wrong the Husbandmen in their person or Cattel, or goods" carried the death penalty. Cutting down fruit trees was also prohibited and punished severely. Interestingly, the Deuteronomic code also specifically protects fruit trees.[98] And Michael Ignatieff notes that a warrior nephew of Muhammad advocated the following: "abstain from killing small children, old men, or women; abstain from cutting palm trees; abstain from slaughtering sheep or cows or camels except to feed yourselves."[99] Arboreal protection seems an odd priority in a martial document of this kind, where all sorts of violent acts and desperate situations are described, but it derives from concern to protect subsistence and supplies in wartime.

Under "Of Duties in Action," the economical language of article V stated that "None shall kill an Enemy who yeelds, and throws down his Armes." The Convention Respecting the Laws and Customs of War on Land, signed at The Hague, October 18, 1907, forbids "To kill or wound an enemy who, having laid down his arms, or having no longer means of defence, has surrendered at discretion." Crimes against humanity, recognized at the Nuremberg Trials, were otherwise covered in the parliamentary army's code in its effort to protect civilians and their means of subsistence. Neither the cavalryman nor mount fed freely. It was forbidden, for example, to let horses "feed in sown grounds" or "endamage the Husbandman any way," as well as it was forbidden, "in his Quarter," to "abuse, beat, fright his Landlord, or any Person else in the Family, " or to "extort Money or Victuals, by violence." This document described rules and procedures, and the penalties for their breach that defined the army. These rules made it both a military and a moral institution. The rules provided for the efficiency of the fighting force. They structured incentives to ensure individuals, officers and men, were committed to winning. They provided for the well-being of individuals serving in the army. These rules also protected the vulnerable from the army.

Rules must be communicated as well as formulated. Announcing rules begins a principal's political control of his or her agents. The articles of war were made known to the soldiers in a weekly routine:

> These Lawes and Ordinances be made more publicke and knowne, as well to the Officers, as to the Common Souldiers, every Colonel and Captaine is to provide some of these Bookes, and to cause them to be forthwith distinctly and audibly read in every severall Regiment . . . And weekly afterwards, upon the Pay-day, every Captain is to cause the same to be read to his owne Company, in presence of

his Officers . . . that none may be ignorant of the Lawes and Duties required of them.[100]

Marching on to Scotland after the battle of Preston, Cromwell issued a proclamation to his troops stipulating that plunderers and those that "abuse the people in any sort" will be tried by a council of war and punished "according to the Articles of War made for the government of the army in the kingdom of England, which is death."[101] He ordered that those in the chain of command communicate this proclamation and that captains must notify their troops.

To maintain control requires monitoring and then following up on the information in the form of consequences for violators. After the surrender of Langford House in 1645, six of Cromwell's soldiers ignored the surrender agreement and plundered the surrendering royalists. The soldiers were arrested, tried, and drew lots. The loser was hanged. Cromwell sent the other five to the royalist governor of Oxford. The governor, acknowledging Cromwell's "noble spirit," reciprocated and set them free.[102] Historians appear in agreement about the high discipline of the parliamentary armies. Barbara Donagan writes that "Fairfax and his officers were noted for their care 'to see Articles always kept, in which they judged their honour deeply concerned.'"[103] It was what the Israeli Kahan Commission referred to as combat morality. According to C. H. Firth, "by the judgement both of friends and foes one of the most striking characteristics of the Cromwellian army was the excellence of its discipline."[104] Even the Earl of Clarendon, the royalist historian, testifies most affirmatively to the discipline of the parliamentary army: "Cromwell had been most strict and severe in the forming of the manners of his army, and in chastising all irregularities; insomuch that sure there was never any such body of men so without rapine, swearing, drinking, or any other debauchery . . ."[105] Observing the similarities between royalist and parliamentary articles of war, Ian Gentles says, "that the armies of Parliament were better disciplined than those of the king is a cliché," and claims that although "England had atrocities . . . it was spared the full horrors of the Thirty Years War, in part because of the restraining effect of the Articles of War adopted by both sides."[106] The distinctiveness of Cromwell's leadership and the parliamentary army is revealed in the incidence of rape. For Cromwell's wars Charles Carlton notes, "one sign of the comparative lack of gratuitous violence was a remarkable absence of rape in the British civil wars."[107] Rape is a barometer of the principal-agent problem in security forces. In contrast to Russian women and the revolutionary Red Army, no English, Scottish, or Irish women were assigned to "wash the barracks" of the victorious New Model Army.

The discipline extended to Ireland. Cromwell understood that it had been common practice for armies in Ireland to pillage and abuse the civilians. He could have simply behaved as the Irish and Scottish Protestant commanders had behaved. He did not. In Dublin on August 24, 1649, he ordered the publishing "throughout all Ireland" of a declaration asserting that his army was a different army. He forbade violations by his men and reasserted the articles of war:

> Whereas I am informed that, upon the marching out of Armies heretofore, or of parties from Garrisons, a liberty hath been taken by the Soldiery to abuse, rob and pillage, and too often to execute cruelties upon the Country People: Being resolved . . . diligently and strictly to restrain such wickedness for the future, I do hereby warn and require all Officers, Soldiers, and others under my command, henceforth to forbear all such evil practices as aforesaid; and not to do any wrong or violence toward Country People, or persons whatsoever, unless they be actually in arms or office with the Enemy; and Not to meddle with the goods of such, without special order."[108]

He hanged two of his men for plundering ten days later. He repeated these proclamations against plunder and the abuse of civilians throughout the Irish campaign and later in the Scottish campaign. In that country too, he also enforced his orders severely. Observers "noticed the perfect order kept among them . . . Cromwell had three soldiers scourged by the Provost Marshal's men . . . and one, for being drunk, made to 'ryde the meir, at the Croce of Edinburgh.'"[109] At the siege of Limerick, in July 1651, twelve Irish prisoners were killed after Colonel Tothill had promised their safety. The commander, Cromwell's son-in-law Major-General Henry Ireton, court-martialed Tothill and released some Irish prisoners.[110] Cromwell and son, through the implementation of the articles of war, ensured that agents conformed to their norms.

It is possible that these norms were also, in part, a product of diffusion. The Swedes under Gustavus Adolphus, king of Sweden, who died fighting the Catholic General Albrecht von Wallenstein at the battle of Lutzen, were reputed to behave well. Yet, the Swedish training of the Scottish general David Leslie did not help the Irishmen who surrendered to him. Leslie accepted the surrender of Montrose's Irish soldiers at Philiphaugh but then apparently gave in to pressure from the Presbyterian ministers who accompanied his army, and his men first killed the camp-following boys and women, and then the Irish soldiers.[111] Gustavus was reputed to carry in his saddlebag a copy of the recently published *Laws of War and Peace* by Hugo Grotius.[112] The pleasure-taking soldiers of Wallenstein characterize service under boring Gustavus in a play:

FIRST MOUNTED RIFLEMAN:
With Gustav, the Swede, the plague of the people.
His camp was like a church with a steeple;
Prayers, by his orders, had to be
Said at retreat and at reveille.
And from his nag he'd preach and prate
If we were inclined to celebrate.
CAVALRY SERGEANT: He was a God-fearing gentleman.
FIRST MOUNTED RIFLEMAN: And girls?—You had to leave them
Alone
Or 'twas off to the church and a wife you'd own
          —*Friedrich Schiller, Wallenstein's Camp*, Act 1, Scene 6

Even Count Tilly, according to historians, could not elicit the level of civilian cooperation through the uncontrolled behavior of his agents that Wallenstein achieved: "The imperial name had more terrors than that of the League, and Tilly was amazed to see cities which had refused entry to his troops open their gates to Wallenstein."[113] But Wallenstein's lack of control of his agents proved fatal. He was finally murdered by his own troops, by Scottish, Irish, and English mercenaries. Wallenstein himself, at least in Schiller's dramatization (1799), returns us to the principal-agent problem in the human rights field:

> The city would become a battlefield,
> Fraternal discord with its eyes aflame
> Would be set loose to rampage through its streets.
> Shall the decision be committed to
> This deadly rage that no command controls?
> There is no room to fight here, just to slaughter;
> The madness of the Furies, when let loose,
> Cannot be called off by a leader's voice.
>
> —*Wallenstein's Death,* Act III, Scene 20

Interestingly, unlike his Tilly, Schiller's Wallenstein is as helpless as Shakespeare's Henry V claims to be before Harfleur. Henry says he might just as well "send precepts to the leviathan to come ashore" as try to control his enraged soldiers. In contrast, parliamentary commanders, notably Cromwell, generally managed to control the "madness of the Furies" and resisted the command temptations of indiscriminate violence.

Beyond its high level of discipline, there were other characteristics of the New Model Army that worked to suppress goal variance and soldiers selfishly seeking their own private benefits. Principal-agent logic forces attention on incentives and the appropriate organizational response. Agents of violence are particularly hard to monitor and control, even when the leader is on the spot. The New Model Army's structure of material incentives were conducive to discipline and low violations. The army was paid regularly. Further, and unlike later British armies up to the twentieth century, in the New Model Army there was the real possibility of promotion from the ranks.[114] Regular pay, and the possibility of promotion reduced the soldiers' temptation to break discipline in order to improve their personal welfare at the expense of the local population.

Compensation takes care of some of the likely goal variance. It cannot directly address the universal soldier's desire for sex and revenge. Less emphasized in principal-agent analysis is a third, and softer, instrument of control. As David Hume observed about the problem facing Roman emperors and the Soldan of Egypt with their praetorian guards and mamalukes, the "opinion" of these agents was critical. Economists themselves recognize that the beliefs of the agents are central, that recruiting properly motivated agents is the priority, and that "reputation" can constitute a reward.[115] This is the solution that David Hume described, and it was something that Oliver Cromwell knew.

The New Model Army had esprit de corps, at least after its first major victory at Naseby. Part of this esprit de corps was the work of the commander. Ian Gentles argues that Cromwell cared for his troops.[116] At the battle of Dunbar on September 3, 1650, Cromwell defeated a Scottish army that was twice the size of the English army and in possession of the high ground. His dawn attack found the Scots unprepared for battle, musketeers without matches to fire their weapons, too few scouts, and officers seeking shelter from the rain. Cromwell saw a relationship between the disciplined good behavior of his men, their commitments, ("men as had the fear of God before them, as made some conscience of what they did"), and their winning. The army embodied Cromwell's values: "Beyond efficiency and order, beyond martial spirit and triumph, the New Model Army possessed one other unique trait: the harmonious coexistence of diverse religions and political opinions."[117] Tolerance was valued by both principal and agents.

"FATE, CHANCE, KINGS AND DESPERATE MEN":[118] A SUBOPTIMAL EXECUTION

One problem brought Cromwell's values to the fore, set limits to his tolerance, raised the issue of political opportunism, and put his convictions at odds with public opinion. It was the same problem that later confronted Lenin: the captive monarch problem. Cromwell did not choose Lenin's solution, although he had the opportunity to do so. The paths not chosen, his refusal to choose Lenin's or Borgia's way, constitute evidence that Cromwell put moral imperatives before political expediency. If he had been motivated by power and building political support, then he would not have had the king publicly executed.

In thinking about historical evidence and explanations, one limitation is that one cannot go back and manipulate the things that one thinks are causal. It would be helpful to go back and have France and Britain intervene for the Republic in the Spanish Civil War, have Neville Chamberlain choose "war rather than dishonour," or have the Germans decide not to give Lenin a one-way ticket to the Finland Station. While appeasement, Guernica, and the Bolsheviks are irreversible, one can design a mental experiment about how things might have been different, as well as simply examine what happened. If we have a good general explanation that provides clear statements about how events are to be connected, then we can compare what happened with what the general explanation would have led us to expect. The technique is sometimes referred to as "counterfactual analysis," but it is a familiar mental exercise: "Those who like to lay down the history book, and to speculate upon what might have happened in the world but for the fatal occurrence of what actually did take place (a most puzzling, amusing, ingenious, and profitable kind of meditation), have no doubt thought to themselves what a specially bad time Napoleon took to come back from Elba . . ."[119] So, suppose we think we have a single goal for leaders, say Machiavelli's power motive, then we ought to be able to identify the policy option that represents the most efficient means for achieving the goal, that is, the option that a rational politician should choose if that person is interested in maximizing personal power. While not approaching the flexibility of the experimental sciences, one can supplement the evidentiary riches of written history by examining history rewritten within a particular explanatory framework. History does not mean you are stuck with what happened in the past.

But we need to know what happened before examining the alternatives. The captive monarch was put on trial. His trial was a show trial. The accused repeatedly questioned the constitutional authority for the trial. Divine right succumbed to profane procedures and political symbolism. The House of Commons, minus 140 politically suspect members who were turned away by the assiduous door keeping of Colonel Pride's regiment of foot, established a stacked High Court of Justice and charged His Majesty with treason. The king refused to plead. The sentence was execution. The warrant to sever

Charles's head from his body had 59 signatures, including Oliver Cromwell's. Later, when they were tried as regicides by the restored monarchy, some signatories claimed that they were pressured into signing. However, others who had disagreed with the execution did not sign, and many named to attend the trial did not. It was difficult to find a judge to conduct the trial, and the one found, John Bradshaw, wore a special metal-reinforced hat and armor under his judicial robe for fear of assassination. The trial proceeded awkwardly to its conclusion, with an uncooperative defendant who laughed at being named a traitor and who received shouted support from the gallery, reportedly from the wife of the absent great parliamentary commander Thomas Fairfax. The king spoke from the scaffold. He asked pardon for his enemies, folded back his hair from his neck, and signaled the incisive moment. A disguised executioner, whose identity has never been established, cut off the king's head. Reluctance rather than eagerness appears to have marked the proceedings from beginning to end. Even the spectators reportedly groaned their sympathy for the man, if not for the passing of the known political order.

Charles, acephalous in Whitehall, was now popular. Pamphlets eulogizing the king and his martyrdom were quickly and widely distributed.[120] Abroad, condemnation from foreign governments who would not recognize the new Commonwealth jeopardized English shipping and trade. In the north, the Scots, upset at the killing of a native son, declared Charles II as the successor.

Death of the king shifted political support from Parliament to the monarchy. It was not a sensible choice for an opportunist. If Cromwell's motivation was enhancing his own personal power, then he was a bungler. In a macabre sort of way, the quasi-judicial execution of Charles I is a suitable decision point for an analysis of the political leader's motivation for political violence.

The public execution of the king plausibly belongs in the category of suboptimal choices for Cromwell, as well as for Charles I. The option chosen detracted from rather than contributed to popular support for Cromwell. He even had difficulty mustering support from his own side from among members of parliament, lawyers, army officers, and the others chosen to judge the king. Of 135 named, only 88 ever attended throughout the course of the trial[121]—empty seats for this truly original political drama. Deciding on death, Cromwell and his associates personally took responsibility for the decision by signing the execution warrant. Then they allowed the king a fine exit, despite the negative consequences for public support: "Cromwell knew that the course they were all embarked on had no precedent," writes Derek Wilson, "He knew that it lacked the support of the people."[122] Biographer Antonia Fraser says: "It was clear that the actions of the Commons were not only inimical to the large majority of the population of England — not one in twenty supported it said Lord Northumberland—but the slender nature of their support was well known to the men concerned."[123] Beyond its consequences in political support, the course of action chosen also carried with it considerable personal risk of royalist reprisal.

To try to repair some of the political damage after the event, John Milton published pamphlets to explain why it was lawful to execute tyrannical kings and to respond to royalist propaganda. In describing a king who "broke" Parliaments at home and betrayed Protestants abroad," he registers what must be one of the first complaints concerning public policy and the fickleness of public opinion. He writes, "an ingratefull and pervers generation, who having first cry'd to God to be deliver'd from their King, now murmur against God that heard their praiers, and cry as loud for their King against those that deliver'd them."[124] With the restoration of the monarchy, Milton served a sentence for his regicidal prose.[125] But he survived.

The execution of Charles created immediate condemnation from abroad and serious uncertainty in the foreign affairs of an untried government. The Scottish Parliament had already condemned the trial and Louis XIV and the Dutch had written urging Cromwell not to execute the king.[126] In Scotland "the execution of the king . . . horrified even those Scots who had hitherto been the king's bitterest opponents, and swung the whole country round into opposition to Cromwell and the Commonwealth."[127] And Machiavelli would not have approved of the conspicuous accountability of the act and the survival of bitter relatives whose vengeance reached into Cromwell's grave.

The public execution of the monarch, publicly decided on by a few of his subjects, was an unprecedented and unpopular course of action in a monarchical system. An opportunist, a power-seeking, self-interested decision maker would have chosen differently. Rather than seek agreement with the king or publicly execute him at serious political cost in domestic and foreign support, the likely choice of the opportunist would be to get rid of the king without being held accountable for the act. Another puzzle of the English Civil War is that Charles was not secretly murdered after midnight and far from the capital, or whilst trying to escape, or did not fall mortally ill or off his horse while hunting. He left his life on a raised scaffold under the executioner's ax at two in the afternoon. The story goes that before stepping outside on that winter day, his executioners extended to him the dignity of an extra shirt so that he would not shiver and appear afraid. The paths of action not taken represent the "nonevidence" to test the hypothesis that Cromwell was an opportunist.[128] Cromwell, in contrast to Lenin, took direct accountability for the action.

In the seventeenth century, removing an opponent without taking responsibility for the action might involve a hunting accident, illness, or the reaction of an overzealous guard to an escape attempt. There is no evidence that Cromwell had any interest at all in these options. Instead, Cromwell first attempted to compromise with the intransigent king. The king's response was a secret deal with the Scots to support their religious agenda for England in exchange for their military help. Parliament paid the price of a second civil war in 1648, that time against the Scots and the English royalists. A biographer describes Cromwell's costs: "In order to maintain the shifty monarch on his throne he had wrestled in prayer, argued with recalcitrant radicals, put his reputation and even his life on the line and finally gone cap in hand to Carisbrooke [where the king was held] to plead for peace. He had been accused of being a royal "creature" by the Levellers . . . Opening doors for the king had cost Cromwell dear and every one had been firmly slammed by Charles."[129] In addition to another war, Cromwell had personally risked losing support within his own ranks by extending to the king opportunities to compromise.

There were alternatives. The disappearance or murder strategy had been done before: King William Rufus was killed while hunting, and Richard II, Henry VI, and Edward V died in custody or were murdered.[130] The strategy was on the agenda. In 1647 in a letter to

Colonel Whalley, Cromwell mentioned rumors of an assassination attempt, "a most horrid act," and ordered the colonel to ensure the king was well guarded.[131] Others had warned the king of army factions plotting to kill him. When the king was transferred to Hurst castle "some Royalists believed . . . that the 'nauseous, pestilential Air' might kill off His Majesty,"[132] but the king did not come down with anything. Neither Fortuna nor *virtù* was to provide a resolution of the problem. Failing an opportune illness, a Borgia option was under active discussion. The contemporary royalist historian, the Earl of Clarendon, says some of the military officers were "for the taking away of his life by poison; which would make least noise; or, if that could not be so easily contrived, by assassination."[133] Clarendon explains why there was support for the disappearance option: "whilst he was alive . . . there would be always plots and designs to set him at liberty . . . and in a short time a faction . . . may be in the army itself . . . Whereas, if he were confessedly dead, all these fears would be over; especially if they proceeded with that circumspection and severity towards all his party as in prudence they ought to do."[134] Clarendon also identifies the risks the king took in trying to escape: "The making of an escape, if it were not contrived with wonderful sagacity, would expose him to be assassinated by pretended ignorance, and would be charged upon himself."[135] While in captivity the king was permitted to hunt, and he did escape temporarily. In summary, the opportunist's preferred outcome was possible, the most efficient policy was a subject of discussion among both royalists and Parliament's supporters, and there were very good opportunities to implement the policy. But Cromwell abjured poison or a seaside strangling on the Isle of Wight, as Cesare Borgia had dealt with his rivals on that New Year's Day by the Adriatic. He chose differently in conformity with his sense of justice and patriotism. The nonevidence as well as the evidence is consistent with value-based risky or imprudent behavior and represents a departure from the opportunist's best strategy. Cromwell declined to have his opponents murdered even though the alternative that he chose cost him political support.

Cromwell made a clear normative distinction between the first and the second civil war. He regarded the king's deal with the Scots as the action of a traitor. The first war had been between the English, as

Cromwell saw it. In the second, the royalists broke their word, were unpatriotic, and acted against God, whose inclination had been revealed with the parliamentary victory in the first war. The leading soldiers of the parliamentary army, Cromwell included, met for three days prior to taking the field in the second war and pledged "to call Charles Stuart, that Man of Blood, to an account for that blood he had shed and mischief he had done, to his utmost, against the Lord's cause and people in these poor nations."[136] They were well aware of their personal risks, as the presiding judge's metal hat testified. Just a few months after the execution, when Isaac Dorislaus, who had assisted in the trial, made a visit to Holland, royalists assassinated him.

Later in 1649, when the opportunist would be securing and enjoying power, Cromwell left London and political life for the mortal dangers of an Irish campaign. As we know from contemporary politics, coup-leaders go abroad at considerable risk, let alone to fight. He survived the siege warfare and sickness in Ireland, unlike his son-in-law, fellow regicide, and comrade-in-arms Henry Ireton, who perished at Limerick. In his battlefield dispatches to Parliament, Cromwell would consistently link what he and his soldiers fought for to a particular set of values: God, country, justice, and toleration.

It is best left to the royalist historian to describe Cromwell's relationship to the "perfect opportunist."

> He was not a man of blood, and totally declined Machiavel's method, which prescribes, upon any alteration of a government, as a thing absolutely necessary, to cut off all the heads of those, and extirpate their families, who are friends to the old [one.] And it was confidently reported, that in the council of officers it was more than once proposed that there might be a general massacre of all the royal party, as the only expedient to secure the government; but Cromwell would never consent to it . . .[137]

An institutional framework of rules and enforcement procedures and the propitious rather than adverse selection of agents combined to build a reputation for Cromwell's army and to effectively address control problems, in keeping with the beliefs and commitments of the leadership. Therefore, the impact of the agents in amplifying or distorting the level of repression was limited. With Cromwell in the field, authority leakage was minimal. He and other leading parliamentarians remade the army, but its main mission remained war, not dirty war, and its operating procedures that protected vulnerable citizens and prisoners were detailed in writing in the articles of war and were communicated and enforced.

Violations in the English Civil War were well below the levels expected by the standard explanation of human rights violations. External costs imposed by the international system or by the economic elite are an unlikely source of restraint. Domestic opposition to violations was only noticeable among those least likely to be able to organize it, the peasantry outside the parliamentary heartland. Where potential international costs and public opinion did signal another course of action, the victorious parliamentary commanders ignored the signal and publicly beheaded the king. Cromwell did not have the king disposed of, did not have a Spanish minister or a local Cheka do the deed to insulate himself from negative public opinion, did not protect himself from filial revenge, and left not his fingerprints but his signature at the scene of the crime. Nor were his other actions consistent with a power-seeking opportunist. In general, his internal commitment to tolerance lowered violations below the levels an opportunist would prudently have employed to enhance his power. Cromwell coped with the repeated attempts to reconstitute monarchical powers by force, and, leading from the front, he left a battlefield legacy for toleration that probably eased the Restoration settlement and the constitutional bargains that followed. Most peasants, most mutineers, and most of the royal family survived, in contrast to the Russian experience.

The Three Horsemen
of Political Violence

Hell is empty, and all the devils are here.
    —William Shakespeare, *The Tempest*, Act I, Scene 2

It is discouraging that the three inexhaustible horsemen of political violence—Machiavelli, the Grand Inquisitor, and Count Tilly—have just visited us with our bloodiest century. Yet, while they traverse the length and breadth of the historical and cultural range, leadership is an optimistic focus, more easily influenced than historical processes and economic structures, and one that directs our attention to the questions of what is motivating the violence and how to arrange things in such a way that good leaders and agents drive out bad.

Violence is done selfishly for the rewards, rationally for power, or *logically* for the faithful, the future, or the Völk. The selfishness or *willingness* of agents is ubiquitous. But the three war stories in this book show that the principals distinguish themselves by the management of this selfishness and by their own motivations. In Israel, violence was and is a means to create and defend the state, readily and opportunistically used. Artifice, deception, and manipulation characterize the management style. Principals seek to reap the political and strategic benefits deriving from the actions of their independently motivated agents. From the state's founding violence, Israeli leaders have used artificial information asymmetry to distance themselves from "calculated atrocities." The Israel narrative illustrates not desert lore and tribal custom, but the operation and outcomes of Machiavelli's imperative to get and hold power under pressure from hostile borders and from the constant presence of a minatory demography, using violence when necessary and deflecting responsibility onto agents when possible.

For Comrade Inquisitor, the Russian violence was the definitive proof of the depth of the revolutionary, rather than spiritual, experience, and so it was desirable in itself. Atrocities were not an instrument adjusted to the measure of the opposition and offset for international criticism. In this motivational environment, the agents were loosed, not managed, to pick up their own unspeakable momentum by an immovable principal.

In England, a commitment to tolerance and a skepticism about the sure efficacy of violence and about hanging for trifles kept violence below the level expected across different episodes, threat levels, and national theaters. With these core beliefs, an accountable principal directly addressed the problems of adverse selection and moral hazard. Cromwell recruited self-governing agents who had the conscience to exercise self-restraint. He monitored and restrained those who proved unable to do it for themselves. In England, Scotland, and even in Ireland the Tolerator was ascendant. Yet, Tolerators were present elsewhere. Sharett and the report of the Kahan Commission in Israel and I. N. Bernstein, the Left Socialist Revolutionary in Russia tried to raise a standard for a different way of managing the use of force during times of civil conflict. Their efforts may not have done much good at the time, but they signaled the possibility of alternative paths, just as Cromwell, who did make a difference at the time, clarified the impact of leadership on the dark side of government.

Studying leadership provides a far better understanding of the patterns of violence in the three wars than does an effort to explain the differences by examining the economic factors, historical circumstances, or threat levels. Centuries, geography, technology, and, most important, the magnitude of violations separate these three conflicts. Population size and the numbers of men mobilized differs, but we know from elsewhere that huge killings can be accomplished in a short period of time with very primitive weapons. As with Israel and England, the Russian Civil War was fought in the context and wake of an extremely bloody international war. Still, these three civil wars did not have uniform consequences for the level of violence unleashed on society. Widespread atrocities are not a necessary feature of civil war; nor are they a spillover or contagion effect from other wars, or a single path preselected by a nondemocratic tradition. One can find a more straightforward explanation in the selfish, strategic, and intentional choices made by the participants.

The mobilization, arming, and movement of large numbers of former civilians will have human costs. Some among these agents will always seek reward even when commanders make a sincere effort to assert responsibility. These sorts of violations do not, however, amount to a "law of civil war" that dictates systematic slaughter. Russia was a combatant in the First World War, but many of those who fought in the English Civil War had seen and had served in the carnage of the Thirty Years' War. The English, Irish, and Scottish soldiers, who presumably behaved badly enough abroad, did not, however, bring continental practices home. The comparison suggests that we cannot explain the high atrocity rate in Russia as a lesson learned from fighting foreigners, although Lenin found trench warfare exculpatory. In his 1918 "Letter to American Workers," he wrote, "the international imperialist bourgeoisie slaughtered ten million men and maimed twenty million in 'their' war . . . If our war, the war of the oppressed and exploited against the oppressors and exploiters, results in half a million or a million casualties in all countries, the bourgeoisie will say that the former casualties are justified, while the latter are criminal."[1] The total for Lenin's war did in the end reach 10 million victims, matching the slaughter of the First World War. He could still defend his war as a just war against exploiters and oppressors and for the Russian proletariat—which at the time was narcissism of a largely imaginary difference in a Russia that lacked a significant industrial sector and had most of its work force still on the farm.

The simplifying assumptions that all governments want to survive and are more or less equally willing to do whatever it takes in order to do so are the theoretical underpinnings to the relationship between civil war and human rights violations. As the level of the opposition threat to government survival rises, it will provoke commensurately nasty deterrence activities from the government. Yet, even with the very high threat levels signaled by full-scale civil war, the interesting question is why leaders respond differently, that is, why they manage threat differently, committing fewer or more killings than are necessary to secure government survival. Either way they are acting imprudently and inefficiently. Either they risk not doing enough to frighten the opposition into abandoning resistance, or with disproportionate violations they literally overkill by employing resources beyond what is required to achieve the goal and risking provocation of further opposition from those with nothing left to lose. A Russian scholar argues that the Bolshevik "de-cossackization" and its requisition and recruitment policies provoked uprisings by the Cossacks and peasants.[2] Slaughtering prisoners may actually have increased the determination of the opposition who knew surrender meant "to be chopped up like sheep."[3] Disproportionate violence stimulated further resistance to the government.

It is difficult to argue that the level of threat in the Russian Civil War was so markedly higher than the level of threat in the English Civil War, or in the Arab-Israeli conflict for that matter. And it is simply implausible to claim that it exceeded the threat level by such a margin as to account for the exponential contrasts in the use of violence. Midrange estimates put noncombat deaths and executions by both the Red Army and the specialized security forces of the Bolsheviks at about 100,000 a year for the Russian Civil War, and the most recent analyses put the figure considerably higher. Ten Deir Yassins in 1948 would still amount to just one-hundredth of the Bolshevik killings, and the English Civil War atrocity rate was lower than the Israeli. Appeasement rather than violence, western front successes, and the armistice contained the very real German threat. The short-term and uncoordinated White armies of 1918 to 1920, seashore foreign intervention from Britain, France, the United States, and Japan, and the sailors of Kronstadt were not conspicuously more threatening to the Communists than the invasions of the Arab armies were to the new Israeli government, or the royalist armies, full-scale and repeated Scottish interventions, and the Levellers were to Parliament in the English Civil War. Add the duration, and therefore the more prolonged uncertainty, of the English conflict, then the claim that the threat was greater in Russia becomes more questionable.

All the same, placing the devils here among us and taking leaders and what they say seriously, both those with a straightforward interest in power and those with ideological convictions, is not an uncontroversial position. Where are the more obvious weaknesses in this argument and in the evidence from the historical record, and what does the argument imply for combating violence?

The argument may seem too individualized and voluntaristic, particularly in a field empirically preoccupied with explanations that rely on impersonal structures and the characteristics of the political, economic, historical, and cultural environment. The standard approach toward a general understanding of political violence, one that endures and travels, is to look to the presence or absence of militarized conflict, or to measurable differences in political regimes, culture, demography, or levels of economic development. Such an approach avoids moral judgments, recognizes the modest role of individuals in the scheme of things, and saves us from caricature: "Louis XIV was a very proud and self-confident man . . . and he ruled France vilely . . . At the end of the eighteenth century there had gathered in Paris a couple of dozen persons who began talking about all men being free and equal. Because of this, over the length and breadth of France men fell to slaughtering and destroying one another."[4] Agents fare no better in this account, aimless at Austerlitz. An account of individuals' motives and intentions is not a narrative filled with the unlimited surprises of the exercise of free will, trivial and significant, and the accidental progress of nations. If we link the personalities to general motivations, then the sequence of events that we are interested in understanding may seem less capricious. After all, it is, as they say, easier to know man in general than man in particular, and the vanity of giving individuals, both principals and agents, the central role does allow us to do something to combat the violence. Think of the alternative. Looking for explanations in the ineffable currents of history or in broad environmental or structural characteristics may suck out the historical personalities, only to leave a void, instead of a link between the structure and the thing we want to explain, and a more fatalistic attitude to political violence. In any case, even the assumption that behavior fits the relevant environmental structure is false for significant historical episodes. Cromwell's behavior defies his autocratic and unenlightened age.

Civil wars, the absence of democracy, or the stage of historical development do not lead to the same violent behaviors. The most notorious campaign of the enormously destructive American Civil War was arguably Sherman's march of 100,000 men to Atlanta and 60,000 men on to the sea in the summer and later months of 1864. The historical record of this campaign does not support Bolshevik appeals to it as a precedent for their murderous behavior. General William T. Sherman, a proud but apparently not so self-confident man, abhorred in Georgia, whose father died when he was young and who was given to funks, defies the law of civil war. It is true that the Confederate General John Hood shared Lenin's later assessment of Union conduct in the American Civil War. As the Union Army besieged Atlanta, Hood protested to Sherman: "the unprecedented measure you propose transcends, in studied and ingenious cruelty, all acts ever before brought to my attention in the dark history of war. In the name of God and humanity, I protest, believing that you will find that you are expelling from their homes and firesides the wives and children of a brave people."[5] The British military historian and strategist Liddel Hart argued that this remark just confirmed that Hood had a deservedly low place on West Point's graduation list and had given little attention to the history of war.[6] Sherman's burning and looting was tame by Russian standards. The single nastiest episode seems to have occurred when one of his general's stranded black camp followers on the wrong side of a river, to be drowned or slaughtered by Confederate cavalry.

The *Instructions for the Government of Armies of the United States in the Field,* prepared by Francis Lieber and promulgated by President Abraham Lincoln in April 1863, regulated the behavior of Union forces. This General Order Number 100 became a landmark in the laws of war. Justice, honor, and humanity were to guide the Union soldier. Soldiers were described as "moral beings, responsible to one another and to God." Removing civilians, as at Atlanta, was provided for in article 18, but article 16 forbade cruelty, torture, and the use of poison. Lieber had himself known imprisonment in Prussia before fleeing to England and then to the United States and academia.

Sherman's men traveled light and lived off the country. Foraging, as in Russia or the Thirty Years' War, brought the soldiers into conflict with the local people. But most of the damage was to property. Sherman's Special Field Orders, No. 120, November 9, 1864, stated:

> Soldiers must not enter the dwellings of the inhabitants, or commit any trespass . . . To corps commanders alone is intrusted the power to destroy mill, houses, cotton-gins, etc; and for them this general principle is laid down: In districts and neighborhoods where the army is unmolested, no destruction of such property should be permitted; but should guerrillas or bushwackers molest our march, or should the inhabitants burn bridges, obstruct roads, or otherwise manifest local hostility, then army commanders should order and enforce a devastation more or less relentless, according to the measure of such hostility.[7]

Despite the severe language, Sherman had an idea of proportionality and a goal of deterrence underlying his order, and he controlled his agents accordingly. Rape, the universal barometer of the quality of the principal-agent relationship in security forces, seems to have been a rare occurrence: "homicide and rape were almost unknown."[8] In his memoirs Sherman says, "No doubt, many acts of pillage, robbery, and violence, were committed by these parties of foragers, usually called bummers; . . . but these acts were exceptional and incidental. I never heard of any cases of murder or rape."[9] In *Sherman: A Soldier's Passion For Order*—noteworthy is the assessment in this title—his recent biographer John Marszalek concurs, "rape and murder were practically nonexistent."[10] The burning of the railway hub of Atlanta blackened Sherman's reputation, but his campaign in Georgia saw success combined with restraint.

As with the English Civil War, we have conduct in the American Civil War that does not fit the environment. An earlier century does not establish an environment that necessitates a less civilized course of action, and it is not that we are judging historical actors by values that we invent and then apply to them. The historical conceit that the living seem to have is thinking themselves so different from the dead, in another country as it were. But they are not so far from us in their taste for brutality or in their capacity for decency. While the formal international human rights regime is a creation of the last century, it reflects advances in the speed of communication nonexistent when the norms of decency that underlie this regime were created. In his sixteenth-century story of the First Crusade, *Jerusalem Delivered,* Torquato Tasso has the Christian knight Godfrey issue a field order: "I ban more rapine and more / Cruelty. / Let the call of trumpets sound / forth my decree."[11] Unfortunately there is no historical record of Godfrey's order. There is evidence that if there was such an order, it was honored very much in the breach, with the Christians delivering their cross to Jerusalem in an unforgivable way. The crusaders comprehensively massacred both the Muslim and the Jewish inhabitants, perhaps seeking reward for their dangers and toils and perhaps as fanatics; historical accounts of the taking of Jerusalem support both interpretations. But the point is that Tasso wanted Godfrey to be a better hero.

Satisfactory explanations of the political world are rarely purely deterministic or voluntaristic. Commitments and beliefs engage individuals with society and with some greater, shared, collective experience such as class or country, and in this way "determine" individual action. Yet, we ordinarily hold individuals accountable for the beliefs that guide them. We select our values not as we choose between soup or salad, but guided by the family and others that we associate with, and from a socially and historically set menu of choices. In this way, we place beliefs on the theoretical crease between voluntarism and determinism—which creates some intellectual discomfort—although we know that the main issue is not the place we give a theory, whether it is voluntaristic or deterministic, but how to balance theoretical elegance with a satisfactory explanation. How can we reduce the causal ingredients without debilitating consequences to our explanatory strength and reach?

BASTARDS AND OTHER DISASTERS

While the Bolsheviks are incorrect in claiming the American Civil War as a precedent for their terror, there are subsequent human rights catastrophes that measure up to their standard. The last century opened with the genocide of Armenians in Turkey and closed with the inquisitorial whirlwind that swept away the hundreds of thousands of Tutsi in Rwanda and the urban bloodbaths of Bosnia.

A young man from Tuzla, Drazen Erdemovic, voluntarily surrendered to the International Criminal Tribunal for the Former Yugoslavia at The Hague. He first initiated contacts with journalists in March 1996, out of anger and remorse for his actions at Pilica Farm on or about July 16, 1995. On that day, from ten in the morning until three in the afternoon, he met busloads of Bosnian Muslim men, took them to a field next to the farm buildings, lined them up, and shot them in the back with a Kalashnikov rifle. He personally murdered between 70 and 100 civilians. His unit, the 10th Sabotage Detachment of the Bosnian Serb Army, altogether murdered 1,200 Muslim civilians ages 17 to 60 years. Some victims were made to kneel as if at prayer in order to be beaten with iron bars. The bus drivers had to shoot at least one civilian in order to align their interest with that of the other agents and to keep them quiet. Distributing culpability is a standard operating procedure for agents of violence.

Later that day, Erdemovic witnessed the execution of approximately 500 Muslims at the cultural hall in Pilica. The prosecution had been unaware of this incident, which was later confirmed by crime scene analysis. The French judicial police superintendent, who worked for the tribunal's Office of Prosecution, interviewed Erdemovic numerous times and testified that Erdemovic was in a state of shock when he recalled the details of the massacre. He said Erdemovic's motivation in coming forward was from remorse and from anger toward the people who had put him in the situation, whom he wanted to name, and from the desire to provide the necessary evidence to bring them to trial. Erdemovic had not been completely trusted by his unit. He had been demoted previously for not fulfilling assignments where there was a risk of civilian casualties. At the farm, he had been told that if he was sorry for the victims, he could join them. He was also worried about the safety of his own family, in part because he was a Croat serving in the Serbian army. For his murders, Erdemovic pled guilty to a violation of the laws or customs of war. He was sentenced to five years imprisonment. The prosecutor agreed that the accused's claim that he was acting under orders was correct, that he had to kill or be killed, that his remorse was genuine, and that his cooperation with the prosecution was excellent. These factors, along with the guilty plea and time served, explain the light sentence. The tribunal decided that duress, the claim to have had no choice, was not a complete defense under international law for a soldier charged with killing civilians.

Erdemovic's orders came from Radovan Karadzic, the president of the Bosnian Serbs, and Ratko Mladic, the Serb army commander. Their indictment for genocide by the tribunal describes the Serb leaders' intention to destroy the Muslims as an ethnic group; an intention that they pursued with little regard for likely cost and one that puts them in the Inquisitor's column, although, interestingly enough not unequivocally. There is the possibility of the Insincere Inquisitor, and Slobodan Milosovic, according to the chief prosecutor of the tribunal, provides a good illustration. In her indictment, Carla Del Ponte describes Milosovic's motivation: "Beyond the nationalist pretext and the horror of ethnic cleansing . . . the search for power is what motivated Slobodan Milosovic."[12] Acceding to this account, Milosovic used inquisitorial rhetoric to mobilize political support. The difficulty for the Insincere Inquisitor is that the rhetoric implies unleashing violence that may then be more problematic to adjust to the changing political situation. The violence may go on longer than Machiavelli would advise, which it did and which then precipitated the events leading to Milosovic's downfall.

The tribunal's indictments provide a graphic and utterly gruesome record of behavior, including torture, cannibalism, and sexual assault, with spectators and familial relationships often used to intensify the pain.[13] The court saw its first genocide conviction in August 2001 with the case of one of Mladic's subordinates, General Radislav Krstic. He received a sentence of 46 years imprisonment for his role at Srebrenica.

Thus Srebrenica was delivered by the heavy armor of the Serbs. They gained the territory, secured the town, and put the inhabitants to death or to flight.

> After Srebrenica fell to besieging Serbian forces in July 1995, a truly terrible massacre of the Muslim population appears to have taken place. The evidence tendered by the Prosecutor describes scenes of

unimaginable savagery: thousands of men executed and buried in mass graves, hundreds of men buried alive, men and women mutilated and slaughtered, children killed before their mothers' eyes, a grandfather forced to eat the liver of his own grandson. These are truly scenes from hell . . .[14]

Instead of ratcheting down the terror, the Serbs followed up with a systematic slaughter. In doing so, far from showing concern about the potential international costs of their actions, they humiliated the representatives of the international community, even donning United Nations uniforms to dupe the Muslims into surrendering.

Under its statute, the International Tribunal has the power to prosecute individuals for crimes against humanity. Rape is explicitly identified as one of these crimes. The crusading Serbs, destroyers of many of the mosques in Bosnia, raped the Muslim women in the towns and villages that they occupied. For the first two years of the war, international investigators put the number of rapes at about 20,000.[15] In addition to the usual motive, some rapists claimed that they were ordered to rape to ensure that the victims and their families would never return. There is also the claim that the intention was to impregnate Muslim women.[16] The expectant mothers were held in custody until late in their term, when it was too late to abort their "Chetnik babies." Beneath the selfish motives of the agents, there is another layer of motives, which suggests that here this crime may not indicate a genuine problem of control.

The secretary-general's report on the fall of Srebenica, requested by a General Assembly resolution, describes and analyzes how his organization could offer safety and deliver terror. One factor emphasized in the report is that the UN did not understand Serb motivations. The Serbs were not just after territory with civilians sometimes caught in the crossfire, as the UN had supposed. The report concludes that the civilians' "death or removal was the very purpose of the attacks upon them."[17] This misunderstanding of the nature of Serb motivations meant that the UN policy responses were totally inadequate: "through error, misjudgement and an inability to recognize the scope of the evil confronting us, we failed to do our part to help save the people of Srebrenica from the Serb campaign of mass murder."[18] As for the

Serbs, their own savagery and the spectacle of the cowed and humiliated UN ironically undermined Serbian power and their strategic position. Srebrenica, followed by the Serb shelling of the marketplace in Sarajevo, raised the stakes for the international community and stiffened NATO's resolve. With the Croat successes on the ground—which General Mladic was late in responding to as he concentrated his forces on the next safe area—came an end to hostilities.

COMBATING THE VIOLENCE

Town dwellers in the twentieth century worry about aerial bombing, not just storm troopers in the heat of the action. Horses have relinquished the harness to mechanized transport, but the motives positioning the caterpillar tracks above a town in Bosnia are little different from those known to Godfrey. And Count Tilly would cynically salute the professionalism of the Free French General in Italy whose Moroccan troops looked forward to raping the local women. Understanding these motivations, as the United Nations came to realize in its painful self-study of its actions at Srebrenica, is the starting point for analysis and action. The victims' names change, and time and place switches victims with violators. It is our "idols," as Dostoevsky called them, that differ, not the leader-directed supervaluation of common identity that provides some collective meaning and simplified, often terrible solutions. The Inquisitor's improvement over Jesus is not having to think for oneself. Thanks to the Inquisitor, we are confident in our own prospects, and we follow the logic of the argument to bravery or cruelty, and to a set of victims defined economically, culturally, racially, regionally, nationally, politically, as well as religiously. Also enduring is the power motive, the opportunistic use of cruelty to get and maintain political office that Machiavelli described with detachment, a motive that provides some self-regulation of the levels of cruelty when principals are aware that excessive violations may jeopardize political office. Finally, the universal soldiers and agents bring their own filthy motivations.

While we are stuck with these motives, we have long condemned the behavior that they produce. Whether deserving it or not, Niccolò

Machiavelli's work and name quickly became synonymous with evil, and Friedrich Schiller's pencil and poetry did hold Tilly accountable. There is a long history of concern and there are clues to progress.

So what are the implications of applying principal-agent logic for correcting behavior and combating violence? This logic suggests particular kinds of intervention. The principal must confront the problem of moral hazard, the hidden actions of the agents, and the temptation and opportunities that the agents have for seeking Count Tilly's reward. What we learn from the general analysis of bureaucracies is that adequate compensation for officials is an important tool in combating private temptations and the problem of corruption. The extra compensation magistrates received in imperial China was called "money to nourish honesty."[19] Financial compensation is a direct response to bribery, the most general form of corruption, and is a partial response to the bureaucracy of repression's use of violence. For the rewards these agents seek are not solely monetary, and nonmonetary rewards are more difficult for principals to address without doing further harm. Compensation in the form of "comfort women" was the Japanese military's response to their soldiers' seeking violence and sex indiscriminately from the local population.

The principal can correct informational disadvantages by monitoring, either through specialized government agencies or by paying attention to the countervailing activity of affected interests. The particular difficulty with government use of violence is that agents in this area are particularly hard to monitor. The principal may not want to know, and the normal organizational genesis of affected interests (that is, the growth of the policy-relevant interest groups) that can provide a substitute for official monitoring may be stunted by fear and intimidation. In hard-to-monitor policy areas, economists' models of out-of-control bureaucracies and corruption suggest that paying higher wages, or simply accepting some level of corruption, are the alternatives.[20] But as noted in the use of violence, nonmonetary rewards are also at stake and accepting violence is morally different from accepting corruption. In other words, there is no substitute for monitoring and accountability in this policy area. A positive dimension of globalization is the increasing ability of the international system to make up for the democratic deficits in domestic political

188 / AGENTS OF ATROCITY

systems. The international system, through the recent growth of human rights advocacy group activity that now has a global reach and through the development of international human rights law and tribunals, compensates for the inadequacies of domestic monitoring and accountability: it forces knowledge and responsibility on the principal where that is necessary. These components of the international system are now making it more difficult to sustain artificial information asymmetry. Individualizing responsibility for human rights violations through international tribunals and international criminal courts is a positive development, very much in keeping with a focus on principals and agents. Yet it is a mistake to assume that the international system weighs in neutrally. While the advocacy groups may emphasize broad human rights concerns across the globe, the major players in the international system bring their own policy biases to their selection of cases for humanitarian intervention.

A less direct consequence of using principal-agent analysis is to think more widely about motivation and leadership. The economist's traditional world of material incentives and costs is an elegant but thin representation of the influences and forces that shape the human condition and the behavior of soldiers and security forces. Reputation belongs in the equation, and notably for the soldier. Remember that as we successively play the parts that make up a life, from crying baby, to whining schoolboy, and sighing lover, we progress to the soldier: "Jealous in honour, sudden and quick in quarrel, seeking the bubble reputation even in the cannon's mouth," according to Shakespeare.[21] Commanders may share this unromantic view of reputation and honor as a motivation; Napoleon is said to have observed that, "it is with baubles that men are led." Still, honor and reputation may counter the reward-seeking of other agents and the opportunism of some leaders. Accompanying Count Tilly on that May day in Magdeburg were the honor guard as well as the reward-seeking agents of violence. And in Israel, citizen-soldier protests and refuseniks had troubled the Lebanese invasion from the beginning: some unit commanders protested the plan to move into Beirut and other military staff anonymously leaked information to journalists. Not all soldiers succumb to Tilly's reward; some may adhere to a notion of combat morality, and this has implications for reducing the likelihood of human rights violations.

The problem for the sincerely information-seeking principal is to know what sort of agents, with what sort of tastes and traits, have been recruited. Given the task at hand, the principal is likely to be inundated with bad risks, with the hard men. One option to address this problem is to universalize selection, the equivalent of the insurance company succeeding in insuring everyone. The state, through its power of coercion, has options not open to the insurance company and could institute conscription, with no special units with special intakes, and so mix good with bad risks and have agents monitoring agents. Alternatively, the principal could select, train, and license the agents. With the difficulties associated with addressing the problem of moral hazard in the area of political violence, propitious rather than adverse selection is likely to be the main lever for the genuinely concerned principal. Propitious selection means careful recruitment combined with a training emphasis on combat morality. As Kenneth Arrow, the Nobel Prize - winning economist, says: "there is a whole world of rewards and penalties that take social rather than monetary forms. Professional responsibility is clearly enforced in good measure by systems of ethics, internalized during the education process and enforced in some measure by formal punishments and more broadly by reputations."[22] Oliver Cromwell knew this wisdom. He actively recruited agents with a conscience, institutionalized a notion of combat morality, and systematically suppressed the filthy motives and the reward-seekers. Here is what we prize in Cromwell: without the prospect of private reward, wherever the campaign, and when there were no external pressures to behave decently, Cromwell's soldiers fought successfully for him while preserving both his and their own reputations and so spoke more clearly than his own letters and speeches to the inspirational nature of his leadership.

The beauty of starting with principal and agent is the prospect of revealing the lines of accountability. It strips the principal of his refuges in ancient hatred, in the exigency of war, in desert lore, or in some other feature of the environment, and pulls him out from behind his "Spanish ministers" and his enraged and uncontrollable agents. No doubt it does not assure perfect control, yet principal-agent analysis itself exposes the likely artifice behind a principal's denials of responsibility, and in this way it reduces the odds of bastards being bastards.

Notes

CHAPTER ONE

1. Quoted in Richard Bernstein, "An Ugly Rumor or an Ugly Truth," *New York Times*, 4 August 2002, sec. 4.
2. Ernst Cassirer, *The Philosophy of the Enlightenment*, trans. Fritz C.A. Koelln and James P. Pettegrove (Princeton: Princeton University Press, 1951), 169.
3. Theodor Meron provides a fascinating legal commentary on this early fifteenth-century siege as well as on the later slaughter of the French prisoners at Agincourt. Meron relates the drama to the historical accounts and to the evolution of the laws of war. Theodor Meron, "Shakespeare's Henry the Fifth and the Law of War," *American Journal of International Law* 86 (1992).
4. Friedrich Schiller, *The History of the Thirty Years' War in Germany*, trans. A. J. W. Morrison. (Boston: Francis A. Nicolls Company, 1901), 178-9.
5. C. V. Wedgwood, *The Thirty Years' War* (New Haven: Yale University Press, 1949), 290; Charles Carlton, *Going to the Wars: The Experience of the British Civil Wars, 1638-1651* (London: Routledge, 1992), 175.
6. Wedgwood, 288-90; Georges Pagès suggests, contrary to Schiller, that Tilly lost control of his troops. Georges Pagès, *The Thirty Years' War, 1618-48* (New York: Harper & Row, 1970), 128.
7. Mikhail Sholokhov, *And Quiet Flows the Don* (London: Putnam, 1934), 62.
8. Anthony Beevor, *Berlin: The Downfall 1945* (London: Viking, 2002).
9. Iris Chang, *The Rape of Nanking* (London: Penguin Books, 1997), 94.
10. Michael Walzer, *Just and Unjust Wars: A Moral Argument with Historical Illustrations* (New York: Basic Books, 1977), 133.
11. Ignazio Silone, "Reflections on the Welfare State," *Dissent* 8 (1961): 189.
12. Ann Marie Prévost, "Race and War Crimes: The 1945 War Crimes Trial of General Tomoyuki Yamashita," *Human Rights Quarterly* 14 (1992): 316.
13. See Prévost.
14. International Criminal Tribunal for the Former Yugoslavia, <http://www.un.org/icty/ind-e.htm>
15. <http://www.un.org/icty/indictment/english/mil-ii011122e.htm.>

16. This criticism of the standard model includes my previous work that lies within this research tradition. See Zehra F. Arat, *Democracy and Human Rights in Developing Countries* (Boulder: Lynne Rienner Publishers, 1991); David Carleton, and Michael Stohl, "The Foreign Policy of Human Rights: Rhetoric and Reality from Jimmy Carter to Ronald Reagan," *Human Rights Quarterly* 7 (May1985): 205-29; David L. Cingranelli and David L. Richards, "Measuring the Level, Pattern, and Sequence of Government Respect for Physical Integrity Rights," *International Studies Quarterly* 43 (June 1999): 407-17; David L Cingranelli and David L. Richards, "Respect for Human Rights after the End of the Cold War," *Journal of Peace Research* 36 (September 1999): 511-34; Christian Davenport, "The Weight of the Past: Exploring Lagged Determinants of Political Repression," *Political Research Quarterly* 49 (June 1998): 377-403; Christian Davenport, "Liberalizing Event or Lethal Episode? An Empirical Assessment of How National Elections Affect the Suppression of Political and Civil Liberties," *Social Science Quarterly* 79 (June 1998): 321-41; Christian Davenport, "Human Rights and the Democratic Proposition," *Journal of Conflict Resolution* 43 (February 1999): 92-116; Conway W. Henderson, "Conditions Affecting the Use of Political Repression," *Journal of Conflict Resolution* 35 (March 1991): 120-42; Linda Camp Keith, "The United Nations International Covenant on Civil and Political Rights: Does it Make a Difference in Human Rights Behavior?" *Journal of Peace Research* 36 (1999):95-118; Neil J. Mitchell and James M. McCormick, "Economic and Political Explanations of Human Rights Violations," *World Politics* 40 (1988): 476-98; Steven C. Poe and C. Neal Tate, "Repression of Human Rights to Personal Integrity in the 1980s: A Global Analysis," *American Political Science Review* 88 (December 1994): 853-72.

17. Caroline Beer and Neil J. Mitchell, "Human Rights in India: Investigating an Outlier," paper presented at the American Political Science Association meeting, San Francisco, August 30-September 3, 2001.

18. Noam Chomsky and Edward Herman, *The Political Economy of Human Rights: The Washington Connection and Third World Fascism* (Boston: South End Press, 1979), 8. See also Clair Apodaca, "Global Economic Patterns and Personal Integrity Rights After the Cold War," *International Studies Quarterly* 45 (2001): 587-602; David L. Richards, Ronald D. Gelleny, and David H. Sacko, "Money with a Mean Streak? Foreign Economic Penetration and Government Respect for Human Rights in Developing Countries," *International Studies Quarterly* 45 (2001): 219-39.

19. Samantha Power, *"A Problem from Hell": America and the Age of Genocide* (New York: Basic Books, 2002), 327.

20. Robert D. Putnam, *Making Democracy Work: Civic Traditions in Modern Italy* (Princeton: Princeton University Press, 1993); Robert D. Putnam,

Bowling Alone: The Collapse and Revival of American Community (New York: Simon & Schuster, 2000).

21. Jeane Kirkpatrick, "Dictatorships and Double Standards," *Commentary* 68 (November 1979), 34-5.

22. Mitchell and McCormick, 1988.

23. Amnesty International, *Amnesty International Report 1982* (London: Amnesty International Publications, 1982), 134.

24. Mark Danner, *The Massacre at El Mozote* (New York: Vintage Books, 1994), 69-71.

25. Amnesty International, *Amnesty International Report 1983* (London: Amnesty International Publications, 1983), 136.

26. William Stanley, *The Protection Racket State* (Philadelphia: Temple University Press, 1996), 225.

27. United Nations, *Report of the United Nations Truth Commission on El Salvador 1992* available at <http://www.derechos.org/nizkor/salvador/informes/truth.html>

28. Charles Anderson, in his criticism of the standard approach to explanation in the field of comparative public policy, argues that "political systems do not make policy. Policymakers do." Charles W. Anderson, "System and Strategy in Comparative Policy Analysis," in *Perspectives on Public Policy Making,* ed. W. G. Gwyn and G. C. Edwards (New Orleans: Tulane University Press, 1975), 226.

29. George Leggett, *The Cheka: Lenin's Political Police* (Oxford: Clarendon Press, 1981), 104.

30. François Furet, *Interpreting the French Revolution* (Cambridge: Cambridge University Press, 1981), 62.

31. Arno J. Mayer, *The Furies: Violence and Terror in the French and Russian Revolutions* (Princeton: Princeton University Press, 2000), 323.

32. See Gary Bass, *Stay the Hand of Vengeance: The Politics of War Crimes Tribunals* (Princeton: Princeton University Press, 2000), 107.

33. Meron, 33.

34. See Anthony Downs, *Inside Bureaucracy* (Boston: Little, Brown, 1967).

35. See Sydney Anglo, *Machiavelli: A Dissection* (London: Paladin, 1971), 47.

36. See Margaret E. Keck and Kathryn Sikkink, *Activists Beyond Borders* (Ithaca: Cornell University Press, 1998) for the development of international networks of advocacy groups that have made human rights violations more transparent. See also Power on the major twentieth-century genocide and the importance placed on international factors; and David P. Forsythe, *Human Rights in International Relations* (Cambridge: Cambridge University Press, 2000) and Jack Donnelly, *International Human Rights* (Boulder: Westview, 1997) for general treatments of international human rights.

CHAPTER TWO

1. The explanatory strategy has been described by Mark Lichbach, *The Cooperator's Dilemma* (Ann Arbor: University of Michigan Press, 1996), 239: "theorists should use narrow or thin theories . . . (i.e., those that assume pecuniary self-interest) as a baseline model; determine how much of the phenomenon under question can be explained by such theories; finally, adopt wider or thicker theories . . . to account for those aspects of the phenomenon that remain inexplicable."

2. I should note that I take Machiavelli's advice to the Prince quite literally. Alternatively, scholars have argued that Machiavelli was not a serious advocate of the use of cruelty. See, for example, Garrett Mattingly, "Machiavelli's Prince: Political Science or Political Satire," *American Scholar* 27 (1958). Others have argued that he was actually trying to undermine the Prince with bad advice. See, for example, Mary G. Dietz, "Trapping the Prince: Machiavelli and the Politics of Deception," *American Political Science Review* 80 (September 1986). Just to be clear, I am not attempting to contribute to the interpretative debate over Machiavelli's intentions.

3. Niccolò Machiavelli, *The Prince,* trans. Robert Adams (New York: W.W. Norton, 1977), 72.

4. Machiavelli, 73.

5. Machiavelli, 90.

6. Machiavelli, 28.

7. Machiavelli, 22.

8. See Scott Sigmund Gartner and Patrick M. Regan, "Threat and Repression: The Non-Linear Relationship Between Government and Opposition Violence," *Journal of Peace Research* 33 (1996); Mark Lichbach, *The Rebel's Dilemma* (Ann Arbor: University of Michigan Press, 1995).

9. Gartner and Regan, 276.

10. Fyodor Dostoevsky, *The Brothers Karamazov,* trans. Richard Pevear and Larissa Volkhonsky (New York: Vintage Books, 1991), 254.

11. Voltaire quoted in Ernst Cassirer, *The Philosophy of the Enlightenment,* trans. Fritz C.A. Koelln and James P. Pettegrove (Princeton, N.J.: Princeton University Press, 1951), 169.

12. Sigmund Freud, *Civilization and Its Discontents* (New York: W.W. Norton, 1930), 68-69.

13. Paul M. Sniderman, Pierangelo Peri, Rui J.P. De Figueiredo, Jr., and Thomas Piazza, *The Outsider: Prejudice and Politics in Italy* (Princeton, N.J.: Princeton University Press, 2000), 58-9.

14. Sniderman, 127.

15. Henry Kamen, *Inquisition and Society in Spain in the Sixteenth and Seventeenth Centuries* (London: Weidenfeld and Nicolson, 1985), 32.

16. Kamen, 39.

17. B. Netanyahu, *The Origins of the Inquisition in Fifteenth Century Spain* (New York: Random House, 2001), xxiii.
18. Netanyahu, 990.
19. Machiavelli, 44.
20. See Michael Walzer, *On Toleration* (New Haven, Conn.: Yale University Press, 1997).
21. See Gartner and Regan.
22. See John Stuart Mill, *On Liberty* (London: Penguin Books, 1974), 76.
23. John W. Kingdon, *Agendas, Alternatives, and Public Policies* (Boston: Little, Brown, 1984).
24. David Hume, "Of the First Principles of Government," in *Hume's Moral and Political Philosophy*, ed. Henry D. Aiken (New York: Hafner Press, 1948), 307.
25. Dostoevsky, 261.
26. Quoted in Hannah Arendt, *Eichmann in Jerusalem: A Report on the Banality of Evil* (New York: Penguin Books, 1994 [1963]), 177.
27. See John Brehm and Scott Gates, *Working, Shirking, and Sabotage: Bureaucratic Response to a Democratic Public* (Ann Arbor: University of Michigan Press, 1997) for an excellent discussion of these issues. See Anthony Downs, *Inside Bureaucracy*, (Boston: Little, Brown, 1967) for a general discussion of goal variance, the role of zealots, the possible goals of agents, and the value of assuming that bureaucracies are reducible to the selfishness of individuals.
28. Kenneth J. Arrow, "The Economics of Agency," in *Principals and Agents: The Structure of Business*, ed. John W. Pratt and Richard J. Zeckhauser (Boston: Harvard Business School Press, 1985), 39.
29. The influence of multiple principals has been a preoccupation of the analysis of American bureaucratic behavior in which bureaucrats are responsible to both the president and Congress. Parliamentary as opposed to presidential systems generally provide simpler lines of accountability between principal and agent.
30. See Benny Morris, *Righteous Victims: A History of the Zionist-Arab Conflict, 1881-1999* (New York: Alfred A. Knopf, 1999), 197.
31. David J Rothman and Aryeh Neier, "India's Awful Prisons," *New York Review of Books,* 16 May 1991, 55.
32. Kamen, 50-52 and 135.
33. Isaiah Berlin, *Four Essays on Liberty* (Oxford: Oxford University Press, 1969), 51.
34. Iris Chang, *The Rape of Nanking* (London: Penguin Books, 1997), 40.
35. Theodor Meron, "Shakespeare's Henry the Fifth and the Law of War," *American Journal of International Law* 86 (1992), 30.
36. Hugo Grotius, *The Law of War and Peace* (1625), trans. Francis W. Kelsey (Indianapolis, Ind.: Bobbs-Merrill, 1925), 657.
37. Priscilla B. Hayner, *Unspeakable Truths: Facing the Challenge of Truth Commissions* (New York: Routledge, 2002), 79.

38. Jeffrey S. Banks and Barry R. Weingast, "The Political Control of Bureaucracies under Asymmetric Information," *American Journal of Political Science* 36 (May 1992).

39. See Murray Edelman, *The Symbolic Uses of Politics* (Urbana: University of Illinois Press, 1964).

40. Brehm and Gates, 202.

41. Downs, 84.

42. Machiavelli, 35.

CHAPTER THREE

1. Tom Segev, *One Palestine Complete: Jews and Arabs Under the British Mandate,* trans. Hiam Watzman (New York: Metropolitan Books, 2000), 442.

2. See Robert Axelrod, *The Evolution of Cooperation* (New York: Basic Books, 1984).

3. Yaacov Bar-Siman-Tov, "Ben-Gurion to Sharett: Conflict Management and Great Power Constraints in Israeli Foreign Policy," *Middle Eastern Studies* 24 (1988): 330.

4. Michael Brecher, *The Foreign Policy System of Israel: Setting, Images, Process* (New Haven, Conn.: Yale University Press, 1972), 231-2.

5. Quoted in Segev, 394.

6. Hannah Arendt, *Eichmann in Jerusalem: A Report on the Banality of Evil* (New York: Penguin Books, 1994 [1963]), 8-10.

7. Uri Bialer, "Facts and Pacts: Ben-Gurion and Israel's International Orientation, 1948-1956," in Ronald W. Zweig, ed., *David Ben-Gurion: Politics and Leadership in Israel* (London: Frank Cass, 1991), 217.

8. Nathaniel Lorch, "Ben-Gurion and Sinai," in Zweig, 308.

9. Quoted in Shabtai Teveth, *Ben-Gurion and the Palestinian Arabs: From Peace to War* (New York: Oxford University Press, 1985), 191.

10. Michael Bar-Zohar, *Ben-Gurion* (London: Weidenfeld and Nicolson, 1977), 206.

11. Brecher provides an excellent discussion of the contrast between Ben-Gurion's and Sharett's foreign policy views.

12. Quoted in Benny Morris, *Righteous Victims: A History of the Zionist-Arab Conflict, 1881-1999* (New York: Alfred A. Knopf, 1999), 287.

13. Quoted in Gabriel Sheffer, *Moshe Sharett: Biography of a Political Moderate* (Oxford: Clarendon Press, 1996), 69.

14. Sheffer, 725.

15. Brecher, 261.

16. Bar-Zohar, 217.

17. Brecher, 255.

18. Thomas Friedman, *From Beirut to Jerusalem* (New York: Farrar Straus Giroux, 1989), 104.

19. Friedman, 91.

20. Friedman, 89.
21. The data is for Israel and the occupied territories and is collected from the annual country reports of the U.S. Department of State, Bureau of Democracy, Human Rights, and Labor, United States Department of State. 2002. *2001 Country Reports on Human Rights Practices: Israel* available at: http://www.state.gov/www/global/human_rights/2001_hrp_report/israel.html. There was a time, notably during the Cold War, when data from this source was less reliable, but there is evidence that the quality of the information improved during the 1990s (see Steven C. Poe, Sabine C. Carey, and T. C. Vazquez, "How are these pictures different? A quantitative comparison of the U.S. State Department and Amnesty International Human Rights Reports, 1976-1995," *Human Rights Quarterly,* 23 August 2001: 650-77). For validation, I compared the number of Palestinian dead with figures from *Amnesty International* reports for six of the eleven years and they were highly correlated. As the *State Department Country Reports* for 2002 will not be issued until 2003, I used figures from a United Nations report, and daily newspaper coverage for the first seven months of 2002 in the *Guardian* and annualized these data. On a cautionary note, it is worth observing that fatalities are only one measure of interaction, that only eleven observations are included, and that it is unclear whether earlier periods fit quite as well.
22. See James Ron, "Savage Restraint: Israel, Palestine, and the Dialectics of Legal Repression." *Social Problems* 47 (2000): 445-72.
23. Morris, *Righteous Victims,* 587.
24. Morris, *Righteous Victims,* 587.
25. Benny Morris and Ehud Barak, in "Camp David and After" (*New York Review of Books,* June 27, 2002, 47), say that the al-Aqsa Intifada was planned months prior to Sharon's visit. Others say there is no evidence to support this claim. See Henry Siegman, "Partners for War," *New York Review of Books,* January 16, 2003.
26. Baruch Kimmerling and Joel S. Migdal, *The Palestinian People: A History* (Cambridge, Mass.: Harvard University Press, 2003), 363.
27. Martin Gilbert, *Israel: A History* (New York: William Morrow, 1998), 616.
28. Sheffer, 734.
29. See Axelrod, 14.
30. Andrew Kydd and Barbara F. Walter, "Sabotaging the Peace: The Politics of Extremist Violence" *International Organization* 56, 2 (Spring 2002): 263-96.
31. See Siegman, "Partners for War," and Avishai Margalit, "The Suicide Bombers," *New York Review of Books,* January 16, 2003.
32. John Masefield, *Cargoes:*

> "Quinquereme of Nineveh from distant Ophir
> Rowing home to haven in sunny Palestine"

33. Teveth, 166.
34. Segev, 382.
35. Segev, 381-3.
36. Segev, 454.
37. Gilbert, 80.
38. See Gilbert, 111.
39. Segev, 385.
40. Morris, *Righteous Victims*, 147.
41. The official *Haganah History Book*, quoted in Segev, 386.
42. Segev, 387.
43. Segev, 387.
44. Segev, 423.
45. Howard M. Sachar, *A History of Israel from the Rise of Zionism to Our Time* (New York: Alfred A. Knopf, 1996), 250.
46. Sachar, 216.
47. Segev, 430-1; John Bierman and Colin Smith, *Fire in the Night: Wingate of Burma, Ethiopia, and Zion* (New York: Random House, 1999), 125.
48. Sachar, 215.
49. U.S. Department of State, Bureau of Democracy, Human Rights, and Labor, *Country Reports on Human Rights Practices: Israel 1997*. United States Department of State: 1998, 1.
50. Sheffer, 191.
51. Gilbert, 142.
52. Segev, 477.
53. Segev, 5.
54. John Bagot Glubb, *A Soldier with the Arabs* (London: Hodder and Stoughton, 1957), 79.
55. See Glubb, 165.
56. Morris, *Righteous Victims*, 208.
57. Morris, *Righteous Victims*, 208.
58. Quoted in Benny Morris, *1948 and After: Israel and the Palestinians* (Oxford: Clarendon Press, 1990), 50.
59. Morris, *Righteous Victims*, 207.
60. Morris, *Righteous Victims*, 198.
61. Quoted in Morris, *1948 and After*, 37.
62. Morris, *Righteous Victims*, 198.
63. Nathaniel Lorch, *The Edge of the Sword: Israel's War of Independence, 1947-1949* (New York: G.P. Putnam's Sons, 1961), 58.
64. Glubb, 81.
65. Meir Ya'ari quoted in Gilbert, 219; Morris, *Righteous Victims*, 240; Sheffer, 376.
66. Quoted in Gilbert, 486.
67. Glubb, 211-12.
68. Morris, *Righteous Victims*, 245.
69. Morris, *Righteous Victims*, 255.

70. Morris, *1948 and After,* 75.
71. Quoted in Morris, *1948 and After,* 133.
72. Gilbert, 229.
73. State of Israel, *Political and Diplomatic Documents, May-September 1948* (Jerusalem: Ahva Press, State of Israel, 1981), 369.
74. Morris, *Righteous Victims,* 257; *1948 and After,* 142-3.
75. Natan Alterman quoted in Sachar, 444.
76. Morris, *Righteous Victims,* 278; Uzi Benziman, *Sharon: An Israeli Caesar* (New York: Adama Books, 1985), 54-8.
77. Quoted in Gilbert, 290.
78. Sheffer, 686; Morris, *Righteous Victims,* 279.
79. Sheffer, 686.
80. Sheffer, 686.
81. Sheffer, 712.
82. Morris, *Righteous Victims,* 280-1.
83. Sachar, 480-1.
84. Sheffer, 960.
85. Sheffer, 738.
86. Sheffer, 743.
87. Brecher, 261.
88. Morris, *Righteous Victims,* 280.
89. Quoted in Sheffer, 788.
90. Sheffer, 788.
91. Benziman, 47.
92. Sachar, 498.
93. Gilbert, 321.
94. Morris, *Righteous Victims,* 295; Sachar, 536 and 595.
95. Avner Yaniv, *Dilemmas of Security* (New York: Oxford University Press, 1987), 128.
96. Ze'ev Schiff and Ehud Ya'ari, *Israel's Lebanon War* (New York: Simon & Schuster, 1984), 215.
97. Schiff and Ya'ari, 216.
98. Schiff and Ya'ari, 14.
99. Friedman, 138.
100. Report of the Commission of Inquiry into the Events at the Refugee Camps in Beirut (The Kahan Commission), February 8, 1983, available at: http://www.us-israel.org/jsource/History/kahan.html, 11.
101. Weston D. Burnett, "Command Responsibility and a Case Study of the Criminal Responsibility of Israeli Military Commanders for the Pogrom at Shatila and Sabra," *Military Law Review* 71 (Winter 1985): 156.
102. Schiff and Ya'ari, 252
103. Burnett, 176.
104. Quoted in Sachar, 914.
105. Schiff and Ya'ari, 285.
106. Benziman, 259.

107. Gilbert, 509; Morris, *Righteous Victims,* 544.

108. Burnett, 159.

109. Kahan Commission report, 20.

110. Quoted in Kahan Commission report, 22.

111. Quoted in Kahan Commission report, 24.

112. Schiff and Ya'ari, 265.

113. Schiff and Ya'ari, 269.

114. Schiff and Ya'ari, 271.

115. Schiff and Ya'ari, 274.

116. Kahan Commission report; others report a figure as high as 2,000 (Gilbert, 509).

117. Burnett, 74.

118. Gilbert, 509.

119. See Gary J. Bass, *Stay the Hand of Vengeance* (Princeton, N.J.: Princeton University Press, 2000).

120. Friedman, 164.

121. Kahan Commission report, 62.

122. Kahan Commission report, 90.

123. Gilbert, 512.

124. Quoted in Gilbert, 512.

125. Brecher, 369.

126. Anne Karpf, "Remember the Pain, Heal the Wounds," *The Guardian,* 26 March 2002.

CHAPTER FOUR

1. Maxim Gorky, 10 November 1917, quoted in Geoffrey Swain, *The Origins of the Russian Civil War* (New York: Longman, 1996), 69.

2. Christopher Read, *From Tsar to Soviets: The Russian People and Their Revolution, 1917-21* (New York: Oxford University Press 1996), 191.

3. Vladimir N. Brovkin states, "largely due to the Bolsheviks' own policies, their former allies turned into foes and cleared the way for Deniken's offensive." Brovkin, *Behind the Front Lines of the Civil War: Political Parties and Social Movements in Russia, 1918-1922* (Princeton, N.J.: Princeton University Press, 1994), 100.

4. Robert Service, *Lenin: A Political Life* (Bloomington: Indiana University Press, 1995), III, 323.

5. Quoted in George Leggett, *The Cheka: Lenin's Political Police* (Oxford: Clarendon Press, 1981), 41.

6. Leggett, 8.

7. Alexander N. Yakovlev, *A Century of Violence in Soviet Russia* (New Haven: Yale University Press, 2002), 106.

8. Quoted in David Shub, *Lenin* (New York: Doubleday, 1951), 327.

9. Vladimir Lenin, "The Russian Revolution and Civil War," *Collected Works* 26 (Moscow: Progress Publishers, 1965), September 29, 1917: 33.

10. Simon Schama, *Citizens* (New York: Knopf, 1989), 788.

11. Quoted in Brovkin, 103.

12. William Doyle, *The Oxford History of the French Revolution* (Oxford: Clarendon Press, 1989), 223. Lenin survived the attentions of Dora Kaplan, his lone female assassin; Charlotte Corday stabbed Marat to death in his bath where he was seeking dermatological relief from a skin complaint. She went to the guillotine for putting Marat out of his misery.

13. Susan Dunn, *Sister Revolutions: French Lightning, American Light* (New York: Faber and Faber, 1999), 95.

14. Dunn, 119. Her account follows François Furet's, who deduces "the Terror from revolutionary discourse" and explicitly rejects an external threat account of violations; see François Furet, *Interpreting the French Revolution* (Cambridge: Cambridge University Press, 1981), 61.

15. Lenin, "Fear of the Collapse of the Old and the Fight for the New," *Collected Works* 26, 24-27 December 1917: 401.

16. Quoted in Leggett, xxxii.

17. I. N. Steinberg, *In the Workshop of the Revolution* (New York: Rinehart, 1953), 119.

18. Lenin to the Nizhni Novgorod Soviet, August 1918, quoted in Robert Conquest, "The Human Cost of Soviet Communism," Subcommittee to Investigate the Administration of the Internal Security Act and Other Internal Security Laws of the Committee on the Judiciary, United States Senate, 92nd Congress, 1st Session (Washington, D.C.: U.S. Government Printing Office, 1971) Doc. 92-36: 8.

19. Lenin, "On the Famine: A Letter to the Workers of Petrograd," *Collected Works* 27, 22 May 1918: 396.

20. Lenin's cable to Trotsky, November 1918, quoted in Dmitri Volkogonov, *Trotsky: The Eternal Revolutionary*, trans. Harold Shukman (New York: Free Press, 1996), 176.

21. Lenin in a note to a colleague, August 1920, quoted in Service, 42.

22. Steinberg, 145.

23. Lenin, "Comrade Workers Forward to the Last Decisive Fight!" *Collected Works* 28, August 1918: 56.

24. Lenin, "How to Organize Competition," *Collected Works* 26, December 24-27, 1917: 414.

25. Iris Chang, *The Rape of Nanking* (London: Penguin Books, 1997).

26. Lenin, "Letter to American Workers," *Collected Works* 28, August 20, 1918: 71.

27. William Henry Chamberlin, *The Russian Revolution* (New York: Macmillan, 1935), 81.

28. Israel Getzler, *Kronstadt 1917-1921: The Fate of a Soviet Democracy* (Cambridge: Cambridge University Press, 1983), 166.

29. See Yakovlev, 55-6.

30. Service, 246.

31. Getzler, 154.

32. Swain, 157.

33. Indicative of this support was an election held in the winter of 1917 in which these more moderate socialists won 267 of the 520 seats and the Bolsheviks received 161. See Edward H. Carr, *The Russian Revolution from Lenin to Stalin, 1917-1929* (London: Macmillan, 1979), 7.

34. Swain, 227

35. Leggett, 327.

36. Lewis Carroll, *Alices's Adventures in Wonderland* (New York: The Modern Library, 2002), 107

37. Diane P. Koenker, "Urbanization and Deurbanization in the Russian Revolution and Civil War," in *Party, State, and Society in the Russian Civil War,* ed. Diane P. Koenker, William G. Rosenberg, and Ronald Grigor Suny (Bloomington: Indiana University Press, 1989), 81.

38. Mary McAuley, *Bread and Justice: State and Society in Petrograd, 1917-1922* (Oxford: Clarendon Press, 1991), 276.

39. Read, 191; Conquest, 11; Evan Mawdsley, *The Russian Civil War* (Boston: Allen & Unwin, 1987), 286-7.

40. "Only under the second Bonaparte does the state seem to have made itself completely independent . . . an adventurer blown in from abroad, raised on the shield by a drunken soldiery, which he has bought with liquor and sausages, and which he must continually ply with sausage anew." Karl Marx, "The Eighteenth Brumaire of Louis Bonaparte," *Selected Works* (London: Lawrence and Wishart, 1970), 170.

41. Leggett, 66; Dmitri Volkogonov, *Lenin: A New Biography,* trans. Harold Shukman (New York: Free Press, 1994), 209; see Mark Steinberg and Vladimir M. Khrustalev, *The Fall of the Romanovs: Political Dreams and Personal Struggles in a Time of Revolution* (New Haven, Conn.: Yale University Press, 1995) for a discussion of the evidence.

42. Chamberlin, 92-4.

43. Sergey P. Melgounov, *The Red Terror in Russia* (Westport, Conn.: Hyperion Press, 1926; reprint 1975), 76.

44. Melgounov, 78.

45. Steinberg, 228.

46. Leggett, 464.

47. Schama, 791; Doyle, 257.

48. Volkogonov, *Trotsky,* 145.

49. Taisia Osipova, "Peasant Rebellions: Origin, Scope, Dynamics, and Consequences," in *The Bolsheviks in Russian Society: The Revolution and the Civil Wars,* ed. Vladimir Brodkin (New Haven, Conn.: Yale University Press, 1997), 173.

50. Quoted in Chamberlin, 80.

51. Elias Heifetz, *The Slaughter of the Jews in the Ukraine in 1919* (New York: Thomas Seltzer 1921), 7.

52. Chamberlin, 80.

53. Chamberlin, 203

54. Volkogonov, *Lenin*, 241.

55. Brovkin, 104.

56. Melgounov, 182.

57. Leggett, 130.

58. Leggett, 73.

59. Quoted in Lennard D. Gerson, *The Secret Police in Lenin's Russia* (Philadelphia: Temple University Press, 1976), 183-4.

60. Quoted in Volkogonov, *Trotsky*, 132.

61. Volkogonov *Lenin*, 327; whether gas was actually used is disputed. David Stone mentions its use in Tambov, see Stone's "The Russian Civil War, 1917-1921," in *The Military History of the Soviet Union*, ed. Robin Higham and Frederick W. Kagan (New York: Palgrave, 2002), 30. Delano Dugarm suggests that technical problems prevented its use: see Dugarm, "Peasant Wars in Tambov Province," in *The Bolsheviks in Russian Society*, ed. Vladimir N. Brovkin (New Haven: Yale University Press, 1997), 192.

62. Lenin, "Meeting of Presidium of the Petrograd Soviet," *Collected Works* 26, 14 January 1918: 501.

63. Leggett, 312.

64. Quoted in Yakovlev, 79.

65. Brovkin, 71.

66. Brovkin, 85.

67. Shub, 320.

68. Lenin, "Report on Foreign Policy," *Collected Works* 27, 14 May 1918: 379.

69. Brovkin, 139.

70. Brovkin, 139.

71. Lenin, "Telegram to Stalin," *Collected Works* 27, 7 July 1918: 533.

72. Lenin to the commander at Penza, 9 August 1918, quoted in Service, 109.

73. Leggett, 309.

74. Service, 109.

75. Quoted in Service, 246.

76. Quoted in Yakovlev, 157.

77. Yakovlev, 156.

78. Francesco Benvenuti, *The Bolsheviks and the Red Army, 1918-1922* (Cambridge: Cambridge University Press, 1988).

79. Leggett, 97.

80. Melgounov, 18.

81. Volkogonov, *Lenin*, 343-4.

82. Gerson, 149.
83. Leggett, 181.
84. Richard Pipes, ed., *The Unknown Lenin: From the Secret Archive* (New Haven, Conn.: Yale University Press 1996), 77.
85. Lenin, "Summing-Up Speech on the Report of the Central Committee of the RCPB," *Collected Works* 32, March 9, 1921: 204.
86. Victor Serge, *Memoirs of a Revolutionary, 1901-1941,* trans. Peter Sedgwick (London: Oxford University Press, 1963), 128-9.
87. Susan Weissman, *Victor Serge: The Course Is Set on Hope* (London: Verso, 2001), 28.
88. Lenin, "Summing-up Speech on the Tax in Kind," *Collected Works* 32, 15 March 1921: 242.
89. Getzler, 243.
90. Yakovlev, 219.
91. Steinberg, 293.
92. Shub, 361.
93. Yakovlev, 220.
94. Getzler, 241.
95. Getzler, 244.
96. Lenin quoted in Leggett, 22.
97. Leggett, 253.
98. Gerson, 38.
99. Leggett, 233.
100. See Mawdsley, 285-6.
101. Lenin to Penza Communists, 11 August 1918, in Pipes, 50.
102. Leggett, 95.
103. Weissman, 35-6.
104. Melgounov, 245.
105. Melgounov, 178-9.
106. Mikhail Sholokov, *And Quiet Flows the Don* (London: Putnam, 1934), 668.
107. Leggett, 201.
108. See Richard Rhodes, *Masters of Death: Himmler's Willing Executioners* (New York: Alfred A. Knopf, 2002); Reich. 2002. "Masters of Death: Himmler's Willing Executioners," *New York Times,* 30 June 2002.
109. Melgounov, 128.
110. Melgounov, 217.
111. Brovkin, 85.
112. Isaac Babel, *1920 Diary* (New Haven, Conn.: Yale University Press, 2002), 28.
113. Babel, 84.
114. Babel, 68.
115. D. Fedotov White, *The Growth of the Red Army* (Princeton, N.J.: Princeton University Press, 1944), 52.

116. A. B Murphy, *The Russian Civil War: Primary Sources* (New York: St. Martin's Press, 2000), 194.
117. Brovkin, 96 and 121.
118. Fedotov White, 112.
119. Fedotov White, 102-103
120. Quoted in Gerson, 60.
121. Chamberlin, 71-2.
122. Leggett, 188.
123. Leonard Schapiro, *The Communist Party of the Soviet Union* (New York: Vintage Books, 1971), 266.
124. Leggett, 145 and 157.
125. Gerson, 71.
126. See Leggett, 190-1; Gerson, 69.
127. Gerson, 65.
128. Boris Levytsky, *The Uses of Terror: The Soviet Secret Police 1917-1970* (New York: Howard, McCann and Geoghegan, 1972), 28.
129. Lenin, quoted in Service, 40.
130. Lenin, quoted in Shub, 326.
131. Lenin, "Report to the 7th All-Russia Congress of the Soviets," *Collected Works* 30, 6 December 1919, 233-4.
132. Levytsky, 37.
133. Pipes, 117 and 128.
134. Steinberg, 120.
135. Lenin, "Telegram to J.V. Stalin," *Collected Works* 30, 16 February 1920: 363.
136. Pipes, 11.

CHAPTER FIVE

1. Charles Carlton, *Going to the Wars: The Experience of the British Civil Wars, 1638-1651* (London: Routledge, 1992), 211-14; Charles Carlton, "Civilians," in *The Civil Wars: A Military History of England, Scotland, and Ireland, 1638-1660,* ed. John Kenyon and Jane Ohlmeyer (Oxford: Oxford University Press, 1998), 273-8.
2. William Shakespeare, *Macbeth,* Act I, Scene IV. This line is not for Macbeth but for the also treacherous earlier Thane of Cawdor, who behaved with dignity at his execution and treated his own life "as twere a careless trifle."
3. Carlton, "Civilians," 272.
4. C. V. Wedgwood, *A Coffin for King Charles* (New York: Time Inc., 1966), 64.
5. Wilbur Cortez Abbott, ed., *Writings and Speeches of Oliver Cromwell* (Cambridge, Mass.: Harvard University Press, 1937), I: 677.
6. John Locke, *A Letter Concerning Toleration* (Indianapolis: Bobbs-Merrill Educational Publishing, 1955), 56.

7. Abbott, I:278.
8. Abbott, II:325.
9. Abbott, II:339.
10. John Stuart Mill, *On Liberty* (London: Penguin Books, 1974), 76.
11. Mill, 119.
12. Abbott, III:459.
13. Abbott, IV:274.
14. Abbott, IV:368.
15. Antonia Fraser, *Cromwell: The Lord Protector* (New York: Alfred A. Knopf, 1973), 490.
16. Abbott, IV:36.
17. W. D. Rubinstein, *A History of Jews in the English-Speaking World: Great Britain* (New York: St. Martin's Press, 1996), 46.
18. Christopher Hill, *God's Englishman* (New York: Harper & Row, 1970), 113.
19. Tom Reilly, *Cromwell: An Honourable Enemy* (Dingle, Co. Kerry, Ireland: Brandon, 1999), 197.
20. J. C. Davis, *Oliver Cromwell* (New York: Oxford University Press, 2001), 109.
21. Hill, 213-14.
22. Maurice Ashley, *Cromwell* (Englewood Cliffs, NJ: Prentice Hall 1969), 5.
23. Fraser, 487 and 704.
24. Roger Hainsworth, *The Swordsmen in Power: War and Politics Under the English Republic: 1649-1660* (Stroud, Gloucestershire: Sutton Publishing, 1997), 161.
25. Ashley, 170.
26. National Gallery, London. The gallery blurb writer sees a "magnificent" horse, but a gallery lecturer pointed out the disproportion.
27. Conrad Russell, *The Causes of the English Civil War* (Oxford: Oxford University Press, 1990), 119.
28. Mark Kishlansky, *The Rise of the New Model Army* (Cambridge: Cambridge University Press, 1979), 92.
29. Abbott IV:471; Thomas Carlyle, *Oliver Cromwell's Letters and Speeches* (New York: Charles Scribner's Sons, 1845), IV:61.
30. Kishlansky, 6.
31. Edward, Earl of Clarendon, *The History of the Rebellion and Civil Wars in England* (Oxford: Oxford University Press, 1849), IV:335.
32. Barbara Donagan, "Atrocity, War Crime, and Treason in the English Civil War," *American Historical Review* 99 (1994):1137.
33. Scott Sigmund Gartner and Patrick M. Regan, "Threat and Repression: The Non-Linear Relationship Between Government and Opposition Violence," *Journal of Peace Research* 33 (1996): 276-7.
34. Fraser, 92; C. H. Firth, *Cromwell's Army: A History of the English Soldier During the Civil Wars, the Commonwealth, and the Protectorate* (London: Methuen, 1902), 15.

35. C. V. Wedgwood, *The Thirty Years' War* (New Haven: Yale University Press, 1949), 217.
36. Wedgwood, *The Thirty Years' War,* 207.
37. Carlton, *Going to the Wars,* 19.
38. Leonard Hochberg, "The English Civil War in Geographical Perspective," *Journal of Interdisciplinary History* 14 (1984), 750.
39. Hochberg, 731.
40. Carlton, *Going to the Wars,* 260.
41. Martyn Bennett, *The Civil Wars in Britain and Ireland, 1638-1651* (Oxford: Blackwell, 1997), 226; Ian Gentles, "The Civil Wars in England," in *The Civil Wars: A Military History of England, Scotland, and Ireland 1638-1660,* ed. John Kenyon and Jane Ohlmeyer (Oxford: Oxford University Press, 1998), 112; Austin Woolrych, *Battles of the English Civil War* (London: B.T. Batsford, 1961), 136.
42. C. V. Wedgwood, *The King's War: 1641-1647* (New York: Macmillan, 1959), 670.
43. Woolrych, 136.
44. Carlton, *Going to the Wars,* 80.
45. Abbott, I:385.
46. Reverend Hugh Peters quoted in Charles Carlton, "Civilians," 283.
47. Carlton, *Going to the Wars,* 178-9.
48. Hainsworth, 70; Hill, 117.
49. Reilly, 170.
50. Nicholas Canny, *Making Ireland British, 1580-1650* (Oxford: Oxford University Press, 2001), 569.
51. Hainsworth, 72.
52. Abbott, II:196-205.
53. Patrick J. Corish, "The Cromwellian Conquest, 1649-53," in *A New History of Ireland, III,* ed. T. W. Moody, F. X. Martin, and F. J. Byrne (Oxford: Clarendon Press, 1976), 382.
54. See Carlyle, III:275.
55. Corish, 291.
56. Canny, 551 and 542.
57. Abbott, I:332.
58. Abbott, II:31.
59. Carlyle, II:166.
60. Corish, 358.
61. John Morrill, *Revolt in the Provinces: The People of England and the Tragedies of War: 1630-1648* (New York: Longman, 1999), 118.
62. Carlton, "Civilians," 273.
63. Clarendon, IV:40.
64. Clarendon, IV:41.
65. Wedgwood, *The King's War,* 429; Morrill, 133.
66. One might argue that this sort of social movement has a restraining affect on the principal. Economist Barry Weingast, interested in under-

standing the stability of democratic politics, argues that the sovereign will exercise restraint for fear of losing public support. He assumes that citizens have views about the legitimate scope of a sovereign's actions. In other words, citizens believe that they have natural or fundamental rights. Weingast assumes also that citizens will be willing to defend those rights, and that there is some way of solving the "coordination dilemma" of citizens getting together to protect those rights in the face of a sovereign threatening to transgress those rights. It is difficult for citizens themselves to solve the coordination dilemma, to agree to cooperate together for mutual protection, because of differences in beliefs, economic circumstances, and other divisions, and because of the individual's propensity to let others take the risks of exposing themselves to a vengeful sovereign. Weingast argues that if there are actual solutions to the coordination dilemma, "it is elites who construct them." Interestingly, for an empirical example he uses the Glorious Revolution of 1689, a bargain between the monarchy and Parliament limiting state powers and providing for toleration (although still not including Catholics). Forty years earlier he would have found some evidence of the more difficult, decentralized, if short-lived, solutions to the coordination problem, but nevertheless might not be persuaded that these rustic associations were the key deterrent protecting England from continental approaches to warfare.

There are several reasons for not giving too much weight to the restraining effect of these associations in explaining the relatively good behavior of parliamentary soldiers in the English Civil War. The west (Cheshire, Herefordshire, Monmouthshire, Shropshire, Worcestershire, Wales), the epicenter of this rural revolt, had royalist political affiliations. If the Clubmen had organized Cambridgeshire, Parliament's heartland, then the political shock would have been of a different order of magnitude. They turned up late in the war, after the parliamentary army and leaders had established reputations for discipline, and after the plans to create a New Model Army. The priority placed on the high discipline of the parliamentary army preceded the peasant revolts. The Clubmen were potentially easy to repress, geographically and temporally limited, and were not taken particularly seriously by parliamentary commanders. A bit like Dr. Johnson's dog that walked on its hind legs, the remarkable thing about the Clubmen was not that they functioned well, but that they functioned at all.

For a fascinating account of peasant insurgency in El Salvador that emphasizes the moral basis for their actions see Elizabeth J. Wood, *Insurgent Collective Action and Civil War in El Salvador* (Cambridge, UK: Cambridge University Press, 2003).

67. Abbott, I:369.
68. Carlton, *Going to the Wars*, 261.
69. Carlton, *Going to the Wars*, 261.

70. Donagan, 1148-9.
71. Gentles, 112.
72. Carlton, *Going to the Wars*, 327.
73. Abbott, I:638.
74. Abbott, I:643.
75. Carlton, *Going to the Wars*, 334; Hainsworth, 94.
76. Abbott, II:476.
77. Corish, 362.
78. Hainsworth, 64.
79. Carlton, *Going to the Wars*, 330; Hainsworth, 66.
80. Carlton, *Going to the Wars*, 330.
81. Abbott, II:126.
82. Bennett, 330; Carlton, *Going to the Wars*, 330; Fraser, 337; Hainsworth, 68.
83. Fraser, 340.
84. Abbott, IV:263.
85. Hainsworth, 10; Jane Ohlmeyer, "The Civil Wars in Ireland," in *The Civil Wars: A Military History of England, Scotland, and Ireland 1638-1660*, ed. John Kenyon and Jane Ohlmeyer (Oxford: Oxford University Press, 1998), 74; Corish, 291.
86. Abbott, II:127 fn.
87. Fraser, 355.
88. The Scottish army under General Robert Monroe killed 3,000 Irish Catholic civilians near Carrickfergus on June 9, 1642 (Reilly, 22).
89. Abbott, II:196-205.
90. Abbott, II:142.
91. Fraser, 254; see Clarendon, IV:428.
92. Fraser, 393; Hainsworth, 105.
93. The Workers Education Association put up a memorial to them on the church wall in the 1970s (see *A Guide to Burford Church*).
94. Ronald Hutton, *The Royalist War Effort: 1642-46* (London: Longman, 1982), 137.
95. Barry Coward, *Cromwell* (New York: Longman, 1991), 105.
96. Firth, 400.
97. Theodor Meron, "Shakespeare's Henry the Fifth and the Law of War." *The American Journal of International Law* 86 (1992):30.
98. See, Michael Walzer, *Just and Unjust Wars* (New York: Basic Books, 1977), 130.
99. Michael Ignatieff, *The Warrior's Honor: Ethnic War and the Modern Conscience* (New York: Metropolitan Books, 1997), 150.
100. Firth, 412.
101. Abbott, I:656.
102. Abbott, I:390.
103. Donagan, 1151.
104. Firth, 276.

105. Clarendon, Edward, Earl of, *Selections from the History of the Rebellion and the Life by Himself* (Oxford: Oxford University Press, 1978), 381.

106. Gentles, 111-12.

107. Carlton, *Going to the Wars,* 259.

108. Abbott, II:111.

109. Abbott, II:349.

110. Firth, 302.

111. Wedgwood, *The King's War,* 498.

112. Donagan, 1143.

113. Wedgwood, *The Thirty Years' War,* 206.

114. See Gentles, 110.

115. Kenneth J. Arrow, "The Economics of Agency," in *Principals and Agents: The Structure of Business,* ed. John W. Pratt and Richard J. Zeckhauser (Boston: Harvard Business School Press, 1985), 50.

116. Gentles, 119.

117. Kishlansky, 218.

118. John Donne, *Death.*

> Thou'rt slave to fate, chance, kings and desperate men,
> And dost with poison, war, and sickness dwell . . .

119. William Makepeace Thackeray, *Vanity Fair* (London: Oxford University Press, 1864), 339-40.

120. Sarah Barber, *Regicide and Republicanism: Politics and Ethics in the English Revolution, 1646-1659* (Edinburgh: Edinburgh University Press, 1998), 133.

121. Abbott, I:728-9.

122. Derek Wilson, *The King and the Gentleman: Charles Stuart and Oliver Cromwell, 1599-1649* (New York. St. Martin's Press, 1999), 415; see John Buchan, *Cromwell* (London: Sphere Books, 1971), 318.

123. Fraser, 278.

124. John Milton, *Eikonoklestes in answer to a book intitl'd Eikon basilike the portrature His Sacred Majesty in his solitudes and sufferings* (London: TN,1650), Preface.

125. The civil war was not wasteful of intellectuals. Thomas Hobbes, who said he was born in fear because his mother delivered him in the year of the Spanish Armada, was fearful of parliamentary reaction to his *Elements of the Law* and fled to Paris (see C. B. Macpherson, "Introduction" to Thomas Hobbes, *Leviathan* (London: Penguin, 1968). In 1646 he was appointed mathematics tutor to the heir to the English throne. Hobbes returned to Commonwealth England in 1651. Although parliamentarians would not find much intellectual or religious comfort in his new book, *Leviathan,* he published rather than perished. He was more fortunate than the French philosopher and mathematician Condorcet,

caught in his country's revolution, who published then perished in a Parisian prison in 1794.

126. Fraser, 284-9.

127. R.C. Mackie, *A Short History of Scotland* (Edinburgh: Oliver and Boyd, 1962), 175.

128. Counterfactual arguments, James D. Fearon writes in "Counterfactuals and Hypothesis Testing in Political Science" (*World Politics* 43 [1991]: 169), "make claims about events that did not actually occur" and are of the form: "If it had been the case that C (or not C), it would have been the case that E (or not E)." Therefore: if Cromwell had been an opportunist, he would have "disappeared" Charles I, not publicly executed him. According to Fearon, counterfactual arguments "are made credible (1) by invoking general principles, theories, laws . . . and (2) by drawing on knowledge of historical facts relevant to a counter-factual scenario" (176). For our purposes, Machiavelli's motive for violence that assumes power as the motive and conceives violations as contributing to power satisfies the first criterion. For the second criterion, there is historical evidence that the contemporary functional equivalent of "disappearance" was on the agenda and part of the policy discourse at the time. So the execution of the king is a suitable case for counterfactual analysis.

129. Wilson, 399.

130. Graham Edwards, *The Last Days of Charles I* (Stroud, Gloucestershire: Sutton Publishing, 1999), xiii.

131. Abbott, I:552.

132. Edwards, 88.

133. Clarendon, *Selections,* 528.

134. Clarendon, *Selections,* 528-9.

135. Clarendon, *Selections,* 287.

136. Wedgwood , *A Coffin for King Charles,* 4.

137. Clarendon IV:110.

CHAPTER SIX

1. Vladimir Lenin, "Letter to American Workers," *Collected Works* 28 (Moscow: Progress Publishers, 1965), 20 August 1918: 71.

2. Taisia Osipova, "Peasant Rebellions: Origin, Scope, Dynamics, and Consequences," in *The Bolsheviks in Russian Society: The Revolution and the Civil Wars,* ed. Vladimir Brodkin (New Haven: Yale University Press, 1997), 164-5.

3. Delano Dugarm, "Peasant Wars in Tambov Province," in *The Bolsheviks in Russian Society,* ed. Vladimir N. Brovkin (New Haven: Yale University, 1997), 187.

4. Leo Tolstoy, *War and Peace,* trans. Rosemary Edmonds (London: Penguin Books, 1982), 1402-3; see Isaiah Berlin, "The Hedgehog and the

Fox," *Russian Thinkers* (London: Penguin Books, 1994) for a discussion of the Tolstoy's theory of history.

5. William Tecumseh Sherman, *Memoirs of General W. T. Sherman* (New York: Library of America, 1990), 593.
6. B. H. Liddel Hart, *Sherman* (Westport, Conn.: Greenwood Press, 1978), 309.
7. Sherman, 652.
8. Liddell Hart, 335.
9. Sherman, 659.
10. John F. Marszalek, *Sherman: A Soldier's Passion for Order* (New York: Free Press, 1993), 306.
11. Quoted in Bernard Knox, "Liberating a Masterpiece," *New York Review of Books* 17 May 2001, 59; Steven Runciman, *A History of the Crusades* (Cambridge: Cambridge University Press, 1987).
12. Ian Fisher, "Power Drove Milosovic to Crime, Prosecutors Say as Trial Opens," *New York Times,* 13 February 2002, 1.
13. International Criminal Tribunal for the Former Yugoslavia, http://www.un.org/icty (9 February 2002).
14. United Nations, "The Fall of Srebenica," Report of the Secretary-General prepared pursuant to General Assembly Resolution 53/35 (1999), 6.
15. Catherine N. Niarchos, "Women, War, and Rape: Challenges Facing the International Tribunal for the Former Yugoslavia," *Human Rights Quarterly* 17 (1995): 656.
16. Niarchos, 657.
17. United Nations, 109.
18. United Nations, 111.
19. Pranab Bardhan, "Corruption and Development: A Review of the Issues," *Journal of Economic Literature* 35 (September, 1997): 1339.
20. Daron Acemoglu and Thierry Verdier, "The Choice Between Market Failures and Corruption," *American Economic Review* 90 (March 2000): 195.
21. William Shakespeare, *As You Like It*, Act II, Scene 7.
22. Kenneth J. Arrow, "The Economics of Agency," in *Principals and Agents: The Structure of Business,* eds. John W. Pratt and Richard J. Zeckhauser (Boston: Harvard Business School Press, 1985), 50.

Bibliography

Abbott, Wilbur Cortez, ed. *Writings and Speeches of Oliver Cromwell.* Cambridge, Mass.: Harvard University Press, 1937.

Abu-Odeh, Adnan. *Jordanians, Palestinians, and the Hashemite Kingdom in the Middle East Peace Process.* Washington, D.C.: United States Institute for Peace, 1999.

Acemoglu, Daron, and Thierry Verdier. "The Choice Between Market Failures and Corruption." *American Economic Review* 90 (March 2000): 194-211.

Alanbrooke, Fieldmarshal Lord. *War Diaries 1939-1945.* Edited by Alex Danchev and Daniel Todman. Berkeley: University of California Press, 2001.

Anderson, Charles W. "System and Strategy in Comparative Political Analysis," in Perspectives on Public Policy Making, ed. W. B. Gwyn and G. C. Edwards. New Orleans: Tulane University Press, 1975.

Arat, Zehra F. *Democracy and Human Rights in Developing Countries.* Boulder: Lynne Rienner Publishers, 1991.

Arrow, Kenneth J. *The Limits of Organization.* New York: W.W. Norton, 1974.

———. "The Economics of Agency," in *Principals and Agents: The Structure of Business,* ed. John W. Pratt and Richard J. Zeckhauser. Boston: Harvard Business School Press, 1985.

Ashley, Maurice, ed. *Cromwell.* Englewood Cliffs, N. J.: Prentice Hall, 1969.

Babel, Isaac. *The Collected Stories.* New York: New American Library, 1974.

———. *1920 Diary.* New Haven: Yale University Press, 2002.

Bailey, Clinton. *Jordan's Palestinian Challenge, 1948-1983: A Political History.* Boulder, Colo.: Westview Press, 1984.

Banks, Jeffrey S., and Barry R. Weingast. "The Political Control of Bureaucracies under Asymmetric Information." *American Journal of Political Science* 36 (May 1992): 509-24.

Bar-Siman-Tov, Yaacov. "Ben-Gurion to Sharett: Conflict Management and Great Power Constraints in Israeli Foreign Policy." *Middle Eastern Studies* 24 (1988): 330-56.

Bar-Zohar, Michael. *Ben-Gurion.* London: Weidenfeld and Nicolson, 1977.

Barber, Sarah. *Regicide and Republicanism: Politics and Ethics in the English Revolution, 1646-1659.* Edinburgh: Edinburgh University Press, 1998.

Bawn, Kathleen. "Political Control Versus Expertise: Congressional Choices about Administrative Procedures," *American Political Science Review* 89 (1995): 62-73.

Beevor, Anthony. *Berlin: The Downfall 1945*. London: Viking, 2002.

Bennett, Martyn. *The Civil Wars in Britain and Ireland, 1638-1651*. Oxford: Blackwell, 1997.

Benvenuti, Francesco. *The Bolsheviks and the Red Army, 1918-1922*. Cambridge: Cambridge University Press, 1988.

Benziman, Uzi. *Sharon: An Israeli Caesar*. New York: Adama Books, 1985.

Bierman, John, and Colin Smith. *Fire in the Night: Wingate of Burma, Ethiopia, and Zion*. New York: Random House, 1999.

Brecher, Michael. *The Foreign Policy System of Israel: Setting, Images, Process*. New Haven: Yale University Press, 1972.

Brehm, John, and Scott Gates. *Working, Shirking, and Sabotage: Bureaucratic Response to a Democratic Public*. Ann Arbor: University of Michigan Press, 1997.

Brovkin, Vladimir N. *Behind the Front Lines of the Civil War: Political Parties and Social Movements in Russia, 1918-1922*. Princeton: Princeton University Press, 1994.

———— ed., *The Bolsheviks in Russian Society: The Revolution and the Civil Wars*. New Haven: Yale University Press, 1997.

Buchan, John. *Cromwell*. London: Sphere Books, 1971.

Canny, Nicholas. *Making Ireland British, 1580-1650*. Oxford: Oxford University Press, 2001.

Carlin, Norah. *The Causes of the English Civil War*. Oxford: Blackwell, 1999.

Carleton, David, and Michael Stohl. "The Foreign Policy of Human Rights: Rhetoric and Reality from Jimmy Carter to Ronald Reagan." *Human Rights Quarterly* 7 (May 1985): 205-29.

Carlton, Charles. *Going to the Wars: The Experience of the British Civil Wars, 1638-1651*. London: Routledge, 1992.

————. "Civilians, " in *The Civil Wars: A Military History of England, Scotland, and Ireland 1638-1660*, ed. John Kenyon and Jane Ohlmeyer. Oxford: Oxford University Press, 1998.

Carlyle, Thomas. *Oliver Cromwell's Letters and Speeches*. New York: Charles Scribner's Sons, 1845.

Carr, Edward H. *The Russian Revolution from Lenin to Stalin, 1917-1929*. London: Macmillan, 1979.

Chamberlin, William Henry. *The Russian Revolution*. New York: Macmillan, 1935.

Chang, Iris. *The Rape of Nanking*. London: Penguin Books, 1997.

Chomsky, Noam, and Edward Herman. *The Political Economy of Human Rights: The Washington Connection and Third World Fascism*. Boston: South End Press, 1979.

Churchill, Winston. S. *Triumph and Tragedy*. Boston: Houghton Mifflin, 1953.

Cingranelli, David L., and David L. Richards. "Measuring the Level, Pattern, and Sequence of Government Respect for Physical Integrity Rights." *International Studies Quarterly* 43 (June 1999): 407-17.

———. "Respect for Human Rights after the End of the Cold War." *Journal of Peace Research* 36 (September 1999): 511-34.

Clarendon, Edward, Earl of. *The History of the Rebellion and Civil Wars in England.* Oxford: Oxford University Press, 1849.

———. *Selections from the History of the Rebellion and the Life by Himself.* Oxford: Oxford University Press, 1978.

Cline, Ray S. *The Power of Nations in the 1990s: A Strategic Assessment.* Lanham, Md.: University Press of America, 1994.

Commission for Historical Clarification. *Guatemala Memory of Silence.* 1999. http://hrdata.aaas.org/ceh/report/english/intro.html

Conquest, Robert. "The Human Cost of Soviet Communism," Subcommittee to Investigate the Administration of the Internal Security Act and Other Internal Security Laws of the Committee on the Judiciary, United States Senate, 92nd Congress, 1st Session. Washington, D.C.: U.S. Government Printing Office, 1971 Doc. 92-36.

Corish, Patrick J. "The Cromwellian Conquest, 1649-53," in *A New History of Ireland,* III, ed. T.W. Moody, F. X. Martin, and F. J. Byrne. Oxford: Clarendon Press, 1976.

Coward, Barry. *Cromwell.* New York: Longman, 1991.

Danner, Mark. *The Massacre at El Mozote.* New York: Vintage Books, 1994.

Davenport, Christian. "The Weight of the Past: Exploring Lagged Determinants of Political Repression." *Political Research Quarterly* 49 (June 1998): 377-403.

———. "Liberalizing Event or Lethal Episode?: An Empirical Assessment of How National Elections Affect the Suppression of Political and Civil Liberties." *Social Science Quarterly* 79 (1998): 321-41.

———. "Human Rights and the Democratic Proposition." *Journal of Conflict Resolution* 43 (February 1999): 92-116.

Davenport, Christian, and Patrick Ball. "Views to a Kill: Exploring the Implications of Source Selection in the Case of Guatemalan State Terror, 1977-1995." *Journal of Conflict Resolution* 46 (2002): 427-50.

Davis, J. C. *Oliver Cromwell.* New York: Oxford University Press, 2001.

Dietz, Mary G. "Trapping the Prince: Machiavelli and the Politics of Deception." *American Political Science Review* 80 (September 1986): 777-99.

Donagan, Barbara. "Atrocity, War Crime, and Treason in the English Civil War." *American Historical Review* 99 (1994): 1137-66.

Donnelly, Jack. *Universal Human Rights in Theory and Practice.* Ithaca: Cornell University Press, 1989.

———. *International Human Rights.* Boulder, Colo: Westview Press, 1997.

Dostoevsky, Fyodor. *The Brothers Karamazov* trans. Richard Pevear and Larissa Volkhonsky. New York: Vingage Books, 1991.

Dow, F. D. *Cromwellian Scotland, 1651-1660*. Edinburgh: John Donald, 1979.

Downs, Anthony. *An Economic Theory of Democracy*. New York: Harper, 1957.

———. *Inside Bureaucracy*. Boston: Little, Brown, 1967.

Doyle, William. *The Oxford History of the French Revolution*. Oxford: Clarendon Press, 1989.

Drobak, John N., and John V.C. Nye, eds. *The Frontiers of the New Institutional Economics*. San Diego: Academic Press, 1997.

Dugarm, Delano. "Peasant Wars in Tambov Province," in *The Bolsheviks in Russian Society*, ed. Vladimir N. Brovkin. New Haven: Yale University Press, 1997.

Dunn, Susan. *Sister Revolutions: French Lightning, American Light*. New York: Faber and Faber, 1999.

Edwards, Graham. *The Last Days of Charles I*. Stroud, Gloucestershire: Sutton Publishing, 1999.

Elster, Jon. *Sour Grapes: Studies in the Subversion of Rationality*. Cambridge: Cambridge University Press, 1983.

———. "Rational Choice History: A Case of Excessive Ambition." *American Political Science Review* 94 (2000): 685-95.

Fearon, James D. "Counterfactuals and Hypothesis Testing in Political Science." *World Politics* 43 (1991): 169-95.

Fedotoff White, D. *The Growth of the Red Army*. Princeton: Princeton University Press, 1944.

Firth, C.H. *Cromwell's Army: A History of the English Soldier During the Civil Wars, The Commonwealth, and the Protectorate*. London: Methuen, 1902.

Forsythe, David P. *Human Rights in International Relations*. Cambridge: Cambridge University Press, 2000.

Fraser, Antonia. *Cromwell: The Lord Protector*. New York: Alfred A. Knopf, 1973.

Friedman, Thomas L. *From Beirut to Jerusalem*. New York: Farrar Straus Giroux, 1989.

Freud, Sigmund, *Civilization and Its Discontents*. New York: W.W. Norton, 1961.

Furet, François. *Interpreting the French Revolution*. Cambridge: Cambridge University Press, 1981.

Furgol, Edward. "The Civil Wars in Scotland," in *The Civil Wars: A Military History of England, Scotland, and Ireland, 1638-1660*, ed. John Kenyon and Jane Ohlmeyer. Oxford: Oxford University Press, 1998.

Gartner, Scott Sigmund, and Patrick M. Regan. "Threat and Repression: The Non-Linear Relationship Between Government and Opposition Violence." *Journal of Peace Research* 33 (1996): 273-87.

Gentles, Ian. "The Civil Wars in England," in *The Civil Wars: A Military History of England, Scotland, and Ireland, 1638-1660*, ed. John Kenyon and Jane Ohlmeyer. Oxford: Oxford University Press, 1998.

Getty, J. Arch, and Oleg V. Naumov. *The Road to Terror: Stalin and the Self-Destruction of the Bolsheviks, 1932-1939*. New Haven: Yale University Press, 1999.

Getzler, Israel. *Kronstadt 1917-1921: The Fate of a Soviet Democracy*. Cambridge: Cambridge University Press, 1983.

Gibson, James L. "Political Intolerance and Political Repression During the McCarthy Red Scare." *American Political Science Review* 82 (1988): 511-29.

Gilbert, Martin. *Israel: A History*. New York: William Morrow, 1998.

Green, Donald P., and Ian Shapiro. *Pathologies of Rational Choice Theory*. New Haven: Yale University Press, 1994.

Glubb, John Bagot. *A Soldier with the Arabs*. London: Hodder and Stoughton, 1957.

Gurr, Ted Robert. "Persisting Patterns of Repression and Rebellion: Foundations for a General Theory of Political Coercion," in *Persistent Patterns and Emergent Structures in a Waning Century*, ed. Margaret P. Karns. New York: Praeger, 1986.

———. *Minorities at Risk: A Global View of Ethnopolitical Conflicts*. Washington, D. C.: United States Institute for Peace, 1993.

Gurr, Ted Robert, and Barbara Harff. *Ethnic Conflict in World Politics*. Boulder, Colo: Westview Press, 1994.

Hainsworth, Roger. *The Swordsmen in Power: War and Politics Under the English Republic: 1649-1660*. Stroud, Gloucestershire: Sutton Publishing, 1997.

Heifetz, Elias. *The Slaughter of the Jews in the Ukraine in 1919*. New York: Thomas Seltzer, 1921.

Henderson, Conway W. "Conditions Affecting the Use of Political Repression." *Journal of Conflict Resolution* 35 (March 1991): 120-42.

Hill, Christopher. *God's Englishman*. New York: Harper Row, 1970.

Hochberg, Leonard. "The English Civil War in Geographical Perspective." *Journal of Interdisciplinary History* 14 (1984): 729-50.

Hume, David. "Of the First Principles of Government," in *Hume's Moral and Political Philosophy*, ed. Henry D. Aiken. New York: Hafner Press, 1948.

Hutton, Ronald. *The Royalist War Effort: 1642-46*. London: Longman, 1982.

———. *Charles the Second, King of England, Scotland, and Ireland*. Oxford: Clarendon Press, 1989.

Ignatieff, Michael. "The Lesser Evil." *Prospect*, March 1998.

———. *The Warrior's Honor: Ethnic War and the Modern Conscience*. New York: Metropolitan Books, 1997.

Kahan Commission. Report of the Commission of Inquiry into the Events at the Refugee Camps in Beirut. 1983. http://www.us-israel.org/jsource/History/kahan.html

Keck, Margaret E., and Kathryn Sikkink. *Activists Beyond Borders*. Ithaca, N.Y.: Cornell University Press, 1998.

Keith, Linda Camp. "The United Nations International Covenant on Civil and Political Rights: Does it Make a Difference in Human Rights Behavior?" *Journal of Peace Research* 36 (1999): 95-118.

Kenyon, John, and Jane Ohlmeyer, eds. *The Civil Wars: A Military History of England, Scotland, and Ireland, 1638-1660.* Oxford: Oxford University Press, 1998.

Kingdon, John W. *Agendas, Alternatives, and Public Policies.* Boston: Little, Brown, 1984.

Kishlansky, Mark. *The Rise of the New Model Army.* Cambridge: Cambridge University Press, 1979.

Koenker, Diane P. "Urbanization and Deurbanization in the Russian Revolution and Civil War," in *Party, State, and Society in the Russian Civil War,* ed. Diane P. Koenker, William G. Rosenberg, and Ronald Grigor Suny. Bloomington: Indiana University Press, 1989.

Lenin, Vladimir I. *Collected Works.* Moscow: Progress Publishers, 1965.

Leggett, George. *The Cheka: Lenin's Political Police.* Oxford: Clarendon Press, 1981.

Levytsky, Boris. *The Uses of Terror: The Soviet Secret Police 1917-1970.* New York: Howard, McCann and Geoghegan, 1972.

Lichbach, Mark. *The Rebel's Dilemma.* Ann Arbor: University of Michigan Press, 1995.

———. *The Cooperator's Dilemma.* Ann Arbor: University of Michigan Press, 1996.

Licklider, Roy. "The Consequences of Negotiated Settlements in Civil Wars, 1945-1993." *American Political Science Review* 89 (1995): 681-90.

Liddell Hart, B. H. *Sherman.* Westport, Conn.: Greenwood Press, 1978.

Locke, John. *A Letter Concerning Toleration.* Indianapolis: Bobbs-Merrill Educational Publishing, 1955.

Lorch, Nathaniel. *The Edge of the Sword: Israel's War of Independence, 1947-1949.* New York: G.P. Putnam's Sons, 1961.

Lustick, Ian S. "History, Historiography, and Political Science: Multiple Historical Records and the Problem of Selection Bias." *American Political Science Review* 90 (1996): 605-18.

———. *Unsettled States, Disputed Lands: Britain and Ireland, France and Algeria, Israel and the West Bank-Gaza.* Ithaca, N.Y.: Cornell University Press, 1993.

Lynch, Michael. *Scotland: A New History.* London: Pimlico, 1992.

Machiavelli, Niccolò. *The Prince,* trans. Robert Adams. New York: W.W. Norton, 1977.

Macpherson, C. B. "Introduction" in Thomas Hobbes, *Leviathan.* London: Penguin, 1968.

March, James G., and Johan P. Olsen. *Rediscovering Institutions: The Organizational Basis of Politics.* New York: Free Press, 1989.

Martinez, Luis. *The Algerian Civil War: 1990-1998.* New York: Columbia University Press, 2000.

Marszalek, John F. *Sherman: A Soldier's Passion for Order.* New York: Free Press, 1993.

Mattingly, Garrett. "Machiavelli's Prince: Political Science or Political Satire." *American Scholar* 27(1958): 482-91.

Mawdsley, Evan. *The Russian Civil War.* Boston: Allen & Unwin, 1987.

Mayer, Arno J. *The Furies: Violence and Terror in the French and Russian Revolutions.* Princeton: Princeton University Press, 2000.

McAuley, Mary. *Bread and Justice: State and Society in Petrograd, 1917-1922.* Oxford: Clarendon Press, 1991.

Meier, Kenneth J. *Politics and the Bureaucracy: Policymaking in the Fourth Branch of Government.* Pacific Grove, Cal.: Brooks-Cole, 1993.

Melgounov, Sergey P. *The Red Terror in Russia.* Wesport, Conn.: Hyperion Press, 1926; reprint, 1975.

Meron, Theodor. "Shakespeare's Henry the Fifth and the Law of War." *American Journal of International Law* 86 (1992): 1-45.

Mill, John Stuart. *On Liberty.* London: Penguin Books, 1974.

Mitchell, Neil J., and James M. McCormick. "Economic and Political Explanations of Human Rights Violations." *World Politics* 40 (1988): 476-98.

Morrill, John. *Revolt in the Provinces: The People of England and the Tragedies of War: 1630-1648.* New York: Longman, 1999.

Morris, Benny. *1948 and After: Israel and the Palestinians.* Oxford: Clarendon Press, 1990.

————. *Righteous Victims: A History of the Zionist-Arab Conflict, 1881-1999.* New York: Alfred A. Knopf, 1999.

Morris, Benny, and Ehud Barak. "Camp David and After." *New York Review of Books,* 27 June 2002, 49.

Murphy, A. B. *The Russian Civil War: Primary Sources.* New York: St. Martin's Press, 2000.

Netanyahu, B. *The Origins of the Inquisition in Fifteenth Century Spain.* New York: Random House, 2001.

New, John. *Oliver Cromwell: Pretender, Puritan, Statesman, Paradox?* New York: Holt Rinehart and Winston, 1972.

Niarchos, Catherine N. "Women, War, and Rape: Challenges Facing the International Tribunal for the Former Yugoslavia." *Human Rights Quarterly* 17 (1995): 649-90.

Niskanen, William A. *Bureaucracy: Servant or Master.* London: Institute of Economic Affairs, 1973.

Norbrook, David. *Writing the English Republic: Poetry, Rhetoric and Politics 1627-1660.* Cambridge: Cambridge University Press, 1999.

North, Douglas C. "Economic Performance Through Time." *The American Economic Review* 84 (1994): 359-68.

————. "Prologue," in *The Frontiers of the New Institutional Economics,* ed. John N. Drobak and John V.C. Nye. San Diego: Academic Press, 1997.

Organski, A. F. K., and Jacek Kugler. *The War Ledger.* Chicago: University of Chicago Press, 1980.

Osipova, Taisia. "Peasant Rebellions: Origin, Scope, Dynamics, and Consequences," in *The Bolsheviks in Russian Society: The Revolution and the Civil Wars,* ed. Vladimir N. Brovkin. New Haven, Conn.: Yale University Press, 1997.

Pagès, Georges. *The Thirty Years' War, 1618-48.* New York: Harper and Row, 1970.

Pierre, Andrew J., and William B. Quandt. *The Algerian Crisis: Policy Options for the West.* Washington, D.C: Carnegie Endowment for International Peace, 1996.

Pipes, Richard, ed. *The Unknown Lenin: From the Secret Archive.* New Haven: Yale University Press, 1996.

Poe, Steven C., Sabine C. Carey, and T. C. Vazquez. "How Are These Pictures Different? A Quantitative Comparison of the U.S. State Department and Amnesty International Human Rights Reports, 1976-1995." *Human Rights Quarterly* 23 (August 2001): 650-77.

Poe, Steven C., and C. Neal Tate. "Repression of Human Rights to Personal Integrity in the 1980s: A Global Analysis." *American Political Science Review* 88 (December 1994): 853-72.

Powell, G. Bingham, Jr. *Contemporary Democracies: Participation, Stability, and Violence.* Cambridge: Harvard University Press, 1982.

Power, Samantha. *"A Problem from Hell": America and the Age of Genocide.* New York: Basic Books, 2002.

Putnam, Robert D. *Making Democracy Work: Civic Traditions in Modern Italy.* Princeton: Princeton University Press, 1993.

————. *Bowling Alone: The Collapse and Revival of American Community* (New York: Simon & Schuster, 2000).

Read, Christopher. *From Tsar to Soviets: The Russian People and Their Revolution, 1917-21.* New York: Oxford University Press, 1996.

Reich, Walter. "Masters of Death: Himmler's Willing Executioners." *New York Times Book Review,* 30 June 2002.

Reilly, Tom. *Cromwell: An Honourable Enemy.* Dingle, Co. Kerry, Ireland: Brandon, 1999.

Rhodes, Richard. *Masters of Death: Himmler's Willing Executioners.* New York: Alfred A. Knopf, 2002.

Richards, David L. "Perilous Proxy: Human Rights and the Presence of National Elections." *Social Science Quarterly* 80 (1999): 648-65.

Ron, James. "Savage Restraint: Israel, Palestine, and the Dialectics of Legal Repression." *Social Problems* 47 (2000): 445-72.

Rothman, David J., and Aryeh Neier. "India's Awful Prisons." *New York Review of Books* 16 May 1991, 44.

Rubinstein, W. D. *A History of Jews in the English-Speaking World: Great Britain.* New York: St. Martin's Press, 1996.

Rummel, R. J. *Death by Government*. New Brunswick: Transaction Publishers, 1994.

Runciman, Steven. *A History of the Crusades*. Cambridge: Cambridge University Press, 1987.

Russell, Bertrand. *The History of Western Philosophy*. London: George Allen & Unwin, 1975.

Sachar, Howard M. *A History of Israel from the Rise of Zionism to Our Time*. New York: Alfred A. Knopf, 1996.

Schapiro, Leonard. *The Communist Party of the Soviet Union*. New York: Vintage Books, 1971.

Schiller, Friedrich. *The History of the Thirty Years' War in Germany*, trans. A. J. W. Morrison. Boston: Francis A. Nicolls, 1901.

———. *Wallenstein and Mary Stuart*. New York: Continuum Publishing, 1991.

Segev, Tom. *One Palestine Complete: Jews and Arabs Under the British Mandate*, trans. Haim Watzman. New York: Metropolitan Books, 2000.

Sen, Amartya K. "Rational Fools: A Critique of the Behavioral Foundations of Economic Theory," in *Beyond Self-Interest*, ed. Jane J. Mansbridge. Chicago: Chicago University Press, 1990.

Serge, Victor. *Memoirs of a Revolutionary, 1901-1941*, trans., ed. Peter Sedgwick. London: Oxford University Press, 1963.

Sheffer, Gabriel. *Moshe Sharett: Biography of a Political Moderate*. Oxford: Clarendon Press, 1996.

Sherman, William Tecumseh. *Memoirs of General W.T. Sherman*. New York: Library of America, 1990.

Sholokhov, Mikhail. *And Quiet Flows the Don*. London: Putnam, 1934.

———. *The Don Flows Down to the Sea*. London: Putnam, 1934.

Silone, Ignazio. "Reflections on the Welfare State." *Dissent* 8 (1961): 185-90.

Sniderman, Paul M., Pierangelo Peri, Rui J.P. De Figueiredo, Jr., and Thomas Piazza. *The Outsider: Prejudice and Politics in Italy*. Princeton, N.J.: Princeton University Press, 2000.

Stanley, William. *The Protection Racket State*. Philadelphia: Temple University Press, 1996.

State of Israel. *Political and Diplomatic Documents, December 1947-May 1948*. Jerusalem: Ahva Press, 1979.

———. *Political and Diplomatic Documents, May-September 1948*. Jerusalem: Ahva Press, 1981.

Steinberg, I. N. *In the Workshop of the Revolution*. New York: Rinehart, 1953.

Steinberg, Mark, and Vladimir M. Khrustalev. *The Fall of the Romanovs: Political Dreams and Personal Struggles in a Time of Revolution*. New Haven: Yale University Press, 1995.

Stone, David. "The Russian Civil War, 1917-1921," in *The Military History of the Soviet Union*, ed. Robin Higham and Frederick W. Kagan. New York: Palgrave, 2002.

Swain, Geoffrey. *The Origins of the Russian Civil War*. New York: Longman, 1996.

Tarrow, Sidney. "Bridging the Quantitative-Qualitative Divide in Political Science." *American Political Science Review.* 89 (1995): 471-474

Thackeray, William Makepeace. *The History of Pendennis.* London: Oxford University Press, 1864.

———. *Vanity Fair: A Novel without a Hero.* London: Oxford University Press, 1864.

Tsebelis, George. *Nested Games: Rational Choice in Comparative Politics.* Berkeley: University of California Press, 1990.

Tuckness, Alex. "Rethinking the Intolerant Locke." *American Journal of Political Science* 46 (2002): 288-96.

United Nations. *Report on Jenin.* Report of the Secretary-General prepared pursuant to General Assembly Resolution ES-10/10, 2002.

———. *The Fall of Srebenica.* Report of the Secretary-General prepared pursuant to General Assembly Resolution 53/35, 1999.

U.S. Department of State, Bureau of Democracy, Human Rights, and Labor. 2002 Country Reports on Human Rights Practices, <www.state.gov/ g/drl/rls/hrrpt/2002/18278.htm>.

Volkogonov, Dmitri. *Lenin: A New Biography,* trans. Harold Shukman. New York: Free Press, 1994.

———. *Trotsky: The Eternal Revolutionary,* trans. Harold Shukman. New York: Free Press, 1996.

Walzer, Michael. *Just and Unjust Wars: A Moral Argument with Historical Illustrations.* New York: Basic Books, 1977.

———. *On Toleration.* New Haven, Conn.: Yale University Press, 1997.

Wedgwood, C. V. *The King's War: 1641-1647.* New York: Macmillan, 1959.

———. *The Thirty Years' War.* New Haven, Conn.: Yale University Press, 1949.

———. *Montrose.* Stroud: Gloucestershire: Sutton Publishing, 1998.

———. *A Coffin for King Charles.* New York: Time Inc., 1966.

Weingast, Barry R. "The Political Foundations of Democracy and the Rule of the Law." *American Political Science Review.* 91(1997): 245-63.

Weissman, Susan. *Victor Serge: The Course is Set On Hope.* London: Verso, 2001.

Wilson, Derek. *The King and the Gentleman: Charles Stuart and Oliver Cromwell 1599-1649.* New York: St. Martin's Press, 1999.

Wood, Elizabeth J. *Insurgent Collective Action and Civil War in El Salvador.* Cambridge, U.K.: Cambridge University Press, 2003.

Woolrych, Austin. *Battles of the English Civil War.* London: B.T. Batsford, 1961.

Zachary, G. Pascal. "Market Forces Add Ammunition to Civil Wars." *Wall Street Journal,* 12 June 2000, sec. A.

Index

The Prince, 3, 31
principal-agent relationships, 5, 11, 15,
    26, 29, 43, 45, 49-54, 62, 81-82, 94,
    134, 158, 160-161, 164, 166, 181,
    187-189
    adverse selection, 45, 50, 91, 123,
        125, 173, 176
    artificial information asymmetry,
        47-48, 63, 78-79, 90-91, 94,
        146, 175-176, 188
    information asymmetry, 45-46, 50,
        51-52, 81-82, 92-93, 160-161
    perverse selection, 91
    propitious selection, 173, 189
prostitution, 98, 101-102, 107, 114
Protestantism, 26, 35, 37, 143, 147, 151-
    152, 154, 156-158, 164, 170
public interest, 3, 35, 52, 98, 117-119
public opinion, relationship to policy, 32,
    52, 59, 139, 148, 150, 167, 170, 174

Qibya, 80-82, 84, 90

Rabin, Yitzhak, 66-67, 77
racism, 37, 39, 140, 158
rape, as instrument of terror, 7, 9-10, 26,
    44, 49-50, 64, 75, 87, 113, 124,
    146, 161, 164, 181, 185
Reagan, Ronald, 15, 17, 41
rebellion, 13, 70, 126
Red Army, 2, 9, 49, 70, 100, 105-107,
    114, 117, 120, 122-125, 127-128,
    130-131, 164, 178
    policy of extermination, 100, 102,
        128
Red Cavalry, 124-125, 128
Red Terror, 20, 106-121, 129
refugee camps, 3, 10, 61-62, 81, 86, 88-
    89
religious differences, as motive for vio-
    lence, 4, 12, 21, 23, 29, 32, 36-37,
    100, 115, 135-136, 139, 141-144,
    151, 158, 167, 171, 186
repression, 6, 13-19, 23-24, 32-38, 41-
    47, 50-53, 62, 66, 68, 73, 93-97,
    104-108, 112-118, 124-130, 146-
    147, 160, 174, 187
restraint, 16, 52, 54, 60, 66, 73, 92, 140-
    141, 146-148, 150, 157, 174, 176,
    181

retaliation, 62-63, 66, 72-73, 83, 113,
    128
retribution, 58, 62, 71, 73, 83, 154
Right Socialist Revolution, 116
Robespierre, Maximilien, 20, 100, 104,
    130
Romanovs, 24, 108, 112
Rupert, Prince, 149, 154, 160
Russian Civil War, 2-3, 19-20, 22-24, 26,
    45, 55, 90, 97, 99-100, 103, 105-
    108, 110, 115, 118, 121-131, 153,
    159, 164, 174, 176-178, 180
    Czech involvement, 102, 105-106,
        116
    synopsis of, 104-106
Rwandan genocide, 42-43, 53, 183

Sabra and Shatila refugee camps, 10, 62,
    85, 87-88, 93
Saramago, Jose, 3
savagery, 5, 8, 66, 95, 106, 145, 147, 185-
    186
Scheinerman, Arik
    see Sharon, Ariel
Schiff, Ze'ev, 89, 93
Schiller, Friedrich, 8-9, 11, 18, 22, 44,
    94, 99, 161, 165-166, 187
Scotland, 23, 36, 43, 133, 135, 140, 142-
    144, 147-148, 151, 154-155, 158,
    163-165, 167, 169-172, 176-178
security, 16, 21-22, 24, 31, 46-51, 59-65,
    68-76, 80-83, 87, 93, 98, 107, 129,
    135, 139-140, 143-144, 164, 178,
    181, 188
Serge, Victor, 118-119
Shakespeare, William, 6-7, 11, 22, 48-49,
    53, 57, 94, 129, 133, 166, 175, 188
Sharett, Moshe, 59, 61-63, 65, 68, 72, 77-
    84, 86, 91, 94-95, 176
Sharon, Ariel, 10, 59, 62-63, 67-69, 81-
    92
Sherman, William T., 180-181
Shertok, Moshe, 65, 72
Sholokhov, Mikhail, 9, 123-124
slaughter, 2, 8, 19, 48, 76, 87-91, 102-
    103, 107-111, 120, 129-130, 133,
    141, 146-149, 154-156, 162, 166,
    177-180, 185
Sniderman, Paul, 36
Soker, Jesse, 86-88
Soldiers Against Silence, 85